Experiencing Recruitment and Selection

Experiencing Recruitment and Selection

Jon Billsberry

John Wiley & Sons, Ltd

Published in 2007 by John Wiley & Sons Ltd, The Atrium, Southern Gate, Chichester,
West Sussex PO19 8SQ, England

Telephone   (+44) 1243 779777

Email (for orders and customer service enquiries): cs-books@wiley.co.uk
Visit our Home Page on www.wiley.com

All stories used in this book have been included with the permission of the subjects.

Other Wiley Editorial Offices

John Wiley & Sons Inc., 111 River Street, Hoboken, NJ 07030, USA

Jossey-Bass, 989 Market Street, San Francisco, CA 94103-1741, USA

Wiley-VCH Verlag GmbH, Boschstr. 12, D-69469 Weinheim, Germany

John Wiley & Sons Australia Ltd, 42 McDougall Street, Milton, Queensland 4064, Australia

John Wiley & Sons (Asia) Pte Ltd, 2 Clementi Loop #02-01, Jin Xing Distripark, Singapore 129809

John Wiley & Sons Canada Ltd, 6045 Freement Blvd, Mississauga, ONT, L5R 4J3, Canada

Wiley also publishes its books in a variety of electronic formats. Some content that appears in print may
not be available in electronic books.

Anniversary Logo Design: Richard J. Pacifico

1005202666

Library of Congress Cataloging-in-Publication Data:

Billsberry, Jon.
    Experiencing recruitment and selection / Jon Billsberry.
        p.   cm.
    Includes bibliographical references and index.
    ISBN: 978-0-470-05731-5 (cloth : alk. paper)
    ISBN 978-0-470-05730-8 (pbk. : alk. paper)
        1. Employee–Recruiting–Great Britain.   2. Employee selection–Great Britain.   3. Employee– Recruiting–Great
Britain–Case studies.   4. Employee selection–Great Britain–Case studies.   5. Organizational behavior–Great Britain.
6. Organizational behavior–Great Britain–Case studies.   I. Title.
        HF5549.5.R44B523 2007
        658.3′11–dc22   2007029094

British Library Cataloguing in Publication Data

A catalogue record for this book is available from the British Library.

ISBN 978-0-470-05731-5 (ppc)   978-0-470-05730-8 (pbk)

Typeset in 11/13pt Times by Aptara Inc., India.
Printed and bound in Great Britain by TJ International, Padstow, Cornwall.
This book is printed on acid-free paper responsibly manufactured from sustainable forestry
in which at least two trees are planted for each one used for paper production.

Contents

List of Stories

About the Author

Jon Billsberry is Senior Lecturer in Organisational Behaviour at the Open University Business School and Research Director in the Open University's Human Resources division. He holds degrees from the universities of Manchester, Birmingham and Nottingham. Before turning to academia, Jon worked as a financial analyst and an executive search consultant. Currently, his research interests lie in the areas of person–organisation fit, recruitment, selection, leadership, cinematic representations of work and organisational life, innovative methods of management teaching, the future of management education, and the psychology of the penalty shoot-out. He teaches organisational behaviour, managing people, leadership and human resource management across a range of levels, from 'openings' courses through undergraduate and Master's levels to PhD supervision.

Jon is the chair of the Organisational Psychology division of the British Academy of Management, in which role he founded the Academy's Organisational Psychology Special Interest Group, and secretary of the Management Education and Development division of America's Academy of Management. He has published three other books. His first book, *The Effective Manager: Perspectives and Illustrations*, is a collection of lively and provocative articles on management. His second, *Finding and Keeping the Right People*, gives practical advice on how to attract, select and retain high-quality people. His third book produced with John Storey and Graeme Salaman, *Strategic Human Resource Management: Theory and Practice*, is an up-to-the-minute collection of articles on the current state of human resource management.

Acknowledgements

The stories in this book were written by students taking the Open University's Professional Certificate in Management. I want to thank all the students who sent me their stories so that I could learn about the reality of contemporary recruitment and selection as viewed by the people involved in it. Unfortunately, I have only been able to include a small percentage of the stories I have been sent.

I am greatly indebted to two men: Professors Stephen Fineman and Yiannis Gabriel. Their book, *Experiencing Organizations* (Sage, 1996), captured my imagination as both a student of organisations and as a teacher. The book tells the stories of their own business administration students during their six-month-long job placements. As these students had little experience of work, their tales capture the reality of organisational life through naïve eyes. By adopting this approach, the authors gathered together revealing accounts of the reality of work that are 'fresh and sharp' (Fineman & Gabriel, 1996, p. 1). I realised that the same methodology would provide interesting and provocative insights into my own area of interest – the study of the reality of recruitment and selection. In particular, I thought it would offer me a way to research the different sides of the recruitment decision and to give a voice to constituencies that are rarely heard. As such, their book is the inspiration not just for this book, but also for the research project that it records. I would encourage all readers of this book to read *Experiencing Organizations* as well. I have unashamedly copied the format of Fineman and Gabriel's book: I hope they forgive me.

Two people were particularly helpful in two important ways. First, they granted me access to students. Second, they helped me find a form of words that allowed students to record their recruitment and selection experiences in a way that would both serve as a useful learning tool in the context of their courses and also give me the data I needed for this study. These people are the late Rosie Thomson and the retired Don Cooper. Both have been companionable colleagues, and both are greatly missed.

A number of other people have been crucial to the progress of this project. First, I would like to thank the Open University Business School Associate Lecturers who encouraged and cajoled their students to send me their stories. Without their help I am sure I would not have received the number of stories I did. Secondly, I would like to thank Jackie Connell and Margaret Marchant for secretarial support. Thirdly, I would like to thank the following people who critically read my draft and offered ideas for improvement: Jitse van Ameijde, Eugene Burke, James Heavens, Richard Kwiatkowski, Philip Marsh, Nathalie van Meurs, Patrick Nelson, Graeme Salaman, Ros Searle and Dannie Talbot. Of course, the blame for any mistakes or inaccuracies lies with me. Finally, I would also like to extend my sincere thanks to Claire Ruston of John Wiley not just for her help, support and encouragement, but also for her belief in my project.

REFERENCE

Fineman, S. & Gabriel, Y. (1996) *Experiencing Organizations*, London: Sage.

Introduction

After getting married, living with bereavement and buying a house, changing jobs is the next most momentous time in someone's life. There are many reasons for this. A new job might offer promotion, excitement and challenge. It might offer relief from the tedium of familiar tasks. It might offer salvation from a poor employer. Or it might offer the chance to work again after months, possibly years, of unemployment. A new job frequently means leaving colleagues and friends behind. It might necessitate moving house. It might mean that children have to move schools. All in all, the decision to change jobs is rarely taken lightly; the consequences are almost always life changing.

Similarly, the decision to recruit someone new is a major decision for an employer. Will the person have the right skills? Will they be motivated? Will they fit in? Or will they just turn out to be a liability and disrupt existing employees? Will they make profitable decisions or costly mistakes?

Recruitment and selection is a many-faceted affair with many players, all of whom have an interest in its conduct and outcomes. This book brings together stories from these different perspectives and gives a voice to constituencies that are rarely heard or considered. The writers of the stories are managers studying management and business administration at the Open University. The stories are the students' reflections on real events, chosen because they have taught their writers a lot about recruitment and selection. As such, the stories offer a lucid and direct glimpse of recruitment and selection practice at the end of one millennium and the start of the next.

MY RESEARCH QUESTION

I conducted this study because I am intrigued by the reality of recruitment and selection. In particular, I am interested in why it appears to be so different from the advice offered by experts. If you pick up a 'standard' American recruit-ment and selection textbook, you will find all manner of interesting material on job analysis, selection criteria, statistical measurement and strategies for assessing reliability and validation. British textbooks tend to offer a more crit-ical view on the comparative strengths and weaknesses of different selection techniques and mostly recommend that recruiters supplement their interviews with 'more rigorous' selection methods such as ability and psychometric tests and assessment centres. However, when you observe how people actually go about recruiting new members of staff, they appear to adopt a completely different approach. They rely on interviews and base their selection decisions on impressions formed from a limited amount of information. Selectors rarely use many of the scientific methods advocated in the textbooks and when they do, they tend to be a supplement to the interview rather than a full-blown selection intervention. Why is there a disparity between theory and practice? That was the question that I hoped this storytelling study would answer.

The discrepancy between the prescriptions in the literature and actual re-cruitment and selection practice is something that has been known for many years. It takes many forms. For example, why does almost every selector choose to use interviews, often in semi-structured or unstructured form, for selection, when the literature is quite clear that structured interviews or other forms of selection are more likely to find higher-performing members of staff? Other discrepancies concern the scarcity of thorough job analysis; the use of questionable selection techniques, such as graphology and astrology, which appear to have no predictive validity at all; and the focus of selectors on finding people who will 'fit in', rather than on knowledge, skills and experience.

In addition, I was interested in trying to understand the experience of people on both sides of the transaction. Almost all recruitment and selection research focuses on one side, either the applicant or the selector, ignoring the interaction between the two. I see recruitment and selection as the first stage in the development of a relationship between the two parties, as much as it is the assessment of the employee or employer. It seems to me that if we are going to understand how this relationship develops, we must simultaneously study both sides.

Finally, I was interested in the consequences of recruitment and selection episodes. What impact do they have on future relationships between employer and employees? What effect do they have on successful candidates? And on unsuccessful candidates? What impact do they have on selectors?

It seemed to me that I might gain a better understanding of these things through listening to the stories of people who had recently been involved in these memorable episodes. I hoped to capture people's own realities, rather than cold 'facts' or 'truths', and thereby make sense of some of the contradictions between theory and practice.

LEARNING FROM STORIES

Conducting research about recruitment and selection through stories is both an exhilarating and a frustrating experience. On the one hand, I found myself reading exciting, lively and compelling stories that resonate; but at the same time, thinking "so what?" A story might capture someone's personal experience, it might be engaging and passionate, but is it the truth of the event? Does it have any greater significance? This is a problem that has dogged storytelling research.

Storytelling seems to work well as a research method when the researcher's focus of attention is on understanding the individual, the meaning they give to events, and the causality of events and actions. In such circumstances, the way stories are told can inform the listener about the thoughts, motivations, prejudices and values of the storyteller. Gabriel (2000) provides an excellent example of this in his book *Storytelling in Organizations*. He recounts two different accounts of the explosion of a fire extinguisher. First, that of a manager, Raymond.

The most memorable thing I can think of was when the emergency fire control system in the computer room blew up. The pressurized system blew a cap off and punched a hole through the glass separating the computer room and went through just over our heads; it nearly took our heads off. A couple of months ago. [How much damage did it cause?] It looked worse than it was; but it was pretty spectacular. The safety officer had just moved the compressed whatever it was, so the cap on the compressed system was facing across rather than up and when it blew off, a fairly substantial piece of brass came off like a bullet and went through the glass, so there was glass everywhere. Of course, the computer went down, the place was then flooded. It was out of operation for a couple of days. It didn't affect the working of my department very much other than the e-mail going down. (Gabriel, 2000, pp. 32–3)

This, largely dispassionate, account of the incident contrasts markedly to the story of Maureen, one of the computer operators in the room.

I suppose they tried to kill me; I was sitting at my desk and the gas cylinder exploded which meant that the cylinder was directed at my desk and the nozzle hadn't been properly fixed. . . and it exploded and the projectile hit the window above my desk and caused an almighty explosion and shattered glass

everywhere. They failed on that attempt to kill me! [Who?] The management.
(Gabriel, 2000, p. 33)

In the case of Maureen, we begin to get a sense of how she relates to the managers of the organisation. She appears as a survivor willing to apportion blame, even when it seems most unlikely that the managers of the organisation were active agents in the way she describes. One imagines that she is only half serious, but still, the way she codes her story reveals much about her.

The stories in this book are interesting because they help us to understand the impact of different strategies and approaches on those involved. A time of recruitment and selection is an extraordinarily memorable period in some-one's working life. It is a moment when people are acutely sensitive to cues that can help them make sense of the new environment. Many of the impressions formed during this period stay with applicants and shape their future behaviour.

The stories in this book also tell us something about the collective folklore of recruitment and selection in Britain at the beginning of the twenty-first century. We all know that interviews dominate recruitment and selection, but we are less sure why this is. Is it anything more than custom and practice? Are there any superstitions, tales or legends associated with recruitment and selection? Who knows, some of the stories in this book (perhaps Marathon Woman or 'the woman who enjoys making men cry') may even become part of our recruitment and selection folklore.

Finally, the stories can help us understand some of the thought processes and decision making of those involved. Why do people accept some jobs and not others? Why do people decide to offer jobs to some candidates and not others? Why are particular recruitment and selection techniques chosen? It might not be possible to generalise too widely from the stories, but one advantage of conducting research through storytelling is the richness of insights they offer. If nothing else, these stories will surface some of the questions that we should be asking about recruitment and selection.

THE STORYTELLERS AND THEIR ACCOUNTS

The people who wrote these stories were studying one of two courses with the Open University Business School. The two courses are *The Effective Manager* and *The Capable Manager*. They lead towards a Professional Certificate in Management. They are 'supported distance learning' courses, mainly studied by managers in the evenings or at the weekends. These students are different from the 'traditional' notion of a student because they are all, by and large, currently in work. So they are simultaneously students and managers.[1]

The goal of these courses is to develop the knowledge and skills of managers and much of the learning is achieved through reflective practice. This involves students thinking about events that have they have been involved in, or witnessed, and trying to learn from them using the ideas in the course. One of the most important passages of reflective learning occurs when students write their assignments. And it was in one of these that I asked my students to reflect on a recent recruitment and selection experience. They were allowed to take any perspective: applicant, selector, third party and so on; and they could choose whether or not they wished to submit their assignment to me for research purposes. They were asked not to send in their story if it contained any fictional elements or was slanted to fit in with course ideas. In the instructions, I asked students to describe both their emotions at the time of the incident and the longer-term consequences.

Over a two-year period, about 15% of the students chose to submit their assignments to me. Although submission was anonymous, 90% of students voluntarily revealed their identity. On every occasion I have given the storyteller a pseudonym and tried to disguise the identity of all parties and the locations. The stories have been reported almost verbatim. I have made small edits where necessary to help the flow of the story, but I have always tried to retain the storyteller's 'voice'.

The stories I have included in this book have been chosen for four reasons. First, they appeared to be saying important things about recruitment and selection. Second, they were representative of a recurring theme in the assignments. Third, wherever possible, I wanted to juxtapose different perspectives on an issue. Fourth, I found the stories compelling, readable and engaging.

Once the stories had been chosen, I set about grouping them into chapters, each with an integrative theme. While it was not necessary to group the chapters, I decided to put them into three groups depending on the underlying paradigm: psychometric, social process and person–organisation fit. These

---

[1] I should note that while these courses had very large enrolments (i.e. well over 1000 students a year on each course) and spanned a broad range of companies, there is a small bias to large companies. In addition, at the time these stories were being gathered several large organisations, most notably the Prison Service, were sending a lot of students on the courses. About half a dozen stories from managers in the Prison Service are included in this book, including the whole of Chapter 13, which focuses on an assessment centre run to evaluate officers for promotion. I have decided not to disguise stories that are obviously from the Prison Service, but I have changed names and locations to protect people's anonymity.

paradigms are explained in the next chapter. For the meantime, it is sufficient to note that they mainly reflect the perspective that is taken towards recruitment and selection: from the selector's viewpoint, or the applicant's, or both simultaneously.

One of the difficulties I had grouping the stories into chapters and sections concerned their considerable overlap. A story about a bad interview, for example, is also likely to have relevance in the sections on discrimination and disrespect. As a result, my grouping reflects how the stories have touched me. This is an important aspect of stories: they say different things to different people. Each of the stories is situated within a discussion of relevant and interesting ideas on recruitment and selection. These discussions are just my interpretations of the stories and I imagine that you, and the original tellers of the stories, will have different opinions. It is one of the fascinating and enduring qualities of stories that they are interpreted and speak to people in different ways.

USING THIS BOOK

First and foremost, I believe this book is an interesting read. It contains many compelling stories that have amused, shocked, angered, frustrated and delighted me. I hope the stories will generate similar emotions in you. However, that said, rather like Fineman and Gabriel (1996), this book sits a little uncomfortably on the shelf. It is unlikely to stand as a recruitment and selection textbook in its own right. It is more likely that it will be used in conjunction with textbooks to highlight and illustrate particular issues. I see many of the stories acting as mini-case studies and, as such, as a prompt for classroom discussion. Given this anticipated role for the book, I have concluded each chapter by suggesting some activities to prompt discussion and some ideas for further reading on the subject, just as Fineman and Gabriel did in their book.

READING ON

If you are interested in finding out more about stories, there are three books I would refer you to. The first of these is *Experiencing Organizations* by Stephen Fineman and Yiannis Gabriel (1996). As mentioned earlier, their book provided the inspiration for this book and the research project that it records. Rather than focusing on recruitment and selection, their focus is on organisational culture and the experience of work. Their storytellers are 'naïve' students on placement. In addition to the engaging stories they capture, the book has an excellent introduction that talks about the importance of stories in organisations. Everything they say in the introduction is relevant to the stories in this book and I would encourage you to read it. I found the structure and format of their book excellent and, rather than reinventing something that works, I have 'borrowed' their format.

Gabriel (2000) provides an excellent review of the use of storytelling as a research tool. Winter, Buck and Sobiechowska (1999) explore some of the difficulties associated with the interpretation of stories. Their approach is less managerial and more generally focused.

The recruitment and selection literature is dominated by textbooks advocating the psychometric approach, which is described in more detail in the following chapter. In this mainstream, the books that I have found most useful are Smith and Robertson's *The Theory and Practice of Systematic Personnel Selection* (1993) and Heneman and Judge's (2005) *Staffing Organizations*. One book providing a thought-provoking alternative vision of the subject is Herriot's *Recruitment in the 90s* (1989), which is still exciting and innovative despite being almost two decades old. Two collections of articles also offer interesting perspectives on recruitment and selection. Anderson and Herriot (1997) include a large number of diverse articles covering many aspects of the subject. In particular, the article by Schneider, Kristof-Brown, Goldstein and Smith (1997) explains person–organisation fit. The other collection I would recommend is edited by Schmitt, Borman and Associates (1993).

Finally, I want to give a mention to my own book, *Finding and Keeping the Right People* (2000). This adopts the psychometric approach, but gives a voice to applicants and includes considerations of person–organisation fit in selection.

REFERENCES

Anderson, N. & Herriot, P. (eds) (1997) *International Handbook of Selection and Assessment*, 2nd edn, Chichester: John Wiley & Sons Ltd.

Billsberry, J. (2000) *Finding and Keeping the Right People*, 2nd edn, London: Prentice Hall.

Fineman, S. & Gabriel, Y. (1996) *Experiencing Organizations*, London: Sage.

Gabriel, Y. (2000) *Storytelling in Organizations: Facts, Fictions and Fantasies*, Oxford: Oxford University Press.

Heneman, H. & Judge, T. A. (2005) *Staffing Organizations,* 4th edn, Boston, MA: McGraw-Hill.

Herriot, P. (1989) *Recruitment in the 90s,* London: Institute of Personnel Management.

Schmitt, N., Borman, W. C. & Associates (eds) (1993) *Personnel Selection in Organizations,* San Francisco, CA: Jossey-Bass.

Schneider, B., Kristof-Brown, A. L., Goldstein, H. W. & Smith, D. B. (1997) 'What is this thing called fit?' in N. Anderson & P. Herriot (eds) *International Handbook of Selection and Assessment,* 2nd edn, Chichester: John Wiley & Sons Ltd, pp. 393–412.

Smith, M. & Robertson, I. T. (1993) *The Theory and Practice of Systematic Personnel Selection.* 2nd edn, Basingstoke: Macmillan.

Winter, R., Buck, A. & Sobiechowska, P. (1999) *Professional Experience and the Investigative Imagination,* London: Routledge.

Overview: Paradigms

Recruitment and selection is an unusual discipline in one important sense: it is dominated by one paradigm that underpins the vast majority of recruitment and selection teaching and research. Most other disciplines have competing paradigms that allow researchers, teachers and students the opportunity to adopt differing positions. But the paradigm governing recruitment and selection, the psychometric paradigm, is so dominant that it dictates the recruitment and selection curriculum and is enshrined in the laws of many countries.

Primarily, this paradigm considers recruitment and selection from the perspective of the organisation and shows how good selection decisions should be made (i.e. selecting the person who best fits the selection criteria; Schmitt & Chan, 1998). The curriculum typically includes legal issues in staffing, economic and labour-market issues, recruitment activities, testing and selection, validity generalisation, new employee orientation, internal movement and placement of employees, and employee retention. In essence, this approach to recruitment and selection assesses individuals against the knowledge, skills, abilities and other attributes (KSAOs) required to perform well in the post. The paradigm is that of a rational decision-making process operated by the employer.

Despite the overwhelming dominance of the psychometric paradigm, two paradigms compete with it for a foothold in the recruitment and selection literature. The better established of these is the social process paradigm that emerges out of social psychology. As the name suggests, this paradigm is primarily concerned with understanding recruitment and selection as a social process rather than as a series of obstacles to be overcome (Herriot, 1992, 1993; Iles, 1999). Because it does not purport to offer an alternative to how staff should be selected, it has not replaced the psychometric paradigm at the core of the recruitment and selection curricula. Instead, it is commonly used as a critical adjunct to explore the impact of the psychometric process.

The second alternative to the psychometric paradigm comes from the emerging domain of person–organization fit (PO fit). Primarily this field is concerned with the relationship between employees and employers, but it has always had a foothold in recruitment and selection processes and it has been suggested that it could become a competing paradigm (Bowen, Ledford & Nathan, 1991; Levesque, 2005). From its base in interactional psychology, PO fit considers the interaction between people and environmental factors and thereby avoids one of the greatest problems with the psychometric approach: namely, that it focuses on recruitment and selection from the organisation's point of view and largely ignores the perspective of the applicants. By looking for a 'fit' between applicants and organisations, the PO fit approach has the potential to treat the two sides of the recruitment encounter even-handedly. It is too early in the lifecycle of the PO fit approach for it to have supplanted the psychometric paradigm on curricula. However, the growing importance of the area, not just in recruitment and selection courses but also in the subjects of organisational behaviour, human resource management and strategic management, means that increasing numbers of management educators are reading about it.

One way of thinking about these three paradigms is to consider them as three different viewpoints on recruitment and selection. The psychometric paradigm views matters from the perspective of the selector, the social process views things from the applicants' perspective, while the fit paradigm attempts to consider the perspectives of the selector and the applicant simultaneously. Although this is an over-simplification because both the psychometric and social process paradigms acknowledge the need to consider all the protagonists' perspectives, it does illustrate a fundamental difference between the approaches.

The stories in this book are grouped together according to these three paradigms. This categorisation is mine and not the storytellers' and refers to my own choice about how I have interpreted the stories. This grouping of stories has helped me understand my own philosophical stance towards them and I hope it also helps you.

In this introductory chapter, I want to relate three stories that capture the essence of these paradigms. To my eyes, these stories illustrate many of their defining features.

BILL'S STORY: A TYPICAL SELECTION PROCESS

With a partner, I ran a small engineering company designing gas compression and treatment equipment. The work involved a high level of engineering design, with the actual fabrication work being subcontracted. We needed additional technical staff in design and project management. My partner and I were totally inexperienced in the fields of management, financial accounting and recruitment skills – in fact everything other than engineering! Being aware of this, we approached the problem of recruitment very carefully, even obtaining books from the local library for ideas and guidance.

We started by writing a comprehensive job description and then tried to translate this into a profile of the person we thought we needed. Assuming we would find people with the same basic value system as ourselves, we concentrated on what we felt were the experience and technical skill attributes required.

As we had a limited budget, we had to advertise locally. We investigated the salary level that would appear appropriate for the position and area by reviewing other job advertisements. This also helped us with wording and layout; we were keen to attract the 'right' type of applicant. Our advertisement was scaled to suit our budget, with several keywords and phrases included to make sense only to those applicants who had some knowledge of our type of work. We felt we had done a good job.

We received about 20 replies and the applications were carefully screened against our requirement profile. Those who did not match were rejected and informed. Four candidates were invited for interview.

We approached the interview with some trepidation, as we did not really know how to conduct it. We fell back on our own experience of being interviewed. The interviews were conducted quite formally and notes taken by me and my partner. We started with a detailed introduction of the company and the work undertaken. This was followed by another detailed description of the actual job on offer, including what we expected from the successful candidate. We then embarked on a review of the candidates' CVs and requested detailed explanations at every stage. The final element was taken up with a discussion of the candidates' current circumstances and an invitation to ask any questions they had. At this point we were worried about sounding too positive in case the candidates went away with unrealistic optimism.

One candidate arrived late for the interview and smelled of beer. He apologised immediately and explained that he had been to a pub with his work colleagues as one was leaving. This seemed a reasonable explanation and, given the quality of his CV, we accepted it. Our secretary later volunteered the opinion that he had a drink problem and was totally unsuitable for our company: 'Nobody goes to the pub immediately before an interview for any reason.' This opinion was discounted as being only female intuition with no logical basis.

*Immediately after each interview, we discussed our feelings and made fur-
ther notes. After all the interviews had been completed, we discussed our
findings with our senior director. On paper, the favourite candidate was the
one who arrived late and smelled of beer. His qualifications were good, his
experience seemed relevant and he appeared to have the confidence necessary to deal with customers and suppliers alike. The fact that he had some
annoying mannerisms, such as insisting on pronouncing the word pneumatic
as 'poomatic', was felt to be unfair discrimination and unscientific, and was
therefore ignored.*

*We had just obtained a fairly large order and needed someone as soon as
possible. We did not feel it was necessary to check the candidate's references
or qualifications and we justified this omission on the basis of time and the
impression we gained during the interview. The job was duly offered and
accepted; again our secretary voiced the opinion that we were making a
mistake and would regret it. My partner and I congratulated ourselves on
handling the whole process in a most professional and competent way.*

*During the first few weeks of the man's employment we began to realise
that training and coaching were necessary. We should not have expected a
newcomer to understand his job immediately, we reasoned. However, as the
weeks went by we began to realise that not only could he not grasp the concept
of our business, he did not look beyond the immediate task. We also began to
appreciate that his technical competence was many levels below that which
we had expected. Within six months it was clear that we had made a major
mistake for the following reasons:*

- *He made no attempt to work with or assist others in the company despite
their assistance to him.*

- *Every task had to be explained in detail, often repeatedly, which did not fit
with the qualifications he claimed to have.*

- *He had no commitment to the job and had to be controlled and monitored
every minute. When he completed a task, he would just sit there and wait
for someone to ask if it was completed.*

- *He did have a drink problem and had to be warned repeatedly about coming
back after lunch smelling of beer.*

*It was almost with pleasure, and certainly relief, that we were able to make
him redundant after about one year. We never calculated the monetary cost*

to the company, but the increased burden on the other members of staff was
significant. But worst of all, our secretary had the opportunity to say, 'I told
you so!'

I find Bill's story interesting on many levels. First and foremost, it is typical
of so many stories I received: managers working in small and medium-sized
companies who only get involved in recruitment and selection occasionally
when they have a specific position to fill. Doing so always seems urgent and
critical to the company's success. People apply because they see an advertisement and make their candidacy known by submitting a CV. The CVs are
haphazardly assessed and magically whittled down to a shortlist of four people. These people are interviewed and the 'best' person is offered the job. In
many ways, this is the classic recruitment and selection model and one that
endures in many organisations.

The second aspect of the story I find interesting is the good intentions of
the recruiters. These are people who were desperately keen to do the right
thing; not just for the company, but because that was what they wanted to do.
They were even prepared to admit their inexperience in recruitment and got
themselves to the library. But like so many who have gone before, these are
selectors who relied on their impressions, despite their scientific bias. They
dismissed the 'data' that they had uncovered (e.g. the smell of alcohol on
the breath or unconventional pronunciations of technical terms), which they
interpreted as quirkiness.

The third reason for relating this story is that, although it could be analysed
from any of the three perspectives, it is a particularly good example of a story
that illustrates the strengths and weaknesses of the psychometric paradigm.
We see a conscious attempt to be deliberate and rational. Those involved
view the task of recruiting someone as a rational, step-by-step, decision-
making process of which they are in control. The selectors developed a job
description and employee profile to help them assess the relevance of the
candidates' qualities. However, their data gathering was fairly subjective and
it did not help them tackle the unexpected, such as the candidate's drink
problem and unusual pronunciation of a technical word. In evaluating these
factors, their positive impression of other evidence clouded their judgement
('He apologised immediately and explained that he had been to a pub with his
work colleagues as one was leaving. This seemed a reasonable explanation
and, given the quality of his CV, we accepted it.'). This type of error is known
as the 'halo' effect and is a perennial problem for selectors.

This story illustrates the crisis in the psychometric paradigm: How can
imperfect human beings make the coldly rational and scientific decisions

required by the approach? What is the selector to do when unexpected evidence appears? What impact does the applicant's impression management (i.e. deliberate or accidental deceit) have on the process? Is the recruitment and selection episode detached from the employment of the successful candidate? The first section of this book addresses issues such as these.

MALCOLM'S STORY: HIS FIFTEEN MINUTES OF SHAME

I was interviewed for a middle management post in the social work department of a local authority in which I was already a junior manager. It was only advertised internally, thus limiting the recruitment net to just existing employees.

On arrival I was told by the receptionist that my interview would commence in 20 minutes. Moments later, a door opened off a corridor and I was taken into the interview room. Without explanation of the missing 20 minutes, and while I was still taking my coat off, the interview began. The chairperson said he would read two questions that I was required to answer without comment or interruption from the three panel members. Then there would be some more traditional questioning by panel members, but they would not take any questions from me. After precisely 15 minutes, the interview would terminate.

I was unnerved at being given 20 minutes for final preparation that then telescoped to seconds. The experience of giving two mini-presentations without advance notice was challenging. The panel received these talks with blank, impassive expressions as though engaged in performance art. The deputy director took over questioning and after a preamble on absence management said, 'I see that two years ago you had an 8-week absence for depression, what is your prognosis now?' I said it was only possible to have a prognosis if one had an illness and that I was now in perfect good health. He then asked why, since I had studied law, I had not become a lawyer. My answer was that I had wanted to be a social worker. He rounded off by asking if my parents had been disappointed in me for not becoming a lawyer, to which I provided, in exasperation, the four-word answer, 'Yes, actually they were'. The 15-minute guillotine had now been reached.

At the time, my emotions and thoughts were of having my inner core laid bare. I thought that the deputy director's interrogation about my sickness record was potentially relevant, but had been insensitively handled. His questioning about my parents was invasive, rude and irrelevant to the current selection process. The interview structure caused feelings of disempowerment, particularly the prohibition on questions from the interviewee. The impassive demeanour of the selection panel engendered a sense of being clinically observed. My emotions now are of still some unresolved anger and of a wasted opportunity. I was not offered the post and the experience weakened my relationship with my employer, influencing a subsequent move to a new organisation.

Just as Bill's story is typical of many of the 'selection' stories I received, Malcolm's story is typical of many of the 'reaction' stories. On one level I am absolutely baffled by the selection process these insensitive people created. What sort of data did they expect to get on which to base their decisions? Fifteen minutes to gather data? But the purpose of including this story here is to illustrate the social process paradigm, which means exploring the impact of this process on the individuals playing roles in it.

Let's start with the storyteller, Malcolm. He makes his feelings very clear in the final paragraph. He was angry at the time and he is still angry now. He did not appreciate being treated in this manner. This sort of treatment would be unacceptable no matter who it was applied to. But Malcolm was an internal applicant who must return to work as soon as his 'fifteen minutes of shame' are over. What must be going through someone's head when they leave such an interview and return to their desk? Do such interviewers realise the importance of these events to the people they are interviewing? Such events are very memorable and deeply defining of what the employer values (or doesn't). Malcolm says that this event influenced his relationship with his employer for the worse and suggests that it may have been a factor in his decision to leave the organisation. If this event signals how people are managed in the organisation, I wouldn't be surprised if it was. But was it a causal factor?

Determining causality in these stories is particularly difficult. There are several reasons for this. My storytellers were asked to think back to a recruitment and selection experience and the impact it had on them. This act of recollection focuses attention on this incident at the expense of other factors. Hence, its influence is likely to be over-emphasised. The effect is further exaggerated by having to record the event as an assignment and by the need to find things to talk about. This is a theme that runs through the stories and should be kept in mind when reading them.

I found myself wondering about one of the invisible players in this drama: the successful applicant. How would it feel to be the 'winner'? Presumably, every applicant was subjected to this process (Harris, 2000). Several responses seem possible. The most natural initial reaction would probably be a sense of elation at gaining the promotion. But what happens after that? The person concerned might be managing some of the people who failed in this process. Or they might be friends or acquaintances of people who did not get the job. There might be quite a bit of gossip in the office about the selection process. The person's new boss may have been on the selection panel. In all of these cases, the successful applicant will have difficulties. Will the person be viewed poorly by their staff? What will their friends' opinion be? Will people question their authority or credibility? Will people be hostile? Will the person respect their boss?

And then there is the impact on the members of the selection panel. It would be very worrying if they did not appreciate the poverty of their own selection process; but, of course, they may not. Did they design it or was it foisted on them? How did they feel about managing this dehumanising process? How would it affect their relations with their staff? What would it do to their reputations?

This story demonstrates a key feature of the social process paradigm: selection is not just about clearing hurdles to get the job, it is also part of the relationship between employee and employer. It represents an important moment when expectations are set, when working relationships are established, and when modes of behaviour are determined. One of the reasons this is so is because these are events of particular salience to individuals that have a great impact on their future. External applicants are keenly attentive to every cue that can help them understand what it will be like to work in this organisation. Internal applicants are taking risks by exposing themselves for internal scrutiny and the possible disappointment that might follow. Accordingly, they remember details and their emotional responses to them. When events go against them, they get angry and this can translate itself into disaffection, anger, rebellion and exit.

EMMA'S STORY: A DAY'S FREE LABOUR

I had applied for the position of office manager with a PC software training company based in Silicon Valley, west of London. I was invited for an interview with the managing director (MD). The interview was different to others I had experienced, as it was quite relaxed and relatively informal. We discussed my previous jobs and what type of role I was looking for, but mainly we discussed my experiences of living in a foreign country; I had just returned from living in Sydney for two years.

The MD said he thought I would be perfect for the job, but, just to make sure, he wanted me to join the company for a one-day trial period. I was very surprised about this as I had never heard of anyone being asked to do this. My initial thought was: Is this his way of getting some work done without having to pay for a temp? He then explained that as the company was a franchise and not a large company, he had to 'ensure that all potential employees would fit in with the rest of the team'. Even though I had my reservations, I said yes. I liked the sound of the company: it was relatively new and I felt it would be a great opportunity for me to get in early and grow with the company.

The trial was arranged for the following day; I don't think I have ever been so nervous. My main concern was my potential colleagues. I knew that every time I said or did anything, they would be watching me. Was I capable of doing the job? Would I fit in with them? When I arrived everyone was already there waiting for me. The MD introduced me and gave me a brief description of who everyone was and what they did. The rest of the morning went by very quickly. I was given a brief induction and then set a few tasks to complete, which was their way of checking that I was up to the job.

To be honest, at the time I had mixed reactions. I was paranoid that I was going to make mistakes, but I was also excited about the prospect of getting the job. After lunch I was formally offered the position; it seemed everyone had really liked me and they wanted me put out of my misery. In the short term it meant I had a job that I was really looking forward to, and when I went into the office on my first day I felt like part of the team already. I also knew that I was liked by my new colleagues, which was a great morale booster. I also felt more relaxed asking questions.

I have included Emma's story here to illustrate the PO fit paradigm of recruitment and selection, although it is equally relevant to the social process paradigm. Emma's story is a particularly interesting example of the paradigm for several reasons. It shows how recruitment and selection can be done well. It highlights the interaction between person and environment. It illustrates the strength of the emotions during recruitment and selection and hints at some of the dangers in the paradigm.

The PO fit paradigm is concerned with the interaction of people and the environments they occupy and asserts that the 'fit' of people to their environments is the best predictor of their behaviour. This puts the selector under a tremendous onus, as this story illustrates. The selector has to ensure that the job is the right one for the applicant; the fact that they have applied is not sufficient evidence to indicate that they will be a 'fit' or that accepting the job is in their best interests. The infancy of this approach is demonstrated by the absence of tools and techniques to assess a person's fit (Karren & Graves, 1994). Probably without realising it, the MD has returned to the theoretical roots of PO fit. His solution appears the most natural and common way to assess an applicant's fit: to put them in the working environment and see how they interact with the people, events, tasks and so forth.

Emma's story reveals how difficult it is for applicants to make sensible, calm, rational decisions during recruitment and selection. For most, the prospect of a new job might be salvation from trying circumstances, a fresh start, an exciting opportunity or the culmination of many years' hard work. Consequently, they are likely to have invested a lot of emotion into their application and may start to treat the process as one in which they must 'succeed' in getting the job, rather than one in which they enter with a sense of inquiry. We see this in Emma's story when she says 'I don't think I have ever been so nervous'. In such circumstances, how can the applicant stand back from the process and coolly judge the suitability of this employer? Does this force selectors into paternalistic (possibly altruistic) roles, such as in this story, where they do what is the best interest of applicants even when this conflicts with their own needs?

I have already mentioned that there is a shortage of tools and techniques to assess PO fit in real situations. The selector in this story opted for a realistic job preview, which places the applicant in the environment to allow both parties time to assess whether there is a 'fit'. Imagine what this must be like. How long does it take to settle? How long does it take for the nervousness and excitement to abate? How long does it take to find out what working in the organisation will really be like? Is a day long enough? A week? A month? Three months? And this is a problem for PO fit approach to recruitment and selection. Theoretically, it is very appealing. But in practice it is still in the cradle and barely able to conceptualise walking (Billsberry, 2006).

THINKING ON

1. Bill ignored two contrary indicators (i.e. the applicant smelled of alcohol and could not pronounce a technical word correctly). How should you handle situations in which data points to different assessments of an applicant?

2. On a related point, good selection advice advocates the production of a job description from which selection criteria are drawn. What should you do when an applicant introduces something that you deem important (e.g. they reveal a skill that you might use, or have particular knowledge or access that would be handy, or demonstrate particular competences that you did not know about but that are relevant) but that is not on your selection criteria?

3. Malcolm commented on the impassive demeanour of his interview panel. Should the selection environment be such a serious one? Could it be more relaxed? What impact might the injection of humour have?

4. Emma said, 'I don't think I have ever been so nervous'. What impact does nervousness have?

5. Compare and contrast the differing experiences of Emma and Malcolm. How does the 'atmosphere' of the process influence (1) the applicants, (2) the selectors, and (3) the organisation?

6. Make a list of five jobs you know reasonably well. How long would it take people to get a realistic preview of each of those jobs to the point where they could determine whether or not they would thrive in them? What factors are important in your time assessments?

READING ON

The three recruitment and selection paradigms you have read about in this chapter are at varying degrees of maturity. The psychometric paradigm is the 'veritable old man'. It is the approach that dominates recruitment and selection and is embedded in the content of recruitment and selection textbooks, the curricula of personnel selection courses and the law. It is all-pervasive. Most textbooks take this approach. I would recommend Heneman and Judge (2005) and Smith and Robertson (1993), which although over a decade old is still very fresh and enlightening. An authoritative, if challenging, book on the subject is *Personnel Selection* by Schmitt and Chan (1999), which sets out the psychometric paradigm from a research perspective.

Although social psychology has penetrated the management literature for many decades, the social process paradigm in recruitment and selection is relatively new. It is perhaps best associated with the work of Peter Herriot. Two papers in the early 1990s (Herriot, 1992, 1993) described the paradigm and explained how it differs from the psychometric approach. These are short and readable papers (by academic standards) and well worth seeking out. Iles (1999) devotes a chapter to the social process paradigm in his book, *Managing Staff Selection and Assessment*. In this chapter, he expands the paradigm to encompass issues of fairness and diversity. Interestingly, in the book he outlines the discourse perspective on recruitment and selection, which is about how we think about the subject and, in particular, about the way in which power and knowledge are central to our understanding of recruitment and selection.

The foundations of PO fit can be found in interactional psychology and in the applied work of Ben Schneider. His seminal article, *The people make the place* (1987), is a good starting place to learn about PO fit. Other good sources are Chatman (1989, 1991), Kristof (1996) and Kristof-Brown, Zimmerman and Johnson (2005). But as a recruitment and selection paradigm, PO fit is a relatively new idea and one that is still being shaped. Possibly the best illustration of the idea can be found in Bowen, Ledford and Nathan (1991), who show how three organisations use ideas of person–organisation fit to recruit 'whole people' who will grow with the company. Levesque (2005) is a more recent exposition of these ideas. In Billsberry and Gilbert (in press), we have teased out the assumptions underlying the PO fit paradigm and compared these to the psychometric and social process paradigms.

An interesting discussion on where these paradigms are heading can be found in Anderson *et al.* (2004). They pose some interesting and fundamental questions (Anderson *et al.*, 2004, pp. 490–91): (1) How can organisations select members for highly changeable job roles, newly created jobs and flexible forms of work organisation? (2) How can future-oriented job analysis techniques be developed to scope the likely future task elements and KSAOs (knowledge, skills, abilities and other characteristics) for changeable job roles? (3) What is the criterion-related validity of measures of cognitive ability in selection for changeable work roles rather than for stable, rule-governed jobs? These questions replicate the desire to subsume the emerging new paradigm of PO fit into the psychometric paradigm in the same way that ideas from the social process paradigm were incorporated.

REFERENCES

Anderson, N., Lievens, F., van Dam, K. & Ryan, A. M. (2004) 'Future perspectives on employee selection: Key directions for future research and practice', *Applied Psychology: An International Review,* 53(4): 487–501.

Billsberry, J. (2006) 'Towards a future where we select for fit', *People and Organisations at Work,* 13: 10–11.

Billsberry, J. & Gilbert, L. (in press) 'Using Roald Dahl's *Charlie and the Chocolate Factory* to teach different recruitment and selection paradigms', *Journal of Management Education.*

Bowen, D. E., Ledford G. E. & Nathan, B. R. (1991) 'Hiring for the organization, not the job', *Academy of Management Executive,* 5(4): 35–51.

Chatman, J. (1989) 'Improving interactional organizational research: A model of person–organization fit', *Academy of Management Review*, 14: 333–49.

Chatman, J. (1991) 'Matching people and organizations: Selection and socialization in public accounting firms', *Administrative Science Quarterly*, 36: 459–84.

Harris, L. M. (2000) 'Issues of fairness in recruitment processes: A case study of local government practice', *Local Government Studies,* 26: 31–46.

Heneman, H. & Judge, T. A. (2005) *Staffing Organizations,* 4th edn, Boston, MA: McGraw-Hill.

Herriot, P. (1992) 'Selection: the two sub-cultures', *European Work and Organizational Psychologist,* 2: 129–40.

Herriot, P. (1993) 'A paradigm bursting at the seams', *Journal of Organizational Behavior,* 14: 371–5.

Iles, P. (1999) *Managing Staff Selection and Assessment.* Buckingham: Open University Press.

Karren, R. J. & Graves, L. M. (1994) 'Assessing person–organisation fit in personnel selection: Guidelines for future research', *International Journal of Selection and Assessment*, 2(3): 146–56.

Kristof, A. L. (1996) 'Person–organization fit: An integrative review of its conceptualisations, measurement, and implications,' *Personnel Psychology*, 49: 1–49.

Kristof-Brown, A. L., Zimmerman, R. D. & Johnson, E. C. (2005) 'Conseqeunces of individuals' fit at work: A meta-analysis of person–job, person–organization, person–group, and person–supervisor fit', *Personnel Psychology,* 58: 281–342.

Levesque, L. L. (2005) 'Opportunistic hiring and employee fit', *Human Resource Management,* 44(3): 301–17.

Schmitt, N. & Chan, D. (1998) *Personnel Selection: A Theoretical Approach.* Thousand Oaks, CA: Sage.

Schneider, B. (1987) 'The people make the place', *Personnel Psychology,* 40: 437–53.

Schneider, B., Kristof-Brown, A. L., Goldstein, H. W. & Smith, D. B. (1997) 'What is this thing called fit?' in N. Anderson & P. Herriot (eds) *International Handbook of Selection and Assessment.* 2nd edn, Chichester: John Wiley & Sons Ltd, pp. 393–412.

Smith, M. & Robertson, I. T. (1993) *The Theory and Practice of Systematic Personnel Selection.* 2nd edn, Basingstoke: Macmillan.

PART I

The Selector's Perspective

The selector's responsibility is awesome. Selectors must make the right decision for the organisation, for the applicants, for those rejected, for those the new recruit will be working with, and for themselves. No matter how we dress it up and assert that applicants make decisions as well, the power relationships and the salvation or opportunity that a new job offers means that recruits are rarely able to exercise their prerogative fully. In most circumstances, the selector makes the selection decision and unless they do something stupid (as we will see), the applicant accepts the job offer.

For many managers, selection decisions are the largest ones they make, although many do not realise this. Imagine the recruitment of someone on a relatively modest starting salary of £20,000. Assuming they stay in the same job for five years, the basic salary costs are £100,000 in 'today's money'. To this, a further 25% should be added for employment costs. On top of these employment costs, the 'costs' of mistakes must be added and the income associated with high performance should be deducted. Any way you look at it, these are big decisions. And yet, despite the size and ramifications of selectors' decisions, the diverse ways in which people tackle recruitment and selection are extraordinary. Some people are so overwhelmed by it that they become 'frozen in the headlights', some seek out training or help and advice from colleagues, while others are so nonchalant that they do no preparation.

When it comes to making the decision of whom to employ, selectors find themselves in a frustrating position. Most do not have the skills, qualifications or time to develop sophisticated new selection techniques such as personality or ability tests, in-tray exercises or assessment centres, and therefore have to rely on interviews, but they realise how weakly based their decisions are. They want more data, they want reliable data, and they want better indicators of who will perform well and who will not. There is a strong sense of frustration in many of the stories in this book.

This sense of frustration is compounded by the nature of the training selectors receive. A common feature of 'fair selection' and 'effective interviewing' courses is that they leave delegates terrified about the legal consequences of making mistakes and of using their own judgement. Many come away from these courses scared rigid about the recruitment task and they vow to ask every candidate exactly the same questions with no variation or follow-up, as we have seen in Malcolm's story.

There is a balance to be struck. While the responsibility is big, selectors must still perform like human beings. They must be sensitive to the people on the receiving end of their actions, while at the same time gathering enough information of a sufficiently high quality to allow them to make an informed decision.

CHAPTER 1

Responsibility

The goal of recruitment and selection is to find someone willing and able to do a particular job in an effective manner. But it is more than this. Recruitment and selection is a process that touches people at a time when they are particularly receptive to the messages about the organisation, the job and the organisation's expectations of them. These messages shape the way people go about their jobs if they are recruited. It is important, therefore, for the people who determine recruitment and selection strategies to think about the atmosphere and nature of the process and how it might shape the future employee's in-role behaviour. When the strategy is right, the consequences can be very advantageous for the organisation, the recruit, the selector and everyone else. When it goes wrong, the effects can be disastrous for all concerned.

The first story in this section shows a selector realising, and then coming to terms with, his responsibility. He would be a saviour for some; but how do you decide whom to save when there are so many desperate people?

TOM'S STORY: REAL PEOPLE

My employer decided to open a manufacturing plant in Glasgow, which would be their first site in Scotland. Part of my remit, as the new plant manager, was to interview and select our new staff. The vacancies were for staff at all levels, from machine operators to team leaders. Employment adverts were placed in the local Glasgow newspapers, with all replies to be sent to our office in Tyne and Wear. In the first week, over 2200 replies were received. The number of replies astounded us.

The advertisements had previously been used for a campaign in Oxford, where there had been issues over attracting suitable candidates. The site manager had lowered the acceptance criteria, and this had led to 45 replies. When the adverts were run in the Glasgow press, the only change made was the removal of any reference to Oxford. The qualifications required were not changed to take into account that the site location was in an area that had traditionally employed a skilled engineering workforce, and we could therefore expect to attract lots of applications from 'persons with mechanical aptitude'.

I started to sort the applications into three lots, labelled 'yes', 'no' and 'undecided'. With this task completed, I took a second look through the 'no' and 'undecided' lots to make a final decision on their contents. However, I was still left with over 400 'yes' applications, although our initial intake would only be 15 employees. I enlisted the help of another manager to shortlist the applicants. We agreed to a shortlist of 35 applicants for interview.

Arrangements were made to interview the shortlisted candidates at a local Glasgow hotel. The interviews were conducted by the company's operations director and me. While the interview room itself was excellent for interviewing, its location on the third floor left a lot to be desired. Getting candidates from the hotel reception to the interview room almost amounted to a forced march. I collected all the candidates myself. On the way up to the interview room, I described the format of the interview and whom else they would meet. Due to time constraints for the operations director, all of the interviews were held over a three-day period.

All through this selection experience, what struck me was that the bulk of the applicants were unemployed and had been for some time. They had been made redundant, or they were, at best, on fixed-term contracts. Until these events, I had never experienced unemployment on such a scale, and certainly had no personal knowledge of it. As I sat looking through the applications, what struck home was that these were 'real' people and I would be responsible for some of them returning to work, in one case after 18 months of job searching. I agonised for hours reading the CVs and covering letters, and in truth let my personal feelings get in the way of my professional responsibilities, which was why I asked another manager to assist in the shortlisting process.

In hindsight, I think that the emotions I felt at the time were partly based on guilt. My own career was taking off. I had a new job, complete with a company car, expense account lunches, great travelling and so on. The short-term impact on me was that for the first time I realised how serious unemployment could be and that it could happen to anyone. I also vowed that no matter what the circumstances, I would never again attempt to interview *so many candidates in such a short space of time. I was drained by the whole experience and still harbour doubts that in every case the right decision was made. In the long term we employed 80 staff, and during this time we changed our recruitment policy to take much closer account of the locality in which we were based. Wherever possible we recruited from areas of high unemployment, using local agencies such as the Govan Initiative and Job Centres for assistance. This policy was so successful in providing quality employees that it became the standard practice for recruiting non-specialist labour within the company.*

Of all the stories I received, few touched me like Tom's. Here is a man confronted by the enormity of his responsibility and who understands the impact his decisions will have: 'I would be responsible for some of them returning to work, in one case after 18 months of job searching.' Tom is clearly quite emotional about the decisions he had to make. This is not just due to the plight of the applicants, but also because of the clash between his upwardly mobile career and their desperation. Tom feels guilty about his own success. To his credit, he sought help. He has learned from the experience and influenced company policy.

Despite the way in which Tom was touched by the stories of the applicants and his desire to help people, it might seem surprising that he found himself designing a selection process that restricted the applicants' opportunity to present themselves: 'Due to time constraints for the operations director, all of the interviews were held over a three-day period.' Interviewing 11 or 12 people a day is quite a chore. Even experienced interviewers who do the job for a living would baulk at this. Among the likely problems are remembering who each person was, tiredness, weakening concentration and fading enthusiasm. Moreover, designing a process involving so many people in such a short period will obviously reduce the amount of time that can be spent with each person.

This story exposes one of the selector's biggest dilemmas: shortlisting. Although Tom was surprised to receive over 2000 applications, such a postbag is not uncommon during periods of hardship. Tom reduced this number to a shortlist of 35. The selection ratio at this point was 1:63. In other words, just 1.6% of the applicants made it through to the shortlist. When this figure is compared to the selection ratio from shortlist to job offer (i.e. 1:2.33 or 42.9%), it highlights shortlisting as by far the most brutal stage in this recruitment and selection process, which is not uncommon. Getting onto the shortlist is the greatest challenge for an applicant.

Historically, the shortlisting process has been poorly supported by selection technology. Selectors have had to rely on a largely subjective assessment of

CVs and application forms. Fortunately for people who, like Tom, receive large numbers of applications, this is one aspect of the process where technology has moved on apace. It is now quite common for applicants to be directed to pre-screening on a computer, often via the Internet. Not only does this pre-screening capture important biographical and contact data, it can also confront potential applicants with some selection tests and decide whom to invite for further selection tests. Tom was looking to fill a range of jobs for which 'mechanical aptitude' was a common requirement. Is an interview the best way to assess this? Would it have been possible to develop a screening test based on this aptitude that could have helped him reduce the initial pile of applications?

Finally, as I reflect on this story, I find myself wondering about the impact this approach to recruitment and selection (i.e. looking to the ranks of the unemployed) might have within the company. Assuming that people with the appropriate knowledge and skills can be found, this source of labour must create a particular organisational culture. I hesitate to inject a note of cynicism into my analysis of the story as I am absolutely sure that Tom and his organisation act from the most worthy of motives, but their actions must influence the internal working environment. Do those 'saved' from unemployment fear losing their jobs again? What impact do these people have on other workers? Is this workforce more compliant than it otherwise would be?

Tom's story is an example of a selector recognising his wider responsibility to society, the unemployed and the disadvantaged. But there are other responsibilities and sometimes they conflict with the nobler responsibility that Tom confronted. Laura's story shows how the pressures to find people to do important work sometimes mean that selectors become less honourable than they might wish.

LAURA'S STORY: THE EVENING SHIFT

At about 10 a.m., two hours into the day shift, a line manager came into the Human Resource (HR) department. This particular manager, like many others, had been with the company for many years; in his case, approximately 20 years. He asked if he could use one of the offices in the department that afternoon to conduct some interviews. Nobody within the HR department knew of any pending recruitment. When the training manager expressed his concern, he was told, 'Schedules have gone up unexpectedly so we need more evening shift workers to start tonight.'

The training manager was visibly shocked and asked the manager to consider the gravity of his words. What were his selection criteria? What training arrangements had been made for these people? Induction? Contracts? Productivity? The long-term costs? The reply is still difficult to believe: 'I haven't got time for all that. I'm going round the shop floor now asking people if they know anyone who wants a job. I'm only asking the good ones though.'

The interviews were conducted that afternoon, each lasting approximately five minutes. The manager was asked again what selection criteria he was using. 'I'm asking them who it was from the shop floor who contacted them to make sure it was a good one. Then I'm asking if they know what it is we make, and if they're nimble fingered, and if they've got kids. I'll make sure they have got someone to look after them.'

It was probably around the time of this incident that I began to realise that some mangers, whom I had felt intimidated by because of their length of experience compared with my own, did not deserve to be held in such high regard. In fact, I began to think that maybe I was a little better than I would give myself credit for. I began to question how an organisation could condone this type of behaviour (this manager was not alone in his shortcomings) and apparently give credibility to managers and supervisors on their ability to 'crisis manage'.

In the short term this process achieved one objective: it let the manager off the hook when the time came to administer a portion of the blame. When production schedules remained unachieved, it must now be the fault of the 'lazy worker'. There were enough of them now – he'd seen to that – so blame, and plenty of it, lay neatly in the lap of the inexperienced, untrained and slightly bewildered new employees.

The long-term cost of this episode must have been phenomenal. Unfortunately, it was not an isolated incident. The culture of the organisation had evolved to accept this as the norm. Staff promotion, historically, was based on an individual's length of service and their ability to instil a little fear in people. Any person not fitting this criteria was considered 'too soft' and so, sadly, did not fit in.

Superficially, this story is about a manager who flouts the rules and apparently has a disregard for proper recruitment and selection procedures. Moreover, Laura paints a picture of an overbearing manager who has little care for people and how they are treated. Indeed, the quotes suggest that he has little respect for his workers ('I'm only asking the good ones'), has sexist attitudes and thinks of employees as lazy. This is a manager for whom we should have no sympathy.

Laura's role as an observer of this episode of recruitment life might trick us into thinking that she is detached from the story and offers us an impartial commentary. However, does this account tell us more about Laura than it does about the players at the centre of the story? Laura is a junior member of the HR team. She clearly sides with the training manager and has internalised the powerlessness of the HR team to prevent practices such as those of this particular manager. Her words reek of discussions within HR about managers in the rest of the company. There is a helplessness and an 'us against the world' quality to this story. What is really going on here?

It is clear that Laura is personalising the event. She sees the manager as an opinionated bully. The training manager, on the other hand, is the victim of circumstance and long-tenured brutes. In effect, Laura has polarised the story into 'black and white'. Imagine how she might view the situation if she were on the other side of the fence. She might view the manager as the victim. Perhaps he is being harangued by his own boss to keep production up or is being hassled by customers for product. The training manager, on the other hand, might be seen as a bureaucrat who is out of touch with the realities of the business environment. The point is that neither of these standpoints provides a full picture; people are seduced into such partial attributions when conflict appears and emotions rise.

I hate to say it, but I find myself mildly sympathetic to the plight of 'this particular manager'. Not to his attitudes and approach to people, but to the difficult situation he has found himself in. He urgently needs to recruit people to do some manual labour in just eight to ten hours' time. This is almost impossible. The natural approach would be to contact employment agencies and find emergency help. This can be quite expensive and is only possible if you are in a major conurbation or centre of temporary work. You would normally do this through your HR department, but in this case it seems that relations have broken down between HR and the managers on the shop floor; close your eyes and you can hear the stilted conversation between the warring factions. So what is this manager to do? Asking existing employees if they know of anyone who wants work seems a perfectly acceptable way of going about things. A five-minute interview might not be the best way of checking people out, but if this is temporary work that just about anyone could do, selection is less of a hurdle and more of a sales pitch. A problem arises if the jobs have any degree of permanence to them. Then the five-minute interview is clearly an inadequate selection test.

The clash between HR and the shop floor in this story is a classic one. It is a clash of bureaucracy and expediency, hard versus soft management, inflexibility and pragmatism, rigidity and responsiveness, the short term against the long term, and a focus on people versus a focus on production. There are times when all of these qualities could be paramount and there are others when compromise is needed. However, when relationships break down, the powerful win.

The recruiting manager in this story appears to put his organisational responsibility above other responsibilities. His focus is to find staff to maintain production and achieve schedules. There will surely be 'people issues' down the line; not just for the new employees, but also for existing employees who recommended the organisation to friends and relations, and for the managers. The long-term impact of the selector's responsibility is explored in the next story.

ANNE'S STORY: 'I WAS HOPING'

When I originally applied for my present job the advertisement featured more about the organisation than the job. The company was portrayed as an exciting and dynamic organisation. This encouraged me to apply. However, the advertisement did not include anything on experience or skills and the details about the job were vague. As a consequence, hundreds of people applied, many of whom did not have the required skills or experience. The sales director later explained to me that it took him days to look at the CVs. He also explained he selected 15 people to be interviewed. This took him three days. He felt this number was too high and he found it difficult to remember the details of each applicant.

When I was interviewed, I was given incorrect information about the role. The director who interviewed me was not familiar with the tasks associated with the job and his interpretation of what was involved was incorrect. At the time of the interview he explained about the various tasks that were involved. He described the job as being varied and challenging and said I would become involved in many areas of the business. He said that the company was a growing and dynamic one: 'We believe in open communication and value people's opinion.' This made me feel I really wanted to work for this organisation. I imagined the job would be very interesting and the function of my department was not only a sales role, but also one that involved coordinating with other departments. I thought I would be able to put ideas forward and people would listen to my opinions. I thought the organisation would be one I could commit to and remain with for several years. Two days after the interview I was offered the job. I was delighted about this and did not hesitate in accepting it.

On the first day the sales director met me. He introduced me to my staff and those in the immediate area of my desk. He then said he was going out for the morning and left me to settle in. This made me feel uneasy and I was unsure what I should actually do. I decided to introduce myself to the rest of the managers and staff. After that I sat with my staff and asked them to explain what they did. When I completed my first day, I remember thinking I was unsure whether I had made the correct decision accepting the job and did not have a clue what my function was within the company. I thought the organisation appeared very unprofessional, which was the opposite image I received at the interview. I found this quite demoralising.

As time went by, I eventually became experienced enough to do my job. I remained with the organisation and made an effort to do my job adequately and tried to listen and motivate my staff. However, I have now been with the organisation two years and have decided we are not compatible. I think my own work is not varied enough and quite often I become bored. I have tried several times to suggest ideas, but the sales director does not consider them. I feel part of the reason for this is lack of time; the other is because he is demotivated and uninterested.

I often think back to my interview and the way in which the job was described. The description of the role and the job I am doing now seem completely different. This has left me feeling misled and had I known the truth about the job I would not have accepted it in the first place. I feel as though the organisation has let me down. When I explained the situation to my sales director he said that 'some errors did occur', but unfortunately it is impracticable to make changes. This has made me feel even more frustrated.

At the interview I explained I was looking for an organisation where there would be an opportunity for promotion. At the time the sales director acknowledged this and said this would not be a problem. Within a couple of days I realised there was not an opportunity for promotion. The next step for me would be a directorship and since all the directors had been with the organisation for years, promotion seemed most unlikely. When I asked my sales director to explain what promotion prospects there were, he replied, 'I said there would be an opportunity for promotion because I was hoping the organisation would grow and eventually there would be an opportunity.' This has made me feel I was deliberately lied to in the interview. I think he said this to recruit a higher calibre of employee. Since I have worked for the organisation it has actually downsized and there is even less of a chance of promotion.

Although this story is told from the perspective of the successful applicant, the key event is the interviewer's over-optimistic assessment of the promotion opportunities: 'I said there would be an opportunity for promotion because I was hoping the organisation would grow and eventually there would be an opportunity.' As I read the story, I gained the sense that this selector did not mean to misled Anne; he just got it wrong and should have been clear to her that this was conjecture. Regardless of whether it was deliberate deceit or not, its impact is great. Anne feels cheated and regrets accepting the offer of the job.

Interactions between selectors and applicants are very powerful in the way in which they influence the future psychological state of successful candidates. Often interviewers forget the impact of their words, especially if they are interviewing many people in the same day. Extracts from Anne's story reveal just how attentively interviewees listen to interviewers' words: 'He said that the company is a growing and dynamic one: "We believe in open communication and value people's opinion." This made me feel I really wanted to work for this organisation.' Two years on, she is able to recall quotes. In shaping Anne's state of mind, it does not matter whether these were the actual words spoken; these are the words she believes were said to her. They have shaped her expectations about the work and she feels let down when they have been shown to be false.

Interviewers easily forget just how attentively interviewees hang on their every word. The words and the way they are spoken are vital pieces of evidence on which applicants base their selection decisions. And when those decisions are to accept job offers, they are the vivid memories of the psychological contract that has been struck with the organisation. When this is breached, people are upset, feel let down and betrayed, may seek retribution and will think about leaving. They certainly will not be contented employees with their minds focused on work.

Wrapped up in all this is the responsibility of selectors towards applicants. Clearly it is unacceptable to lie to applicants. Most would accept that interviewers can be upbeat about work in the recruiting organisation, but when does a 'positive spin' become deceit? At what point do selectors cross the line and mislead applicants? Much depends on how you conceptualise applicants. Are they like ramblers out for a Sunday stroll who are responsible for their own conduct? Or are they akin to shoppers and should benefit from all the protection we afford retail purchasers? The answer lies in the incomplete nature of the information applicants have on which to make their decision. Unless they are internal applicants, they will know very little about the recruiting organisation, what the work will be like, how they will get on with the people and what the atmosphere will be like. This is why they are so attentive to every small piece of information they can glean from the selection process. These are signals about what the work will be like.

Ironically, in Anne's case the pleasantness of the process, the upbeat description of the promotional prospects and professional manner in which she was handled all painted an attractive picture of the organisation that she bought into. Her own excitement prevented her from being more critical. And this draws us full circle to Tom's story, because the more desperate the applicants are, the less they will be able to make an informed decision. To my eyes, the more desperate the applicants are, the greater the selectors' responsibility to them.

THINKING ON

1. Do organisational selectors have a moral duty to recruit people from the ranks of the unemployed whenever possible?

2. Given a choice between two people with apparently equal knowledge and skills who both look like they will be motivated and fit in well, one of whom is unemployed and the other employed (but immediately available), who would you appoint? Why?

3. Attribution theory says that when we explain our own actions we over-emphasise environmental factors (e.g. things outside our control, things that happen to us, external pressures), whereas when we judge other people we over-emphasise personal factors (e.g. their personality, their values and their nature). For example, 'I have been working 12-hour days for the past month and I was unable to get the report finished because I was too tired' as opposed to 'he didn't get the report finished because he is lazy and didn't work hard enough'. Given that selectors have to make assessments of other people, what impact is created by this natural tendency to attribute causality to personal factors?

4. Is the selector's main responsibility to the organisation? Is the primary responsibility to recruit someone who has the knowledge, skills, abilities and other attributes to do the work well? How can the selector's other responsibilities be reconciled with this?

5. What responsibilities do selectors have to applicants?

6. What responsibilities do applicants have to selectors and recruiting organisations?

READING ON

The first couple of stories in this chapter focus on how people are attracted to jobs and how employers can tap into sources of labour. Currently, much of the attention of researchers is on the use of the Internet and other computerised methods to do two things: to make the application process easier; and to assess or screen people as they apply. There are many difficulties associated with the use of the Internet for processing people's applications. How do you verify identity? How do you ensure that people do not practise any screening tests you set them, perhaps using different names? According to Bartram (2000), problems like this are all solvable. However, his main solution – the use of test centres to supervise submissions – removes many of the benefits of letting people apply and be screened online from the comfort of their own homes.

As one might expect, studies that have been conducted on applicants' reactions to the use of technology have demonstrated that, generally, they are favourable. However, Anderson (2003) has criticised these studies for their over-reliance on graduate respondent pools, who are more likely to be accustomed to such methods than other types of applicants, and for their descriptive nature. Provocatively, he writes:

> Should we be that surprised if applicants presented with better designed web sites react more positively to poorly designed ones? Or that reactions to computer-based and Internet-based tests are generally favourable if we limit our subject pool only to undergraduate students who have been brought up using computers as part of their everyday lives? Or that applicants prefer to sit Internet-based tests in the comfort of their own homes as opposed to having to attend an organisation's offices for group testing sessions?
>
> (Anderson, 2003, p. 128)

Although the use of computers in personnel selection is still very much in its infancy, it is attracting an increasing amount of research attention. Computerised versions of paper-and-pencil tests have some clear advantages. The software can do the calculations and provide initial feedback instantly and it can tailor questions to applicants' responses. In addition, such tests reduce some of the administrative burden and they give the impression of professionalism. Reassuringly, van der Vijver and Harsveld (1994) found that computerised tests produced similar results to their paper-and-pencil counterparts, but noted that although completion time was shorter, people were less accurate in their answers. For the latest information, I would direct you to the *Journal of Applied Psychology*, *Personnel Psychology* and the *International Journal of Selection and Assessment* for academic studies and to *Personnel Review* and *People Management* for more applied work in this area.

Shortlisting is one of those Cinderella subjects that has not attracted much research attention, which is a little surprising given that this is usually where the severest culling of applications occurs. Bright and his colleagues (Bright & Davies, 1999; Bright & Hutton, 2000) have looked at the use of curriculum vitae (CVs) in shortlisting and found that one error or misrepresentation is sufficient to reject an applicant. The other main stream of shortlisting research centres on the development of application forms that use biodata to help with the screening of applicants. This subject is well covered in Searle's book (2003), *Selection and Recruitment: A Critical Text*.

An excellent primer on attribution theory, showing how it can be applied to recruitment and selection, is a chapter by Herriot (1989) in Eder and Ferris's (1989) collection *The Employment Interview*, which contains a series of excellent reflections on selection interviews. Herriot's work is based on the work of Eiser (1986), which, although a little dated, is also recommended as a social psychology text.

Psychological contracts are strongly associated with the work of Rousseau. A good starting point to learn about this subject is her seminal book, *Psychological Contracts in Organizations* (1995). Any good organisational behaviour textbook that has been recently updated will discuss advances in this subject.

REFERENCES

Anderson, N. (2003) 'Applicant and recruiter reactions to new technology in selection: A critical review and agenda for future research', *International Journal of Selection and Assessment*, 11: 121–36.

Bartram, D. (2000) 'Internet recruitment and selection: Kissing frogs to find princes', *International Journal of Selection and Assessment*, 8: 261–74.

Bright, J. E. H & Davies, F. (1999) 'You did WHAT in 1983?!: The effects of explained and unexplained gaps in career history presented in resumes', *Australian Journal of Career Development*, 8: 12–17.

Bright, J. E. H. & Hutton, S. (2000) 'The impact of competency statements on résumés for short-listing decisions', *International Journal of Selection and Assessment*, 8: 41–53.

Eder, R. W. & Ferris, G. R. (eds) *The Employment Interview: Theory, Research, and Practice*, Newbury Park, CA: Sage.

Eiser, J. R. (1986) *Social Psychology: Attitude, Cognition, and Social Behaviour*, revd edn, Cambridge: Cambridge University Press.

Herriot, P. (1989) 'Attribution theory and interview decisions', in R. W. Eder & G. R. Ferris (eds), *The Employment Interview: Theory, Research, and Practice*, Newbury Park, CA: Sage, pp. 97–109.

Rousseau, D. M. (1995) *Psychological Contracts in Organizations*, London: Sage.

Searle, R. H. (2003) *Selection and Recruitment: A Critical Text*, London: Palgrave Macmillan.

van der Vijver, F. J. R. & Harsveld, M. (1994) 'The incomplete equivalence of the paper-and-pencil and computerised versions of the General Aptitude Test Battery', *Journal of Applied Psychology*, 79: 852–9.

CHAPTER 2

Professionalism

Recruitment is one of those moments in an organisation's life when it puts itself on show. It advertises to the world that it has a vacancy and invites people to join it. Large organisations spend a lot of money to make themselves look attractive during the advertising period; a good example would be the Armed Services, who produce high-quality television advertisements to entice applicants. On a lesser scale, job advertisements in the trade press are seen by rivals and customers as well as potential applicants and may influence attitudes towards the company. This is one of the reasons many organisations often dedicate more words in their job advertisements to promoting the company than they do to describing the job.

Organisations are also on show during the assessment of applicants. During this phase of the process, applicants get the opportunity to see the organisation from the inside: they can see what it is really like. They are keenly attentive to everything they see. These are clues about what it will be like to work for the organisation. Once the organisation decides whom it wishes to appoint, it has to make itself appear attractive if the person is to accept the offer of a job. For this reason, if for no other, organisations need to be on their best behaviour during selection so that they can land their catch.

The three stories in this chapter illustrate the different ways in which selectors' professionalism is assessed and the impact this assessment can have on applicants' attitudes and decisions. These stories also demonstrate how professionalism is derived from good planning and preparation. The first shows just how wrong someone can get recruitment and selection when left high and dry by her colleagues and without any training or selection experience to fall back on.

SARAH'S STORY: MARATHON WOMAN

This was the first time I have interviewed a person for a job. It was the first week at my current job. There had been a succession of dental nurses previously, and the last nurse had walked out in the middle of a session and never returned. The week before I started, my boss had placed an advertisement in the local paper. Unfortunately there had only been two people from the respondents that were suitable for calling for interview. One of the candidates cancelled as she had accepted a position elsewhere.

I had to carry out the interview in my surgery and without anyone else to assist. My dental surgery was not the ideal place to conduct an interview. The candidate had to sit on the dental chair while, due to the layout of the room, I was forced to sit behind it. This, I felt, did not help put the interviewee at ease.

I had no idea how to prepare myself for the interview. I could only think of a few questions to ask the candidate. In my preparation, I did not think of anything that the candidate might need to gain from the interview. I had not studied the candidate's curriculum vitae in detail, so I found it very difficult to ask questions related to her previous experience. The candidate had never been a dental nurse and had little knowledge about the job (although very keen to learn). I tried to explain what the job would involve, but this also proved difficult as I had myself only been at the practice two days. During the course of the interview, there were many pauses of silence, during which I found it difficult to think of suitable questions to keep the interview flowing. I decided to employ the candidate for a month's trial, and I am happy to say that one and a half years later, she is a trained dental nurse and we work well together.

At the time of the interview, I was very nervous about conducting it as I had never personally recruited my own staff before. I was also trying to find my position in the new practice and trying to 'fit in' with the other employees. I had no idea whether the person I chose would fit in at the practice. I was also very conscious of the previous poor track record of dental nurses and wanted someone for a long-term commitment in order to build rapport, as we would be working closely together for eight hours a day. But being a new arrival at the practice, I had not found out the reasons the previous staff left; was it due to the previous dentist, that the nurses were not suited to the job, or was it due to the organisation itself? I was also aware of the fact that I would be teaching the dental nurse and this was another aspect that I had never carried out before.

When I look back on the incident, I am ashamed of how poorly prepared I was for it. I could have chosen another room to use for the interview. As I am not directly responsible for paying the dental nurse, I had no idea of the wages, holidays, sick leave and pensions, for example. Therefore, I was not very helpful in encouraging her to join the practice.

At the time of the incident, I was very stressed about my job and maybe I should have asked my boss, receptionist or the other dental nurse to assist in the interview, in order to see whether the candidate would fit in; they had been at the practice longer and would be working with the new dental nurse. The short-term impact was that I felt I may not have chosen the correct person for the job and practice as I was the only one who made the decision. Also I felt that the candidate would think poorly of me due to the poor interviewing skills I had. In the long term, the candidate I chose is still doing the job and we work well together. My only reservation is that she does not get on well with the receptionist and other dental nurse. There may be some resentment that they were not consulted in the choice of person.

Sarah's story is one of the funniest and most shocking recruitment and selection tales I have ever heard. On one level, it has a laugh-out-loud quality to it as you imagine the reaction of the applicant being asked to sit in the chair. I find myself conjuring up images of Laurence Olivier's Dr Mengele picking through the interviewee's mouth while casually asking in his dodgy German accent, 'And so vot made you apply for zis job?' Being asked questions by someone behind you is strange enough. But when you factor in the terror of going to the dentist, it is hard to think of a more unsuitable location. 'This, I felt, did not help put the interviewee at ease.' That Sarah thought this location might be suitable is, possibly, the most amazing aspect of this whole episode. Do people really enter into the task of interviewing people with such little thought to applicants' reactions?

Other important issues are highlighted by Sarah's story. She is typical of the huge numbers of people who have to recruit others in small companies. She does not have access to an HR department that organises courses on effective interviewing. She is not surrounded by people who have a lot of experience of recruitment. In her firm, recruiting new staff is an occasional and rare experience that is tackled afresh every time there is a vacancy. Where can she go for advice? But even before she can ask herself this question, she has to realise that she requires help and advice. If you have not interviewed before and your colleagues do not see the need to offer their help, you might assume that this is a straightforward task. Even if you realise that you are unprepared for the task, where do you turn for help? In an earlier story, we saw how Bill and his partner, when faced with a similar problem, got themselves off to the library. Other options are scarce and busy managers are likely to rely on their own judgement, which is what Sarah did.

Naturally enough, her approach to selection was to interview the candidates. Obviously, the interview would be a crucial element of this selection process. But should it be the only one? Coming to recruitment and selection with little knowledge does not just mean that your interviewing skills may be poor, it also means that you are unaware of some of your options. If you think about the selection process for this job with a clean slate and with awareness of all the possible options, you might design something different. Yes, the interview will play a part in the process – although a different environment would be preferable – but other tests might assert themselves. How would you assess a dental nurse's capabilities? How about asking applicants to spend an hour or two doing the job? Or setting up some simple tests? Not only would these help Sarah determine whether or not the applicant had the required skills (or could learn them), but they would help the applicant understand what work would be like in this company.

Sarah freely admits how her lack of preparation left her unable to answer the interviewee's questions. Her lack of knowledge undermined her in three ways. First, as she states, she was unable to persuade the applicant to join because she cannot give her the information she needs to make a decision. Second, the fact that Sarah could not supply this information was likely to influence the applicant's perception of Sarah and the recruiting company and appear quite unprofessional. Third, if the applicant does accept the job, her attitude towards Sarah is likely to be tainted by the unprofessional selection process.

What is particularly interesting about this story is that although these failings are likely to produce these dire consequences, in this case they did not. The only negative legacy of the weak selection process appears to be the new employee's relationship with the other dental nurse and the receptionist. In all other ways, the episode appears to have been successful. This is important, because it illustrates one of the reasons causing the separation of theory and practice. The fact that poorly performed selection can have perfectly fine outcomes can lead to the replication of poor behaviours ('It worked last time so let's do it again') and it makes the complex and elaborate prescriptions in the literature seem pedantic, unnecessary and a waste of time. As a counterbalance, the next story shows how the mistakes of inexperienced and untrained recruiters can influence the psychology of the applicant.

RONALD'S STORY: THE CHARITY CASE

A small advertisement appeared in the Sunday Times *inviting CVs for the CEO of a major animal charity. The name of the charity was not disclosed. There was no detail of the size and exact business of the charity. The salary was advertised as 'generous'. There was a closing date for applications, but the interview date was not advertised. From the address I guessed what the charity was and decided to send my CV. I felt bemused that they did not advertise their name. I received an Annual Review and a job description with a covering letter a few days later.*

When I did not hear again after approximately three weeks I assumed I had been unsuccessful. However, six weeks later I received a phone call from the personnel manager. She explained that I was on the shortlist but that they still had not decided on a date for the interview. She promised to ring back the following week.

Three weeks later, I had not heard so I phoned her. She told me that she found it impossible to determine a date for the interviews that would suit all 20 trustees! I suggested to her that perhaps it would be better to limit the interview panel to three or five. She responded that this was 'a very good idea and she would discuss it with the chairman'. At this point I started to wonder how competent and organised the people were in this charity.

When she finally came back to me with a date, I asked her about the format of the interview and whether I would need to give a presentation. She responded, 'Well, you'd best think of something, because if you don't it will be a very awkward occasion as the trustees haven't got a clue; so you'd better lead them.' I thought this was a very improper statement to make as it undermined the position of the trustees in the eyes of the applicant, who could possibly become the new CEO. I would need to raise this with her if I got the job.

For the interview I was collected from the waiting area by the chairman. When we entered the room there were four other people (trustees) seated behind a table. The chairman 'waved' me towards a chair and while neither he nor I were as yet seated, he asked, 'So tell me, why do you want this job?' I remember having an immediate sense of 'so this is what the Personnel woman meant; they do not have a clue'.

One of the panel members interrupted him and asked if they could be introduced to me. Throughout the interview only two out of the five panel members ever spoke. The interview was completely unstructured and questions appeared to be 'made up' on the spot. The panel was unable to answer the questions I asked, such as 'Is there a business plan?' 'What are the current priorities?' 'What is the current financial position?' 'What is the salary range for the post?' Panel members would look at each other; the chairman would eventually laugh loudly and suggest that 'these matters could be discussed at a later stage'. I felt amazed and frustrated by the lack of information. The overwhelming emotion was 'they are completely incompetent'.

After the interview I was told that I would hear later that evening whether or not I had been successful. A week later I was informed that they would not appoint anyone, but would re-advertise and automatically reconsider my application. I felt very irritated by the delay in informing me of this decision. They did re-advertise in January and I was informed in April that someone had been appointed. I was amazed that it had taken them so long to appoint. My feelings about the charity were very negative as a result of the recruitment process. I felt that the trustees were 'hopeless' and that the personnel manager either did not have any influence at all, or was equally incompetent. I wondered what else was not right and on the whole the charity went down very much in my estimation.

I have since learnt that the previous CEO left 'under a cloud', that the next CEO left very soon after his appointment, and that a new CEO has been appointed recently.

Regrettably, this episode was yet another example of the incompetent manner in which many trustees are managing their charities. In the past year I have had considerable experience of being interviewed by trustees and the vast majority of the interviews were handled very badly.

The short-term and increasingly long-term impact of such experience is that I seriously question whether I wish to be employed by, and be directly accountable to, amateur trustees. This is a major issue as I have been employed in the voluntary/charitable sector all my working life. I am primarily motivated by the 'cause' and cannot picture myself in a commercial setting. I am at a loss about what to do next.

Ronald paints a picture of a shambolic organisation. If this is what the organisation is like when it is on its best behaviour, what must it be like to work for? Who would want to work for this organisation? Presumably, someone desperate or incompetent. But someone good? Ronald is grateful that he was not put in the position of having to decide whether or not to accept this job.

This story is a vivid portrayal of unprofessionalism. Just about everything that could be done poorly was. The anonymity of the job advertisement seems unnecessary, especially when someone in the know can work out which organisation is recruiting. The time delay in responding to applicants creates a bad impression and this is made much worse when specific dates are later missed.

The personnel manager appeared incompetent in many ways. She could not design a suitable selection process, or prepare the interviewers, or know what the interviewees would be expected to do. She reneged on her promises and, to make matters worse, bad-mouthed the interviewers. The niceties of introductions were not attended to. The role of the interviewers was unclear. The interviewers were unable to answer some predictable questions. A further promise to inform the interviewee of the decision was again reneged on.

These failures clearly had an impact on Ronald: 'I wondered what else was not right and on the whole the charity went very much down in my estimation.' Given his anger and irritation, I doubt that he would have accepted the job. Interestingly, Ronald is clearly involved in the charity community associated with this particular enterprise. He is applying for CEO jobs in these organisations, he is aware of the gossip associated with the new CEO, and reports having a lot of interaction with trustees of charities. So the invitation to attend an interview was an important opening up of the organisation to an 'industry insider', someone who might have influence over the way others perceive it.

Lest Ronald's story creates the perception that the charity status of organisations is a cause of unprofessional recruitment and selection behaviour, the next demonstrates a thoroughly professional approach in very similar organisational circumstances. A comparison of Ronald and Paul's stories helps identify the factors that influence professionalism in recruitment and selection.

PAUL'S STORY: THE PANEL MEMBER

The 'incident' was the first external interview panel on which I sat in the voluntary sector, and it was one of the best. We had to appoint a project manager for a homelessness scheme run by a small housing association. I worked for a partner organisation. I was first consulted in relation to the job description, person specification and advert, and then invited on to the interview panel as the external member. I agreed not to be involved in shortlisting candidates, but was sent the application forms of the six shortlisted candidates a week before the interview date. I was invited to go down to the organisation the afternoon before the interviews for a two-hour meeting to discuss the interview format, the questions for the next day and the marking scheme. I initially thought this a bit excessive, but valued the preparation the next day. I had dinner with the chair of the panel that evening.

All candidates arrived at 9.30 a.m. and were offered drinks. The chair of the panel first introduced each member of the panel, and then gave a 20-minute presentation on the aims and work of the housing association, and explained where the new post would fit into the organisational structure. The whole group of candidates was then asked to discuss between themselves a specific question relevant to the job. The panel observed the round-table discussion from different positions around the room and its members were allowed to prompt further discussion if necessary. The discussion lasted half an hour. Each candidate was scored for the content and manner of their contribution. I thought this must be a psychologically hard way to start an interview day, especially for those who had to come back much later in the day for their individual interview.

At the start of their individual interviews, candidates were advised that panel members would be taking notes. The panel member who asked a question concentrated on listening to the candidate without taking notes. Each interview started with a 10-minute presentation that the applicants had been asked to prepare. The information sent out to candidates had said that they were to be scored according to content and presentation skills. The panel then asked each candidate six prepared questions. It had been agreed that prompting was allowed if a candidate did not seem to have understood a question. At the end of the interview each candidate was asked whether they wanted to revise or add anything to one of their previous answers. Each candidate was then asked if they wanted to ask the panel any questions and told that the panel hoped to make the decision that day and would let people know as soon as possible. After the interview, each member of the panel had time to go back over the notes they had taken and to score the candidate on each answer. Again, at the time I felt this might be too structured, but realised its importance on reflection.

After all candidates had been interviewed, scores were added up and compared. Although scores were different, each member of the panel had marked the same candidate highest and the chair was very happy that this person would not only be able to do the job very well, but also fit well into the organisation. The person was phoned and offered the job.

The fact that the whole process had been very well planned and led by the chair had enabled me as a panel member to relax, enjoy the process, engage with each candidate and concentrate on selecting the best. For the first time I understood how important it was to involve all panel members in setting the questions and agreeing the sort of answers we were expecting. We came up with simple but well-thought-out questions, which enabled us to differentiate between candidates who could talk a good interview and those who actually had the relevant experience for which we were looking.

The short-term impact of the process was that we were able to select the best candidate fairly, without discriminating against any group or individual and without disagreement between panel members. The long-term impact has been that the project itself has been a huge success, because a very able and talented manager was recruited through the selection process. The fact that I was invited on to the panel has cemented the relationship between the two organisations and led to a very constructive relationship between us.

Clearly, the organisation in this story appears to have designed and implemented a professional recruitment and selection process. The recruiting organisation in this story is very similar to the one in Ronald's: a small charity run by a small team with trustees guiding strategy. If two such similar organisations can project such a different image of themselves during recruitment and selection, it suggests that it is not organisations' charitable status or their relatively small size that causes the difference. The stories are told from different perspectives: interviewer and applicant. Possibly that explains the difference. Perhaps the external member of an interview panel wants to find a professional process and approaches the event positively, whereas the interviewee who is bemused and questioning the competence of the organisation before he arrives approaches the interpersonal aspects of the encounter negatively. It seems likely that these perspectives will have some influence on the telling of the stories, but if we accept that these are reasonably accurate recollections of events and that the storytellers have not tried to misrepresent their feelings, there is sufficient detail in the stories to reassure us that the storytellers' perspectives are a small factor in the different quality of these processes.

In reading these two stories several factors come to mind. First, there is a marked difference in the attitudes of the participants. In the first, a couple of key players on the side of the organisation seem to show little respect towards their colleagues and the applicants. They do not bother to return calls, they treat applicants carelessly, and they bad-mouth each other. In the second story, the chair, in particular, goes out of their way to make sure that everyone in the process understands their role, has time to do what they need, is properly informed and has the opportunity to ask questions. I get the sense of someone who is doing more than going through the motions; this is a person who wants to do things correctly and believes it is important to treat people in the way that they would want to be treated. This is someone who respects all of the people in this episode regardless of their role.

Secondly, I found myself wondering whether the actions of the participants told us more about them or about their employers. Is the poor behaviour of the personnel manager in the first story a reflection on her, or is this how staff are expected to behave in this charity? Is the chair in Paul's story merely a lone voice of professionalism in an otherwise unpleasant and disorganised company? Of course, we cannot tell from these stories and this reflects applicants' inability to know whether these actions represent 'normal' organisational behaviour. More often than not, the behaviour of individuals does reflect the culture they work in, but not always.

Thirdly, in addition to having an attitude that respects people, the chair in the second story clearly has some experience of recruiting staff. I imagine that the chair has also undertaken some recruitment and selection training. This is reflected in the production of a job description and a person specification, the choice of selection methods, the structuring of the interview and the rating scheme. The outcome is a thoroughly professional recruitment and selection process that will impress all of those involved. This must reflect positively on the company and increase its chances of finding an employee who performs well.

THINKING ON

1. Close your eyes and imagine yourself being interviewed for a job sitting in a dentist's chair with the interviewer sitting behind you. What emotions and thoughts come to mind?

2. How would you react if an interviewer could not answer any of your questions about the job?

3. If you were treated in the same manner as Ronald, what conclusions would you draw about the nature of the recruiting company?

4. Under what circumstances would you accept a job from a company that indulged in the selection practices described in Ronald's story?

5. What is the impact of having someone from another organisation on a selection panel?

6. To what extent does an organisation's culture influence the way it goes about recruiting staff?

READING ON

Many of the themes raised in this chapter have not received much research attention. Just like shortlisting, these are Cinderella topics. Most recruitment and selection writers take it for granted that recruiters will respect people, get the proper training, make appropriate preparations, honour their promises and design a professional process. However, as these stories show, some recruiters are not able to do this, especially if their organisational culture is not amenable or if they are dropped in the deep end. Even in Paul's story, it is clear that considerable time and effort has to go into the development of a thoroughly professional experience.

In looking through the textbooks, other than asides and the odd sentence, I could find no reference to the 'culture' of the encounter. None of the major writers talks about the attitudes or mindset of selectors or how professionalism is achieved. Discussions that mention the interactions of applicants and selectors do so with the context of measurement, equal opportunity or legal constraints. The closest stream of research is the one that deals with selection as a social process. According to this view, selection is not a hurdle to be jumped before joining the organisation. Instead, it is part of the relationship between employer and possible new recruit. As a result, the culture or atmosphere of the encounter plays a key role in setting expectations. If you wish to find out more, the best starting place is the work of Peter Herriot (e.g. 1989a, 1989b).

Closely related is the applicant reactions' literature, which Ryan and Ployhart (2000) summarise into three distinct streams. The first is an examination of how the various components of selection processes influence the attractiveness of an organisation to applicants. The second stream centres on social justice theory and how applicants form their impressions of fairness during selection. The third examines differences in the perceptions of selection processes between majority and minority group members. It is the first of these three streams that maps best onto the themes in this chapter.

REFERENCES

Herriot, P. (1989a) *Recruitment in the 90s*, London: Institute of Personnel Management.
Herriot, P. (1989b) 'Selection as a social process', in M. Smith & I. T. Robertson (eds), *Advances in Selection and Assessment*, Chichester: John Wiley & Sons Ltd, pp. 171–87.
Ryan, A. M. & Ployhart, R. E. (2000) 'Applicants' perceptions of selection procedures and decisions: A critical review and agenda for the future', *Journal of Management*, 26: 565–606.

CHAPTER 3

Interviews

Two techniques dominate selection. The first is the sifting of CVs and application forms. This is when most applicants 'bite the dust'. The second is the interview and, more specifically, the unstructured or lightly structured interview. These two selection techniques play a part in almost every recruitment process. They are what applicants expect and also what they prefer. They are also what selectors feel most comfortable doing. Even though other selection techniques have encroached on the dominance of these methods, by and large the final decision about whom to employ is made as a result of information gleaned through the interview.

There are many problems with interviews as a selection technique. Interviewers place too much emphasis on individual pieces of information. They infer other qualities or weaknesses from these snippets. Poor interviewing can allow interviewees to misrepresent themselves. Frequently, interviewers make decisions based on their 'gut' feeling and are unable to explain the strengths and weaknesses of their preferred applicant. Sometimes the qualitative process becomes too 'scientific', causing decisions to be reached in spurious ways. There are fears that some interviewers unwittingly (and sometimes wittingly) make biased and unlawful decisions, which is facilitated by the interview's free format and unclear decision criteria. And that is just the tip of the iceberg.

But all is not doom and gloom with the interview. It continues to dominate personnel selection and recent research indicates that it is a lot better at predicting future performance than was once thought. Moreover, organisational recruiters are moving away from some psychometric tests that are disadvantageous to protected groups and are relying more heavily on interviews. Also, both scholars and practitioners are more aware of the importance of social processes in recruitment and selection and the way in which these episodes influence the future relationship of the employee and employer. Interviews, it seems, are here to stay.

As you would expect, interviews were the most commonly occurring theme in the stories I received, particularly bad interviews. There were so many that I could probably have devoted the whole book to the topic. In this chapter I have chosen to relate six interview stories that focus on the interviewer. Later in the book, other stories will reveal interviewees' perspectives and many other interview stories are integrated into discussions on other topics. The first story in this chapter reveals many of the mistakes and prejudices that can creep into an interview.

ALAN'S STORY: THE EFFEMINATE CANDIDATE

One of my first tasks in my current job was to recruit a replacement to fill my previous role. As this was a common role in the company, there was a person specification. There was also an interview assessment form based on the person specification, which was designed to reduce the risk of any prejudices influencing our judgements. It was also company policy to use a panel interview format to reduce the risk of prejudice further.

My first involvement with the process was at the second shortlisting stage. Shortlisting had already been carried out by our Personnel department. We had to produce a list of four people to interview from the twelve identified as 'possibles' by Personnel. In fact this was a fairly simple process as the standard of applications was not that high! There were no female applicants for the job. Interviews were to be conducted by me, my manager and his manager. We allowed one hour for each interview, with a half-hour after completion to recap and choose the successful candidate; four-and-a-half hours in total.

The first two candidates were non-starters. The first didn't have a strong enough character and there were doubts over how reliable he would be. The second candidate just didn't want to be there; on paper he looked a good possibility as his father works for a customer of ours (though that had no bearing on his being shortlisted) and I think he was there to please his father. His disinterest wasted our time and also prevented a potentially good candidate being shortlisted. This was most annoying.

On first impressions, the third candidate appeared a bit effeminate for what is a fairly robust environment and this probably clouded our judgement at the start of the interview. My own reaction was 'No, definitely not', but as the interview progressed I was turned round: he was very personable, had relevant experience, and from his work history would have been reliable and willing to work flexible hours (a necessity in the job). After this interview we were unanimous in our opinion that our initial prejudices had been misplaced and that the candidate had gained all our respect for having turned our initial thoughts to make him a possibility; he scored highly on our assessment form.

The fourth candidate was a totally different character from the third. He was very well spoken and very confident in the interview. In fact, this was slightly annoying as he would occasionally lead the interview. But he had taken the time to find out a little about us and asked plenty of questions. He had very little in the way of work experience, a succession of part-time and seasonal jobs, having spent most of his time in education. He had dropped out of a degree course in Sports Studies (albeit with good reason), and was looking for a job with a career structure. He had all the right answers to the criteria we had set ourselves; he scored equally highly on our assessment form.

After all the interviews were completed, we set about choosing the successful candidate. The first two were quickly dismissed as being unsuitable. Since the remaining two candidates were equal on points, albeit scoring highly in different areas, the decision would be made on personality and the most desirable attributes.

My own interest would be served by someone whom I could develop over the next three to five years as a potential replacement for my current job, so allowing me to progress further along my own career path. For this reason I chose the fourth candidate. My own reasoning was that with his confident, well-spoken manner he would be more capable of implementing decisions and controlling situations. He would also be able to represent the department with a 'louder' voice.

Alan is clearly a person who has thought deeply about his own involvement in the selection process and tried to surface his decision-making criteria. He is able to note some of his biases and can argue why he prefers the fourth interviewee. However, his story reveals many of the fallacies, misconceptions and biases that interviewers hold. His story is a commonly heard one: a weak interviewer who thinks he has done a good job, but who has actually made almost every mistake in the book.

Not all of the mistakes were Alan's. He was the junior employee on this selection panel and I wonder how much influence he had over the design of the process. The panel's acceptance of the existing person specification and the interview assessment form seems to have taken place without much assessment of their current relevance. Presumably, they were written some time ago. Since then, many things may have changed: for example the tasks, the technology, the relationships and the location. The selectors might also have explored how well these documents worked last time the vacancy had to be filled.

The unquestioning acceptance of the person specification is concerning because of the central role this plays in selection decisions. Also, I get a sense of these interviewers either under-estimating the importance of their roles or fail to understand the impact of their actions, or both. Alan seems to think that dedicating four-and-a-half hours to this process is quite sufficient. When the time of the other interviewers and people in the Personnel department is factored in, the total is probably in the region of 20 hours. This is not a lot when so much is at stake for the selectors, the organisation and the applicants. When faced with deadlock in the assessment of the final two applicants, they did not consider the option of additional tests or interviews and instead made a subjective judgement.

One aspect of Alan's story shocked me: the way he talked about the second candidate. The weakness of this candidate was seen to be the candidate's fault. Alan found this applicant's apparent disinterest 'most annoying'. This applicant had taken the trouble to apply and attend the interview. He was invited to attend as a result of a shortlisting exercise by the company. The recruiting organisation, therefore, invited this person to come along for an interview. Perhaps Alan's ire should be directed inwards at those doing the screening, rather than towards the applicant. Organisations, after all, have a duty towards applicants and should not needlessly waste their time if they can help it.

Alan is quite right to acknowledge a prejudice: the effeminate voice. However, he does not develop this further. What is it about this voice that makes him think this applicant could not operate in his 'robust environment'? Is this something to do with how seriously this person will be taken? Or was some weakness detected? Or is it something more sinister such as homophobia? By not considering this prejudice fully, the danger is that Alan's bias remains unconscious and unchallenged.

This bias asserts itself when the two candidates are scored equally. The decision is made following negotiation between the three interviewers. Interestingly, the word 'voice' reappears and becomes a powerful factor in the decision. A 'louder' voice was seen as being preferable to an 'effeminate' voice. Here we see spurious assertions based on the unconscious biases: 'My own reasoning was that with his confident, well-spoken manner he would be more capable of implementing decisions and controlling situations.' This is supposition and based on nothing more than a prejudice. These factors do not appear to have been on the person specification. Should they have been? Worse still, Alan seems to care more about the impact of the applicant on his own advancement than on the applicant's or the organisation's interests. I admire his honesty, but not the way this selection decision was made. The next story explores interviewers' decision making in unstructured interviews in more depth.

CAROLINE'S STORY: SQUASH

The memorable recruitment and selection experience I would like to describe occurred last year during my term of office as a governor of a primary school. As head of the Human Resources Committee, I was invited to chair the interviewing panel of three for the recruitment of a teacher. The panel comprised the head teacher, the deputy head and me.

Six candidates were interviewed over the course of the day, and the recruitment process appeared to be going smoothly. By mid-afternoon, the interviews had been completed and we took a break before reconvening to decide which candidate we thought would be most suited to the post. Our next few hours together were to prove less productive.

To my horror, after the short interlude, the head teacher announced, 'Well, none of those seemed brilliant, but I think I could work with the fifth candidate; so let's go for her.' The deputy head added, 'Oh no, I liked the second candidate better – much more lively – so I think we should choose her.' I was then asked if I had a preference for either of the two candidates named so that we could make a decision and go home! I expressed my amazement that four candidates had effectively been rejected without any consideration. With a feeling of irritability, I prepared to confront my colleagues. I explained that I felt their judgements were subjective and without foundation, and no consideration had been given as to whether the candidates were capable of doing the job. How would they have been able to justify their decisions if challenged?

In my role as chair of the panel, I insisted that we took time to consider each candidate separately with a view to making a rational and objective judgement that could be justified on scrutiny. What I hadn't foreseen was that my colleagues had assumed that a 10-minute discussion would give ample time to reach a decision, as they had arranged to play squash within the next half-hour! I was extremely frustrated at their attitudes but, as they were clearly not prepared to stay to discuss the matter further, I arranged for them to return to my house after their game to discuss the interviews over supper. In the short term, the arrangement caused us all inconvenience: the process of selection was lengthened as we did not finalise our decision until 8.30 p.m.

Caroline's exasperation is perfectly understandable. You only have to put yourself in the shoes of the applicants to realise that this is not how selection decisions should be made. On one level, the head and the deputy head disappoint because of their evident lack of respect for the candidates. No matter how poor they might be deemed to be, the panel has a responsibility to the applicants to consider them seriously. They have, after all, taken the time and trouble to apply and, on the panel's request, attend an interview. On another level, the poor quality of the selectors' decision-making skills raises issues about their managerial abilities and their arrangement to play squash raises issues about their level of professionalism. However, I did not include this story to have another side swipe at disrespectful interviewers; I chose it because it is typical of the format of many interviews and it highlights some common dilemmas that confront selectors. The dilemmas are important because the way in which selectors address them can have a considerable impact on their decision making.

This panel decided to interview six people for one post. Four is more common, but six is not unusual. Once breaks are taken into account, six people is about the maximum number that can be interviewed in one day assuming about an hour for each person. But interviewing six people is an exhausting challenge. It is also quite taxing on the memory. Trying to recall the comments of people spread throughout the day is difficult and requires good note taking. It is inevitable that the interviewers will recall different amounts and different types of information about the candidates simply because of the time lags and the way ideas grow, fade and change in the memory throughout the day. Not surprisingly, therefore, many panels opt to shortlist a smaller number of people for purely practical reasons.

Another practical issue concerns the organisation of the panel. In Caroline's story, the three people constituted one panel. They interviewed one candidate at a time and 'ploughed through' all six applicants in order. There are alternative arrangements. They might, for example, have organised themselves as 'lone' interviewers, each spending an hour with each candidate. Given some of the fears concerning the idiosyncrasies and abuses of lone interviewers, few organisations adopt this approach. However, it does have the conceptual advantage of potentially generating three times as much data on each applicant; that is, each applicant has three one-hour interviews with a single interviewer rather than one one-hour interview with the whole panel. Despite worries about unfairness, it has long been known that interviewees prefer one-to-one interviews and find them less daunting. A common alternative is to find an even number of panel members and to pair them up as two-person panels. In this case, this would have doubled the amount of time for which each applicant was interviewed. Moreover, the panels are forced to discuss their views of each applicant and to explain to one another each person's qualities. This may still result in disagreement, but as we see in Caroline's story, people who share the same experience may also not agree.

Caroline's panel members appear to have fallen into one of the most common selection traps. When the head said, 'Well, none of those seemed brilliant, but I think I could work with the fifth candidate; so let's go for her' and the deputy head continued, 'Oh no, I liked the second candidate better – much more lively – so I think we should choose her', the interviewers were seduced into making preference judgements about the interviewees. In effect, they were choosing which one they most liked. This preference-based approach is further demonstrated by Caroline's reflection: 'I was then asked if I had a preference for either of the two candidates named so that we could make a decision and go home!' If you are new to recruitment and selection you might be forgiven for wondering what trap these selectors fell into. After all, they have to choose someone. The psychometric approach is a rational approach to finding someone who will do the job well. The idea is that the selector should begin the process by determining the knowledge, skills and other abilities required to perform well in the role. These are known as the selection criteria. They are used as the benchmarks against which all applicants are judged. To be considered appointable, an applicant should satisfy all the criteria. Only when two or more applicants satisfy all of the criteria is any form of comparison of applicant to applicant conducted and only then against the selection criteria. This is an evidence-based approach that should result in the appointment of someone who can do the job well. The upshot is that each person should be considered against the selection criteria, not against each other. This is the mistake that this panel made.

Caroline was quite rightly concerned that her colleagues were making subjective decisions. 'Subjective' is one of those demonic words in recruitment and selection that is always viewed as a bad thing. However, it is a very difficult word to define. In common parlance, subjective is used to signify a decision based on 'gut feeling' or intuition; it is commonly employed to describe an emotional, non-systematic, non-scientific or irrational method of making a decision. Instead, selectors should make objective, emotion-free decisions based on science and systematic thinking. In practice, this rejection of subjectivity is a call for thoughtful rather than thought-free assessment.

But in reality, there is more here than first meets the eye. Can data be considered truly subjective or objective? Can people function in this manner free from all emotion and intuition? All 'data' that a person receives is processed in some way in their brain, where it is subject to all manner of unknown and unconscious influences and biases. Selectors receive many different types of data, some of which they are aware of (e.g. the words interviewees say, mannerisms, physical appearance, test results) and others that they are not (e.g. subtle inflections of voice, subtle interpersonal behaviours). Selectors are subject to a continual stream of conscious and unconscious data that they 'process' in largely unknown ways. Hence, it can be argued that what looks like objective or rational decision making is still strongly influenced by unconscious and unknown influences. One of the psychometric paradigm's greatest strengths is that it encourages selectors to list their selection criteria and then to list the evidence they have for each candidate against each one. In this way, it helps selectors surface their unconscious decision making so that they can reconsider the quality of the evidence they are using to make decisions. Although there are risks of pseudo-science, the basic approach is simply to help selectors make robust and defendable decisions because they surface the factors influencing their judgement.

JEAN'S STORY: ONE INNOCENT LITTLE QUESTION

At the beginning of the year, I was a member of a team who interviewed people for the position of assistant information officer, which required the incumbent to provide document management services to company staff and contractors. There was an existing job description from which we produced a new job specification. As there were no internal applications, my department head instructed three outside agencies to put forward candidates. The quality of the CVs that were presented varied greatly. A senior colleague and I checked through them purely on skill levels, applicants' previous experience and 'gut feeling'. We decided to interview three people from the 20 or more applicants.

On the day of the interviews, the colleague with whom I was working was off sick and another colleague stepped in to assist. I had prepared a short list of questions that I wanted to ask. After preliminary introductions and trying to relax the candidates, I described the sort of work that they would be expected to perform in detail and then asked my questions:

- *What keyboard skills do you have?*

- *What projects, if any, have you been involved in at your current job?*

- *Why have you left your previous employers?*

- *What interests do you have?*

The final candidate's answers were quite short and guarded and it was becoming harder to assess her. About half way through the interview, in an effort to relax her and find out some general details, I said, 'I see that you are married, do you have any children?' She instantly replied, 'What difference does that make?' I assured her it didn't make any difference and that I was just making conversation, but she was obviously upset by the question. My colleague interrupted and tried to alleviate the situation by explaining that we had several members of the team who had children of all ages and we were just trying to determine what might be common ground. This did not help and the candidate continued to be defensive during the rest of the interview. It was as if she was looking for a hidden agenda behind every question. Finally, when asked if she had any questions, she was only interested in whether we did overtime and how many others I had asked whether they had children or not.

Two aspects of Jean's story attracted my attention. The first, of course, was the unfortunate unprepared question to the final candidate about whether she had children. The second aspect concerned the nature of her prepared questions and the type of data they might garner. These two types of question illustrate common problems in interviews. Jean says that her question about children was meant innocently to help break the ice with the interviewee. Many interviewers do this sort of thing and most of the time it helps the atmosphere of the interview. But occasionally, as in this case, the comment is taken badly and seen as containing more meaning than it was meant to have. Asking about children is a particularly sensitive area as interviewees may, correctly or incorrectly, assume that the interviewers are drawing inferences such as the increased likelihood of inordinate amounts of time off work due to the need to care for the children. In almost all circumstances, questions on this issue are likely to be sexist, as male and female answers may be interpreted differently. To prevent such problems arising, many interview panels develop a script that they do not move away from. Some will refrain from asking follow-up questions and may not answer interviewees' questions for fear of making a mistake. Obviously, there are many 'costs' to such rigid approaches and ultimately they can be self-defeating, with selected candidates refusing to work for such a formal and impersonal organisation.

Although prepared questions might reduce the risk of unlawful questions being posed (although Jean's fourth question illustrates how innocent-looking questions could become a minefield), it does not mean that they will be effective at assessing the candidates against the selection criteria. Jean's first question – 'What keyboard skills do you have?' – illustrates the problem. I imagine that there is a line in the selection criteria stressing the importance of keyboard skills, so the panel need to assess applicants' keyboard skills. But asking a question like this is a disaster waiting to happen. I can just hear the answer: 'I'm an expert with word processors and good with spreadsheets and databases. I'm also quite good with PowerPoint, e-mail and on the Internet.' Fine. What have we learnt? Simply that this applicant knows the names of a few computer software programs. Nothing is learnt about their keyboard skills. Sadly, such questions are typical of those asked by inexperienced interviewers.

The solution is easy. If it is not possible to test applicants' skills in these areas with tests, then questions should be framed that can only be answered by someone with the required skills. So I might ask, 'Explain to me how you would change the style sheet in a Word document' or 'How would you search for a company's financial details on the Internet?' Interviewers form bonds with interviewees and, as mentioned earlier, transfer positive or negative vibes from one answer to another. One way of correcting this bias is to ask questions that can only be answered if the interviewee has the required KSAOs, thereby providing 'objective' data that might count as evidence. It sounds rather pessimistic about the human spirit, but interviewers need to keep in mind that everything an interviewee says might be untrue or 'managed'.

ALUN'S STORY: SPARKS FLY

About a year ago, I, along with some others in my workplace, were called on to do interviews for general operative positions. The interviewing process we used was a panel, which consisted of two people, one from Human Resources (HR) and me. The candidates had already been interviewed by a recruitment agency. The interview we were carrying out was meant to be an informal one, which was just to be for our peace of mind that we were getting the right people from the recruitment agency. However, I wanted to make sure that I was well prepared and I produced a job specification. Because of the ever-changing environment in the electronics industry, I wanted to make sure that we were asking the right questions. The other person on the panel was a woman with a wealth of experience in recruitment, or so I thought. Her name was Sylvia and she had worked in many companies in a senior human resources role. She was well respected by her colleagues; this came about after a relatively short period. Although Sylvia had only been with the company for two months, people in her department looked up to her because of her experience.

We were to conduct 10 interviews that day. I met Sylvia at the start of the day and we found a room just off the reception area. The room had no windows and it was fairly dark. We had not booked a room in advance and this was all we could get.

The first candidate's name was Tim. He was a man in his mid-20s who seemed quite composed when I met him at reception. I always do this as I feel it puts the candidates at their ease; being interviewed can be a nerve-wracking experience at the best of times. I greeted Tim with 'Hello' and I thanked him for coming. He seemed quite composed and he smiled back as he said, 'Thanks for taking the time.' We chatted briefly on the way to the room where Sylvia was waiting. I asked, 'Did you have any trouble finding us?' The response was, 'No, Alun, it was fine.' I opened the door for Tim and introduced him to Sylvia. This is where I'm afraid it all started to go wrong. Sylvia did not even make an effort to stand up as Tim put his hand out to shake hers, and she didn't even look at Tim while I introduced him. Along with this, she had repositioned the chairs in my absence. Before I had left the room to go to the reception area for Tim, I had positioned the chairs in such a way that they would not become an obstacle. Sylvia had moved the chairs so that she was at the furthest point away from Tim.

'Do you want to move up here, Sylvia, a bit closer?' I asked.

'No, Alun, thank you. I want to take notes and I don't want people to see them.' I could not believe somebody could be so stupid. She said this right in front of Tim, who looked on in disbelief. I tried to make out that Sylvia was joking, but at that stage the damage was done and the tone was set for the short time we would spend together.

I explained to Tim that the interview was informal and that the notes Sylvia would be taking would just be used for reference and not to worry. 'The interview will be made up of three parts, Tim. I will ask you some questions about the company, what you have heard we do and so on.' He seemed a little more relaxed with this, so I felt he had probably done some research. 'Sylvia will then ask you some general questions, and at the end you can ask us anything you like about the role we are offering. How does that sound, Tim?'

Tim looked at me with a smile and said, 'That's fine, Alun.'

I proceeded to ask Tim a few questions about the company; he seemed to have a good understanding of what we did. While I was asking Tim these questions, Sylvia was writing notes furiously and without hiding it either. Tim did not seem too bothered, as he appeared to know he answered the questions well.

'It's very warm in here, isn't it?' he asked.

'It is actually, Tim, now that you mention it,' I replied. There was no air conditioning and we couldn't leave the door open as people walking by reception would distract us. So as a consolation I asked Tim if he wanted some water; I needed some myself and promised not to keep him too much longer. With that we proceeded with the interview.

Sylvia had a copy of Tim's CV and was looking at his job experience. 'I see you have a lot of experience in bar work,' she said.

Tim responded, 'Yes I have, Sylvia.'

'I see also you worked in London for some time. So did I,' Sylvia said. I felt maybe at last she was coming around. 'I had to get out of it though, I hated it and the people can be so rude and ignorant,' she continued. 'Why did you leave London, Tim?'

'I left because my parents were opening a bar in Ireland.'

'Your parents were coming home so. . . ?' asked Sylvia.

'No, my parents are English,' he replied. I could tell by his tone that he was not impressed with the line of questioning. 'What has that got to do with this role?' was his next question, and to be honest I was asking myself the same.

'Just making conversation,' Sylvia said. We then went through Tim's CV, which had been sent to us from the agency. Nothing I asked Tim about on his CV matched his answers. The CV said he had a diploma when he really had a degree, for example.

'These people are meant to be professionals and they have butchered my CV!' he roared. I asked him to calm down and that it was irrelevant what was down on the CV as he could explain the discrepancy. But Tim just did not relax after that and everything he said was in an angry tone. Every now and then he would give Sylvia a nasty look. Shortly thereafter I brought the interview to an end and thanked him for his time.

After this, I came back to the room and had a massive row with Sylvia. She could not believe I was questioning her interview technique. Tim was not hired, as I felt he was a fiery character who does not keep a cool head under pressure. I let the agency give him the feedback and apparently he abused the agency people as well. He also told them that he was considering legal action, as he felt the line of questioning was not in line with the position being offered and that he felt one of the people interviewing him didn't like the fact that his parents were English. Nothing came of this, and it was just as well as he may have had a case.

When I look back now I feel I was conscious of what was going on, but I had a horrible sick, uneasy feeling for a day or two afterwards. I tried to defuse what was a very turbulent situation, and I could not believe that somebody working in HR could have so little regard for a potential employee.

Interviews vary greatly between companies. The manner in which they are conducted varies from relaxed to rigid and from informal to formal. Neither extreme is any better than the other, nor is anything in the middle. But it helps interviewees if the interviewers adopt a reasonably consistent style that accords with the culture of the organisation, as this assists them in their assessment of what it will be like to work in the organisation. One explanation for the contrast in Alun and Sylvia's interviewing styles is Sylvia's newness to the company. She may have been acting in the way that was customary in her previous organisation. But judging from Alun's annoyance at her behaviour, it was unacceptable in this organisation.

For someone claiming to be an experienced interviewer, some of Sylvia's comments and questions are a little worrying. The phrase 'Just making conversation' seems to expose a degree of naivety. The line of questions about leaving London might be relevant, but her comments about rude and ignorant Londoners suggest a personal agenda rather than a thought-out line of questioning. She seems rudderless, which the interviewee noticed and challenged. But events may have given Sylvia the last laugh, as her meandering approach raised Tim's hackles and revealed a side of his personality that he would have preferred to keep hidden.

ISOBEL'S STORY: BLINDED BY THE LIGHT

My first job interview was an incident that was an extremely nerve-wracking exercise. When I walked into this room, all I could see were silhouettes of people. They were sitting with the light shining from behind their heads. I was temporarily blinded and could not see them. Once my eyes were accustomed to the brightness of the room, I managed to focus and immediately I noticed a pair of friendly and smiling faces, which helped to ease the tension a bit. I looked at the others; their eyes were doing their best, I thought at that time, to frighten me. However, I managed to stay on and went through the terrorising process of answering questions. What kept going through my mind was the fact that I needed to get the job that was on offer.

I must have stammered badly on countless occasions during the interview. I remembered many times wondering whether I was putting my answers across to them clearly and whether they understood me. I was so nervous and frightened that perspiration started to pour down from my forehead, hands and feet. Moreover, the panel must have thought I was hard of hearing, for I kept asking that they repeated themselves as they took it in turn to ask me questions. But it was all nerves. Nevertheless, I persevered with the interview, at the same time consoling myself with the thought that these people in front of me, asking me questions now and being very professional about the whole thing, must have had their turn and been through what I was being subjected to at that very moment.

In retrospect, my fear of the whole situation came about because of my fear of the unknown. I did not know who the interviewers were, or anything about them; whether they were understanding people, for instance. Do they have teenage children who would be looking for employment in the near future? Perhaps I could then appeal to their sense of parenthood. I knew this much, though, that they were going to ask questions regarding work. But this would seem an unfair thing to do to someone who has just left school. All I knew then about work was starting at a certain time in the morning, an hour's break for lunch and finishing off at a certain time in the evening. I had a rough idea of what the organisation stood for, but I did not know the intricate details of how the organisation was run.

At the time, I was enveloped with an uncomfortable feeling of negativity. The feelings of uneasiness, nervousness and stress, which I felt during the few days before the incident and on the actual day itself, were incredible. I could not compare it with anything since. There were times when I thought of withdrawing from the interview, but I did not have a valid reason and this chance might not come around again. Also, I did not want to be known as a coward. It was a great relief when things were over.

Of all the stories I received, none captured the nervousness of the interviewee as well as Isobel's. This was her first job interview and she did not know what to expect. She mentions the uneasiness, nervousness and stress she felt before the interview. Interviews can be traumatic affairs at the best of times, but when the world of work is a mystery to you, the job interview is a step into the unknown. When Isobel became blinded by the light, her language evokes that more commonly used to describe torture scenes: 'I looked at the others; their eyes were doing their best, I thought at that time, to frighten me. However, I managed to stay on and went through the terrorising process of answering questions.' She depicts herself as the tortured soul who 'needed the job' and who had to hold out until the end of the interrogation: 'There were times when I thought of withdrawing from the interview, but I did not have a valid reason and this chance might not come around again.'

Isobel's description of her physical reaction to being interviewed is very graphic. She mentions stammering, difficulty hearing, and the perspiration on her forehead, hands and feet. Clearly, she was very aware of all this happening, which must be very off-putting when trying to present your best side to the interview panel. More than being off-putting, it must influence what she thinks and this will translate into what she says. The interview panel must also be aware of her nervousness, wonder what is causing it and what inferences to draw. Should they feel sympathy for someone in an unusual or stressful situation or should they judge her harshly for her inability to cope with pressure? Isobel's reaction is more extreme than most, but it highlights how stressful the selection environment can be. In such situations, how should selectors judge the behaviour and utterances of interviewees? How relevant to performance on the job is performance in this artificial and surreal world?

Nervousness and stress are not confined to interviewees. As the final story in this chapter illustrates, interviewers have their worries too.

JEREMY'S STORY: MUDDLING THROUGH

I work in a prison and run the health-care facility. We had built a new house block and were expecting 120 new inmates. I was assisted by two civilian nurses and one health care officer. I was told I could recruit one more nurse to cope with the influx. I felt elated that my department was going to get a 25% increase in staff and another pair of skilled hands to tend our ever-demanding patients. Although I'd never done it before, I didn't panic about the recruitment process; we are a large organisation with a well-organised personnel department. I could leave it to them.

But the questions seemed endless. Where did I want to advertise? What did I want in the advertisement? What type of nurse did I require (general or mental)? Then, my own doubts and inexperience raised questions. What type of person did I require? What qualities should I be looking for? What qualifications, skills and attributes should I look for? How would they fit into the existing team and work pattern?

As I sifted through the application to produce a shortlist, I wondered what I should look for. They all seemed suitable to me. My own line manager helped me shortlist four applicants. A date for interviews was set and now I was worried: I had to sit on the interview panel as the specialist member. The day arrived and I was more anxious than any of the candidates. What if my questions were not appropriate? What if I gave the wrong impression? And I was going to be their boss.

That was two months ago and plainly I muddled through. Clearly, my fears were exaggerated by a situation for which I was totally unprepared. With no training or experience in recruiting, I was thrust into the process because the organisation saw me as the specialist. Although having worked in the prison service for 20 years, I knew next to nothing about recruiting civilians.

Jeremy's story reminds me of Sarah's: his is also a tale of an unprepared and inexperienced recruiter thrown in at the deep end. Where the stories differ is in the degree of nervousness and self-doubt that Jeremy experienced. He appreciated the importance of his role and knew he did not possess the necessary skills. When confronted with real applications, he did not know how to assess them. Fortunately, he had the good sense to ask for help.

I found myself thinking about Jeremy's anxiety over sitting on the interview panel. He readily confesses his degree of nervousness and thinks he may be more anxious than any of the candidates. He has a big decision to make and he does not want to make a mistake. He is so aware of his own shortcomings that I wonder what he will be thinking about during the interview. Will he be as attentive to the interviewees as he should be? What happens if he thinks he makes a mistake? What happens if he is confronted by a candidate as nervous as Isobel? As I dwelt on these questions, I found myself returning to the nature of the selection environment. It is a nerve-wracking and emotional place: a place where people think about themselves and how they come across. It is unlike most other work environments that people experience. It is populated by actors playing roles. And the decisions made during these episodes are vital to all concerned. I wonder how relevant selection in such highly charged, surreal and egotistic environments can be to the real world of work.

THINKING ON

1. How long does it take to 'know' an applicant? How much data do you need before you can make an accurate assessment of someone?

2. How would you decide between two applicants who both appear to satisfy the selection criteria?

3. If someone is obviously unsuitable for the job, should the interviewers still try to surface all the information they have on the person against the selection criteria?

4. *'Reports that say that something hasn't happened are always interesting to me, because as we know, there are known knowns; there are things we know we know. We also know there are known unknowns; that is to say we know there are some things we do not know. But there are also unknown unknowns – the ones we don't know we don't know'* (Rumsfeld, 2002). How does this quote relate to the data gathered by interviewers?

5. There are also unknown knowns: things we do not know that we know. How might these be relevant in selection interviews?

6. Why do interviewers ask questions like, 'What keyboard skills do you have?' How can they be avoided?

7. Everything that someone says in an interview might be untrue. What constitutes useful information?

8. Should interviewers try to put interviewees at ease? What can interviewers do to help put interviewees at ease?

9. Does the interviewer have a responsibility to help interviewees perform at their best in the interview?

10. To what extent should interviewers be in harmony with each other? Does the 'good cop, bad cop' approach have a place in selection interviewing?

11. Put yourself in the position of an interviewer. What inferences would you draw about an interviewee who was clearly very nervous?

12. Can the assessment of people during recruitment and selection episodes ever better the assessment of people doing 'real' work?

READING ON

The interview dominates the recruitment and selection literature. It has attracted a large amount of research interest and there is also a large 'professional' literature that offers practical advice to interviewers. Perhaps the primary question is: Are unstructured interviews (the sort we have been looking at in this chapter) any good at selecting people who will perform well in the job? For decades researchers believed the answer to this question was a definite 'No'. Hunter and Hunter's (1984) meta-analysis is commonly cited as the apotheosis of this stream of research. However, since the mid-1980s refinements in meta-analysis methods (i.e. ways of combining studies to produce a more definitive answer) suggest that the unstructured interview is nowhere near as bad as people once thought. In fact, it might even be quite a good selection technique (Wiesner & Cronshaw, 1988). Interestingly, Wiesner and Cronshaw (1988) looked at the interview type and found that structured interviews (these are not just prepared questions but much more elaborate forms of structure involving scenarios and the empirical testing of questions prior to their use) were better than unstructured interviews. They also found that panel interviews (i.e. two or more people interviewing together) were better at predicting future work performance than one-to-one interviews.

If you are interested in exploring some of the themes related to halo and horns effects, decision making or relationships between interviewers and interviewees, I would recommend two books devoted to the subject of the interview. Eder and Ferris (1989) contains a collection of essays on the interview that is particularly strong on decision making. Dipboye (1992) is more of a textbook and provides the most authoritative account of research into the interview. All other recruitment and selection textbooks devote chapters to interviews, but these are probably the best specialist sources.

If you want to improve your own interview skills, naturally I recommend my own book, *Finding and Keeping the Right People* (Billsberry, 2000). One of the strengths of the book is that it shows you how to analyse jobs and how to construct your selection criteria. In addition, it shows you how you can 'select for fit' in a structured and defendable way. Another recommendation is *Successful Selection Interviewing* by Anderson and Shackleton (1993). This book is an interesting hybrid between textbook and self-help book that offers a thorough and informative treatment of the subject. I would also advise you to have a look at the non-academically grounded books. Some of these are very good indeed. My favourite is Beatty's *Interviewing and Selecting High Performers* (1994).

You might also want to look at interviewing from the interviewee's perspective. There are libraries full of books giving advice to the interviewee on how to answer the 'toughest' questions. Hodgson's *Brilliant Answers to Tough Interview Questions* (2002), Yate's *Great Answers to Tough Interview Questions* (1992) and DeLuca's *Best Answers to the 201 Most Frequently Asked Interview Questions* (1997) are all worth a look.

REFERENCES

Anderson, N. & Shackleton, V. (1993) *Successful Selection Interviewing*, Oxford: Blackwell.

Beatty, R. H. (1994) *Interviewing and Selecting High Performers*, New York: John Wiley & Sons Ltd.

Billsberry, J. (2000) *Finding and Keeping the Right People: How to Recruit Motivated Employees*, 2nd edn, London: Prentice Hall.

DeLuca, M. J. (1997) *Best Answers to the 201 Most Frequently Asked Interview Questions*, New York: McGraw-Hill.

Dipboye, R. L. (1992) *Selection Interviews: Process Perspectives*, Cincinnati, OH: South-Western Publishing.

Eder, R. W. & Ferris, G. R. (eds) (1989) *The Employment Interview: Theory, Research, and Practice*, Newbury Park, CA: Sage.

Hodgson, S. (2002) *Brilliant Answers to Tough Interview Questions*, Harlow: Pearson Education.

Hunter, J. E. & Hunter, R. F. (1984) 'Validity and utility of alternate predictors of job performance', *Psychological Bulletin*, 96: 72–98.

Rumsfeld, D. H. (2002) Department of Defense news briefing, February 12.

Wiesner, W. H. & Cronshaw, S. F. (1988) 'A meta-analytic investigation of the impact of interview format and degree of structure on the validity of the employment interview', *Journal of Occupational Psychology*, 61: 275–90.

Yate, M. J. (1992) *Great Answers to Tough Interview Questions*, 3rd edn, London: Kogan Page.

CHAPTER 4

Structure

In the previous chapter, I related six stories that featured unstructured interviews. Although academic research has shown that unstructured interviews are not as bad at predicting future job performance as once thought, they are by no means perfect. One of the failings of the unstructured interview is the relatively haphazard way in which data is gathered. More often than not, the use of unstructured interviews causes interviewers to have uneven data on candidates; that is, they know about the related skills of one candidate but not that much about their motivation, and vice versa for another candidate. To rectify this situation, some selectors choose to add structure to their assessment of candidates so that the same information is gathered on every applicant. With similar data on every applicant, selectors are better able to assess the applicants against the selection criteria as well as being better able to compare 'like with like'. Some selectors go so far that they exclude all data that has not been introduced during the selection process in order to create a 'level playing field' that is thought to be fair to all concerned. However, I fear that this 'higher common denominator' approach frequently translates into a 'lowest common denominator' approach in the hands of some selectors, as the stories in later chapters will show.

From a practical point of view, when selectors add structure to their selection practices, it usually means that they have thought quite deeply about what they are about to do. It takes a lot of time and thought to put together an assessment centre or analogous test. Developing a rigorous structured interview also takes a great deal of effort. In the previous story we saw how Jean developed some interview questions such as 'What keyboard skills do you have?' This question might be prepared, but it has a 'back of a fag packet' quality to it. Properly structured interviews are much more elaborate affairs that employ piloted or tested questions that expose applicants' KSAOs.

Another way to increase the structure of selection systems is to include other forms of assessment. For example, if you want to discover how good someone's keyboard skills are, why not ask them to do something at a keyboard? The results of tests such as these tend to be used for screening applicants. That is, they are used to determine whether someone should be considered for employment, rather than in the final decision of whom to employ, which usually rests with an interview. In reviewing the stories I was sent, I was astonished by how few references there were to analogous or other forms of tests (e.g. personality, intelligence) in selection processes. Perhaps they do not register in people's consciousness and are not thought worthy of a mention, or perhaps they are not used as often as some people think; there is a known trend away from 'objective' tests of all forms due to the adverse impact they can be shown to have on protected groups.

It was more common to receive stories about assessment centres, both for recruitment and staff development. The words 'assessment centre' conjure up a typical two-day residential assessment at a plush hotel or training centre, where 16 or so applicants are subjected to a range of tests including psychometrics, an in-tray exercise, a group exercise and a series of interviews. But an 'assessment centre' can be any selection process where a number of techniques are combined to provide an 'all-round' assessment of candidates. One of the greatest challenges for selectors is the dilemma of making decisions about applicants when the different tests give contrary indicators, as they invariably seem to do.

BRITANY'S STORY: A TOUGH LESSON

On entering the interview room, I discovered that the panel was made up of six men, seated formally round a table. There was a seat for the candidate some three or four feet from the table. The chair introduced each panel member by name and title. The interview consisted of a list of prepared questions, asked in blocks by each of the interviewers bar one, who I had been told was an independent assessor. The questions mainly related to NHS supplies theory and practice; many of them required a short, factual answer. No supplementary questions were asked.

I found the size of the panel and the formal questioning intimidating. I instantly forgot the names of those on the panel, and wished that they had nameplates. I waited in vain for some questions related to my personal experience. Although I had considerable practical experience of NHS supplies, my theoretical knowledge was limited. On a couple of occasions I admitted I didn't understand the question and the panel politely moved on to the next question without making an attempt to clarify what I had not understood. No encouragement was given to expand on any answers. After 10 minutes, I knew I had failed and that I was being unintentionally humiliated. I wondered why I had been asked to attend the interview.

In retrospect, I can see that I was under-prepared for the interview and was not experienced or mature enough to take on the job. The result was that I quickly felt intimidated, insecure and defensive. I now feel that the advertisement and information pack should have been designed in such a way as to deter me from applying; particularly given that the usual practice is to shortlist all internal candidates regardless of suitability.

Needless to say, my application was unsuccessful. The short-term effect of this on the NHS was that they picked the right person for the job. I, however, felt humiliated by how poorly I had performed. I stopped applying for promotion and started looking for positions outside the NHS. However, there were some positive effects for me. I learnt to prepare better for interviews and to find out more about a post before applying.

Britany experienced the full force of a structured interview. In fact it sounds more like an examination than a job interview. This panel had developed some well-thought-out questions that could only be answered by people with the required knowledge. This sort of structured interview is a very different type of event to the unstructured and semi-structured interviews that are commonplace in recruitment and selection. The power of this approach, as Britany herself points out, is that 'they picked the right person for the job'. Perhaps it would be better to say that they picked someone with excellent knowledge of NHS supplies theory and practice. This is an important qualification, because one of the drawbacks of this approach is that it can over-emphasise knowledge and skills and under-emphasise softer issues such as interpersonal skills and psychological states. Structured interviews can include questions on such matters, but the inclusion of this kind of question after such a hard grilling is often problematic given the extreme changes required in atmosphere, interaction and attitude. Nevertheless, structured interviews such as the one described by Britany have been shown to be highly effective at selecting people in particular types of jobs.

It is to Britany's credit that she was able to learn from this experience and recognise the need to prepare for interviews. Sadly though, it seems to have had an influence in her decision to leave the NHS. The interview made her aware of her shortcomings in relation to NHS supplies theory and the difficulty she would have in getting promoted. Her reaction illustrates an interesting paradox regarding the accurate assessment of internal candidates. She experienced a selection process that has a high level of procedural justice; in other words, she viewed the process used to assess candidates as fair. She is happy to admit that this selection process discovered omissions in her knowledge and skills and it made clear the level of competence that would be necessary to gain promotion. The initial thinking of a person in this position runs something like this: 'I was at fault. I did not have the skills. Who am I kidding? I'm not very good.' The initial reaction may be a sense of uselessness, insecurity, lower self-esteem and defensiveness. Once the person moves out of this slough of despair and self-pity, the thinking will probably change: 'Why am I so useless? Why was I not developed properly? Why was I allowed to put myself in this situation? ' We see this reflected in Britany's comments when she says, 'I now feel that the advertisement and information pack should have been designed in such a way as to deter me from applying.' Hence, there is a paradox in rigorous selection: the better the selection process, the more failed applicants attribute failure to their weaknesses. And this can have serious consequences such as those described by Britany. The irony is that when selection procedures are seen as weak, ineffective or unfair, the more applicants attribute the reasons for their failure to external causes and away from themselves.

STEVE'S STORY: A TESTING TIME

I felt I was ready for a change of job; an advertisement in a leading electronics publication for the position of area sales manager stood out as particularly promising. Applications were invited in writing accompanied by a CV. I duly responded. I received a call from the recruitment company a few days later; this took the form of a mini-interview and lasted about 15 minutes. I was invited to attend an interview with the recruitment company. After discussing my background and why I wanted the job, I was given a psychometric test. This took about 20 minutes and appeared very obscure. The meeting seemed to go well and the interviewer felt he could recommend that I attend the more formal company interview.

I met the field sales manager at the company's head office. He had the results of my psychometric test and we discussed these at length, particularly my apparent strengths and weaknesses. These were very accurate and after about one hour we moved to the managing director's office. I decided to make a presentation about my plans and objectives for the area I would be responsible for. This seemed to go down well and my confidence was high. During the interview, it seemed to me that a product specialist position would be perfect for my skills and experience. I did comment that the position would be interesting should it become available.

I left the interview quite sure that I had made a good impression and felt sure I would at least be shortlisted. I was disappointed to discover that the job had been offered to an employee of the company's main distributor. They felt that as he knew the company through regular contact, he would be best suited; otherwise I would have been successful. This seemed an odd reason, given the various and expensive methods used during the selection process.

Ironically within two months of this, the product specialist's job became vacant. I was invited to attend a very informal interview and subject to me accepting relocation to the South East, the position was mine. No other candidates were interviewed.

Steve's story illustrates one of the main ways in which psychometric tests are used in recruitment and selection: to assess particular qualities of applicants that are followed up in an interview. Used in this way, they allow selectors to explore key features of the individual that are known to be relevant to the job. Steve does not say what the test he took measured, just that it 'appeared very obscure'. He seems somewhat indifferent to the test and apparently took it in his stride. This selector followed best-practice guidelines and gave feedback to Steve on the test. This was well received and Steve notes that the test's ability to surface his strengths and weaknesses was 'very accurate'. Despite the accuracy of the testing, the selection panel did what most panels do and made their decision at the end of an interview; the test data was probably used for interview prompts, to check for major mismatches and to verify subjective impressions.

In the end, this panel chose someone they already knew. They chose the 'safe' option. They chose a person who understood their business better. Applicants from closely related firms and internal applicants have an advantage in interviews because their knowledge of the industry, the market environment, the business culture and so forth makes them sound informed and well researched. They have disadvantages, as we will see later, but this knowledge advantage can play an important role in selection decisions, as appeared to happen in this case.

The tone of Steve's story is interesting. It has a 'matter of fact' quality to it; it reads like a dispassionate chronicle of events. Even when he misses out on the job through an apparent unfairness, he takes it in his stride and does not get inflamed. Perhaps his subsequent recruitment by the same firm has mollified his temper, perhaps he is naturally sanguine, or perhaps the professional design of the selection system with its multiple tests and 'accurate' assessment of him offset any annoyance. Sadly, not everyone is so calm in the face of selection tests. In the following story, applicants react badly to selection tests that exist only in their own minds.

LIAM'S STORY: THE GREAT ESCAPE

Since joining my current employer a year ago as a corporate management graduate trainee, I have been actively involved in the whole graduate recruitment process. I have helped interview prospective graduate employees, aided in the running of assessment centres and attended a graduate forum at which the experiences of our recruitment process were described and commented on by this year's intake in order to identify areas that require improvement. This story is about an event that occurred at the assessment centre where I was selected.

The assessment centre represents the final hurdle for all prospective graduate employees. To be invited to the final centre, the candidate has survived the application form reduction, passed an initial screening interview and probably an in-depth structured interview as well. Although intended to be challenging, the assessment centre is not designed to try to catch candidates unawares, or to test them to the point of breaking. There is plenty of scope for candidates to demonstrate their talents and a great deal can be prepared in advance.

Prior to attending my own assessment centre, I was sent a timetable highlighting the times at which I would be carrying out the various parts of the final assessment. For example, I knew that I would have a panel interview on the second day of the centre and that I was to give a presentation entitled 'The challenges facing the Leisure Industry'. This timetable answered a lot of my questions.

The first session of my own assessment centre went very well; all the candidates seemed to be quite relaxed. We were invited to an evening meal where we had the chance to meet various current employees whom we could quiz about working in the company. This meal marked the end of the first day's activities, but everyone had at the back of their mind that the group presentation was the first event of the following day. Nevertheless, all the candidates met up in the hotel foyer and proceeded to catch taxis to the chosen restaurant. On arrival at the restaurant, it was discovered that not all the candidates had actually caught taxis. Some had been left behind at the hotel. Arrangements were made for the others to travel to the restaurant, but they were inevitably some 30 minutes later than the others. The rest of the event went well, and as far as I was concerned, nobody seemed too bothered about the incident as no comments were made.

However, during breakfast the following morning, it became apparent that some of the candidates – indeed, all those who had missed the initial taxi run to the restaurant – had left the assessment centre in the middle of the night leaving only a note to say why they had departed. We were later told they had written that they felt the taxi run was part of the assessment centre and that their apparent failure to make it to a restaurant was likely to mean they would fail the assessment centre.

My initial emotions were those of amazement and surprise that they could have felt so strongly that they had to leave in the middle of the night. I could not believe that they honestly thought the taxi ride was part of the assessment. The next set of emotions I felt revolved around feelings of guilt and anger that they had acted in this way. By only leaving a short note, I felt they had acted rather rudely towards the company, and they had not fully contemplated the action they were taking, as well as the effort the company had spent in order to arrange the whole assessment centre. I was even asked during my own panel interview what I thought of the actions of the other candidates, at which time I had no hesitance in replying that I was amazed and that I thought it, at the very least, inconsiderate and rather rude.

The short-term impact of the incident centred on the assessors rallying to reassure the other candidates that the restaurant meal was not an assessed exercise and verifying that none of the others had the intention to walk out imminently. The timetable of events for the day obviously had to be rearranged, but even at this early stage it was evident that the assessors were rather concerned that they had given the image that the candidates were being assessed on every little thing they said.

In the longer term, and certainly after the beginning of my employment with the company, there has been a more concentrated effort to involve the newly employed graduates in the recruitment process. For example, at every assessment centre a graduate is always present to answer any questions the candidates might have and to act as an intermediary between the candidates and the assessors.

Liam's perspective as a 'poacher turned gamekeeper' provides a fascinating insight into the dynamics of an assessment centre. He realises the impact the centre has on its attendees who are suspicious of everything that happens (or does not). They fear that any mistake will condemn their application, so much so that simply missing a taxi to a restaurant results in applicants absconding in the dead of night.

Now on the other side of the fence, Liam is able to tackle some of the apparently unfounded fears of the applicants by having recent graduate entrants attend the centres to answer questions and act as an intermediary between the attendees and the assessors. This is an admirable step, but what are its chances in this climate of fear, mistrust and suspicion? It seems to me that the graduate entrants will simply be viewed with suspicion. Are they there to trap the unwary or the naïve? Are they just other assessors? Are they wolves in sheep's clothing?

Liam tells us that the graduates were not being assessed at the evening meal and that they had nothing to fear: 'I could not believe that they honestly thought the taxi ride was part of the assessment.' With Liam's insider status we can be confident that the evening meal was genuinely an opportunity to meet other employees and that no assessment was taking place at the dinner. However, I find myself wondering who is kidding who here. The evening meal may not be a formal part of the assessment, but the assessors would not be human if they did not pick up some insights about the applicants during the dinner. Even if they consciously try to distance themselves from noting behaviours and comments, it is inevitable that their impressions of the applicants will be influenced, albeit very subtly, by the experience. If the assessors were not present at the dinner, it will still have an influence on the assessment processes, as the interaction between participants will shape and change behaviours. This is important if team or group activities form part of the assessment. Perhaps they are right to be wary of this informal moment in the assessment centre.

Liam's indignation towards the escapees deserves some comment. Are they the ones at fault here? They have been subject to a process that has led them to believe that missing a taxi is sufficient to default them. Such was their dejection that they fled the scene in the middle of the night. This is quite an extreme reaction and does not reflect well on the escapees, but I want to point the finger at the company. Its staff designed and ran the assessment centre, they assessed applicants and chose whom to invite and they were responsible for the safety of people at the venue. Although they are trying to rectify the situation with the graduate advisers, perhaps they need to look more closely at how the applicants' misperceptions were created rather than blame them for the calamity.

THINKING ON

1. Should selectors be concerned with the paradox of rigorous selection? If yes, how can they reduce its impact on those applicants whose weaknesses

they ruthlessly expose? If no, how can selectors effectively switch from questioning of applicants' knowledge and skills to softer issues in an effective manner?

2. Would you want to join an organisation that runs its recruitment and selection processes in a clinical fashion? To what extent can you accept being the target of tests?

3. Should a selection process be 'impersonal'?

4. What would you regard as the acceptable limits of selection testing? Would you accept having your blood tested? Would you accept having your DNA sampled? Would you accept being hooked up to a lie detector?

5. Should selectors try to improve the climate of trust between applicants and themselves?

6. What can selectors do to reduce the amount of impression management that applicants indulge in?

READING ON

Structured interviews come in many forms. The best known are the pattern behaviour description interview (Janz, 1982) and the situational interview (Latham *et al.*, 1980). The Pattern Behaviour Description Interview assesses four types of data from interviewees: (1) verifiable information about past achievements, (2) descriptions of current and past work and jobs, (3) self-reports on their strengths and weaknesses, and (4) descriptions of work and non-work experiences. The situational interview presents interviewees with scenarios that are developed from critical incidents in the job. There are many other forms of structured interviews. Cook's text, *Personnel Selection* (2004), provides a thorough review of these methods, while Heneman and Judge (2005) offers advice on how to develop your own structured interview should you be so inclined.

Assessment centres are covered in most recruitment and selection textbooks. Interestingly, while it is natural to think of an assessment centre as a two-day battery of tests in a training centre or hotel, the technical definition of an assessment centre is the use of two or more selection tests at the same stage of selection. This definition is important, because it highlights the difficulties of combining the results of two or more tests. Good books on assessment centres include Ballantyne and Povah (2004), Sawardekar (2002) and Woodruffe (2007), which tend to take a practical approach. You should refer to a good recruitment and selection textbook (e.g. Heneman & Judge, 2005) for information on academic studies of the effectiveness and impact of assessment centres.

REFERENCES

Ballantyne, I. & Povah, N. (2004) *Assessment and Development Centres*, 2nd edn, London: Gower.

Cook, M. (2004) *Personnel Selection: Adding Value through People,* 4th edn, Chichester: John Wiley & Sons Ltd.

Heneman, H. G. III & Judge, T. A. (2005) *Staffing Organizations,* 5th edn, Mendota House, WI: Irwin McGraw-Hill.

Janz, T. (1982) 'Initial comparisons of patterned behaviour description interviews versus unstructured interviews', *Journal of Applied Psychology*, 67: 577–80.

Latham, G. P., Saari, L. M., Pursell, E. D. & Campion, M. A. (1980) 'The situational interview', *Journal of Applied Psychology*, 65: 422–7.

Sawardekar, N. (2002) *Assessment Centres: Identifying Potential and Developing Competency*, London: Sage.

Woodruffe, C. (2007) *Development and Assessment Centres: Identifying and Developing Competence*, 4th edn, London: Human Assets.

PART II

The Applicant's Perspective

Recruitment and selection form a linear and rational process. This begins when a need to recruit is sensed. Once it is agreed that there is a need to recruit someone new, an analysis of the role should take place with a view to understanding the factors that contribute to success. Applications are invited and sifted, the shortlisted applicants are assessed more thoroughly, and the person who best satisfies the criteria is offered the job. This linear and rational paradigm underpins almost all research and practical prescriptions in Europe and North America.

This linear approach assumes that recruitment and selection are mainly about how the organisation makes decisions on whom to offer jobs to. Of course, this is a vital aspect of the episode, but such is the focus on making the right selection decision in a fair manner that other important considerations get forgotten or downplayed. Two of these considerations are the facts that applicants also make decisions, and that applicants' experience during recruitment and selection shapes their subsequent relationship with their employer. The stories in this section remind me how important these two considerations are because when selectors get it wrong, applicants walk away or start work with a negative mindset.

An interesting aspect of recruitment and selection episodes is how memorable they are for applicants. People remember these experiences. Perhaps this is because applicants are particularly keen to pick up on anything – sometimes incredibly minor things – that informs them about the organisation, the job and the people they will be working with. Not surprisingly therefore, these episodes are a very strong force shaping the successful applicant's psychological contract: 'individual beliefs, shaped by the organization, regarding terms of an exchange agreement between individuals and their organization' (Rousseau, 1995, p. 9). These psychological contracts shape subsequent behaviour and failure to attend to the way in which these are being shaped can have powerful and unhelpful consequences.

The stories in this section take the perspective of the applicant and explore the impact of recruitment and selection on applicants. Why do people need the job? What impact does failing to get the job have? How are they treated in the process? How do they evaluate fairness? The first set of stories explores the way internal applicants feel about having to compete against external applicants and vice versa.

REFERENCE

Rousseau, D. M. (1995) *Psychological Contracts in Organizations*, Thousand Oaks, CA: Sage.

CHAPTER 5

Source

In addition to my qualitative analysis of the stories in this book, I was able to retrieve some quantitative data. One piece of quantitative data I was able to glean was the source of applicants. Whereas applicants did not always know or reveal where other applicants were from, more often than not selectors gave away this information (see Table 5.1).

Table 5.1 Composition of the applicant pools

Composition	Occurrence	Percentage
Internal applicants only	20	16%
External applicants only	59	48%
Both internal and external applicants	40	33%
Uncategorisable	4	3%

Several aspects of these data warrant comment. First, the source of applicants was not identifiable in just four of the selectors' stories. This seems a very low figure, especially given that the students' courses made no mention whatsoever of the internal and external split of applicants. It seems that selectors see the source of applicants as something worthy of note, perhaps as an important division that is essential to the telling of their recruitment and selection stories. The second aspect of these figures that prompts comment is the substantial size of all three categories. While this percentage split cannot be taken as typical of recruitment practice in Britain – the study was not designed as a reliable survey of this question – it does suggest that each of the three categories is commonly found.

Most advice to organisational selectors when they find themselves with applicant pools containing a mix of internal and external candidates is to treat everyone the same. By creating a 'level playing field', the hope is that this is seen as fair to all applicants, as it allows everyone an equal opportunity to present themselves at their best. However, as the stories in this chapter demonstrate, such simple advice fails to recognise the complexity of occasions when internal and external applicants find themselves in competition against one another.

LINDA'S STORY: MAKING UP THE NUMBERS

This report describes a series of incidents that occurred when I was short-listed and interviewed at a national non-profit-making organisation with 21 branches throughout England.

The interview started 50 minutes late, with no explanation other than a terse 'they're running a bit late' from the receptionist on arrival. I waited in the busy reception area; no refreshments or facilities were offered. The receptionist was busy and there was no conversation. I began to wonder whether a mistake had been made or I had been inadvertently missed out.

Eventually, I was shown, without an apology for the delay, into a small, long, narrow room. During the interview I was asked questions about the size of the budget I managed. Despite the answers being on my application form, the questioner showed disappointment with my answers. During my presentation another interviewer shuffled papers and read other application forms. This not only seemed discourteous, but was off-putting and did not help me perform well. Afterwards I wished I had stopped at this point and offered to leave, as I felt I was obviously not what they wanted. At the end of the interview I was asked whether I had any questions about the organisation, but these were answered in a perfunctory manner.

I came away thinking that the decision had been made before I was interviewed. I did not feel I had had a fair opportunity to show my skills and experience. My overall impression was that I had been invited to interview to make up numbers and that the job was already earmarked for an internal candidate. After two days I was told the post had indeed been offered to an internal candidate. I was not surprised, but was annoyed about the time that my research, preparation and interview had taken and that I had been treated so discourteously. It took five weeks of chasing before the expenses I had been offered arrived, which compounded the sense of grievance. I was offered feedback, but the person responsible did not return my three telephone calls.

Linda was far from happy about her selection experience with this organisation. She felt like she was applying for a job to 'make up numbers'; a job she never had a chance of getting. Several factors suggested this to her: the missing directions to the venue, inattention during her presentation, questions about things that were already answered by data on her application form, perfunctory answers to her questions, delays in getting expenses to her, and the fact that the job was offered to an internal candidate. All of these factors combined to create the impression that her application was a distraction from the main event.

Linda, of course, may be completely wrong in her assessment of the inevitability of the outcome. She might just have performed poorly and quickly lost the interest of the panel. But in one way this is irrelevant. What matters is Linda's perception of events. She believed that the organisation had wasted her time and never intended to give her a real chance to compete for the vacancy. Linda's story is not an unusual one. Many of the stories I received from external candidates who were competing against internal people felt they were at a severe disadvantage. Some simply felt disadvantaged by a combination of the panel's increased knowledge of internal candidates and internal candidates' better suitability for the role based on their understanding of the organisation, the terminology, ways of doing things, insider information and acquaintance with selectors.

Other storytellers shared Linda's belief that their application was a complete waste of time and that decisions had already been made against them. Most of these people were applying to public sector and not-for-profit organisations such as councils, charities, government agencies and further and higher education establishments. In the 1990s and early 2000s, organisations such as these tended to favour the practice of 'benchmarking' all senior (and many more junior) appointments. In practice, this benchmarking entailed opening up all vacancies to both internal and external applicants. The idea was that this would reduce nepotism, ensure that only suitably qualified people were promoted, improve access to jobs for people with disabilities or other protected groups, and audit the KSAOs of the organisation. Unfortunately, in many circumstances external benchmarking of vacancies that would normally have been filled through promotion processes wasted a lot of people's time, especially that of external applicants. Ironically, some organisations used external benchmarking to get around rigorous internal promotion procedures, because it was easier to show that an internal candidate was the 'best applicant' of a shortlist of four than to demonstrate to a panel that their work had reached a particular standard. Able internal applicants do have some considerable advantages over external candidates as they have a track record of success with the organisation, an understanding of the culture and well-developed networks. External applicants believe and expect that these factors reduce their chances. In many circumstances they are correct.

All is not doom and gloom for the external candidate, though. When up against a good internal candidate, the external applicant is an unknown quantity. The panel members realise that they would be making a brave decision not to appoint someone they know is good and instead import someone about whom they know very little. However, when the internal candidates appear weak, the tide turns and external candidates have some powerful advantages. They are usually able to mask weaknesses and shortcomings. They are able to boost their own influence over successes. They are something new and different; 'the grass is always greener on the other side of the fence'. They may be attractive because they are employed by someone else and they may be perceived to bring freshness and new ideas into the organisation. In such circumstances, being an external applicant will be an advantage.

FATIMA'S STORY: JUST A FORMALITY

When I started working as a personal assistant to one of the senior managers in a public-sector organisation on a temporary basis, I received little by way of induction; I was on a temporary contract and had a scant job description. As the personal assistant to the MD I had to deal with a lot of administration and clerical work of the department, even though it wasn't in my so-called job description.

A similar job to my own was advertised in the local newspaper. It invited candidates for the position, requesting them to send a copy of their CV. I was responsible for placing the advertisement and sending out the information pack, which included a job description and job specification. Since I had become familiar with the organisation and was interested in the post itself, I decided to apply for the position. The MD informed me that according to the company's recruitment policy, I needed to apply for the post like any other candidate outside the organisation.

The most negative aspects about this episode were that on the day of the interviews I was asked to take the candidates into the interviewing panel, even though I was a candidate myself. Also, I kept thinking about the test that I was expected to do. I did not mind so much about the interview itself, but I found the test a bit of an insult to me. I felt I had already gone through the testing stage through my trial period with this organisation; the MD always praised my work and had said that she was very pleased with my performance. When I asked why I had to do the test, she said it was, 'just a formality'.

I felt disappointed because, despite the MD's comments, she did not trust my competence. At the same time, I was thinking that employers always took the feelings of their employees for granted. They think they have the right to treat employees in any way they see fit. With all these feelings of hurt and disappointment, I finally went through some skill tests, which were specially designed to see how one would tackle difficult situations. During them I kept thinking that I had already gone through all these tests and the MD is fully aware of my competence and capabilities. And I was thinking: What happens if I don't do well in my test – is she going to get rid of me?

I could hear the MD and the other woman on the interviewing panel going through the discussions they had earlier with the candidates and were laughing loudly. However, when my interview time came and I was asked to go in, they both looked very cheerful. I was told that I had been successful and they offered me the position. At this point I was not interested in working for this organisation any more, turned down their offer and left the organisation.

Should an internal applicant's track record with a company count for nothing? Should they be forced to prove themselves from fresh? Should they be treated like someone with whom the company has no relationship at all? Are the results from a selection test better than an established record of performance? What is the impact of having to apply for a promotion (or, in Fatima's case, a permanent position) on an existing employee's motivation, commitment, reputation and confidence? These are the sorts of questions that Fatima's story raises.

Just as Linda's story represented many others in a similar vein from external applicants, Fatima's story is representative of an even bigger pile of stories from internal applicants aghast at how they have been treated by their employers. A few internal applicants did write stories supporting a competitive approach, but in every case these were people who benefited from the process by having their promotions accelerated. Most, though, were merely angry that their employers had treated them so callously. I kept reading phrases like: 'I was told that everything I wanted the panel to take into account had to be introduced by me during the interview. I had been working there 12 years. How do you encapsulate that in 50 minutes?' or 'Emotionally, I no longer wanted to work for the company. I had lost the immense sense of pride and security I once had' or 'I feel like I've been treated like a commodity'.

Fatima's reaction to this style of attitude towards employees was to walk away. She was a temporary member of staff and, presumably, was accustomed to job change. She was able to leave and find work elsewhere. That is not the case for many other internal applicants; they return to work with an altered perception of the company's values. An interesting aspect of Fatima's story is the reaction of her MD to her annoyance at having to do the test: 'just a formality'. Fatima might have asked, if it is 'just a formality', why is it part of the selection process? But the phrase 'just a formality' carries a flippant air with it. In her storytelling, Fatima conveys a sense that her MD was unaware of the deeply felt nature of her concerns and her sense of betrayal. Perhaps her decision to leave was not based on having to jump through more selection hoops, some of which she had already cleared, but was instead caused by the MD's attitude towards her.

NICOLA'S STORY: CONFIDENCE

Following the promotion of the incumbent, I participated as a member of an interview panel to find a secretary. When the job fell vacant, the job was enriched by the incorporation of some of the work of three officers. The panel members included the three officers, a representative from Human Resources and me. The job was advertised internally and externally.

Only two of the four shortlisted candidates turned up for the interview, one external and one internal. The external candidate, Briony, who had been recommended by the previous incumbent, was offered the job and she accepted. The internal candidate, Ann, who was more qualified, was rejected. This was a result of how both candidates presented themselves during the interview. Briony, who had limited experience having only worked in a small office, was very alert and answered all of the questions promptly and with confidence. Ann, on the other hand, had over 10 years' secretarial experience and was familiar with organisational policies, but did not respond convincingly to the questioning. She seemed to lack confidence and answered most of the questions in monosyllables. When given a chance to ask questions, she was vague and said that she understood the secretarial aspects of the job.

Afterwards, Ann felt that she had been treated unfairly. This was made worse by the fact that Ann saw Briony at work and it was clear to her that she did not deserve the post; Ann became quite resentful. Briony's weaknesses were obvious and her job had to be redesigned again to give her some assistance.

Among other things, this short story illustrates the information asymmetries that exist when internal and external applicants compete against each other. Assuming that Ann's 10 years of experience are with the recruiting company, she has a long track record of performance in the organisation. The organisation should know, or could easily find out, her strengths and weaknesses and compatibility for the role. Should this be ignored? Briony, on the other hand, is a completely different kettle of fish. Nothing is known about her. This extreme information asymmetry is commonplace and an inevitable consequence of comparing internal and external applicants.

If Nicola was considering only internal candidates and which one to promote, she might approach the task very differently. She might consult work records, ask managers about the applicants, or give the candidates a trial period in the role. However, if she received only external applicants, she might design some work tests (for example typing or shorthand tests), she might use personality tests to assess how well suited the applicants are to the work, or she might use group activities to see how well the applicants interact with other people. The point is that the generic information asymmetry associated with internal and external applicants presents organisational selectors with a major problem: some of the tests they would naturally use for one group are not suitable for the other. The common way to reconcile this dilemma is to treat all the same and to find one way to assess everyone; in this case the interview. An alternative way might be to accept the differences between the two applicant pools (internals and externals) and to redesign the selection process. There are many options. The more obvious include a two-stage approach where jobs are advertised to internals first and only opened out to externals if there are no suitable internal candidates. Another is to use different selection tests for the different cohorts, recognising that the selection criteria must stay the same for all[1].

The information asymmetry between internal and external applicants is not just concerned with the different volume of information available to selectors. It is also possible to identify generic differences in the type of information available for each constituency. As I shall demonstrate in the next chapter, internal applicants usually apply for promotions, as in the case of Ann. In such cases, the organisation knows how well the applicants have performed in previous roles and should be well informed about their motivation, commitment and fit. What is not known is how the internal applicants will perform in the higher-level job – whether they have the skills, can handle the extra responsibility and so forth. With external applicants all of this data is missing, but there is an advantage for the selector in knowing that all the data is missing. They know that they must assess the applicants' skills, motivation, fit and so on.

---

[1] It is important to note that this second option is unlawful in some countries. An example is the USA, where this approach would constitute disparate treatment.

Interestingly, again as I shall show in the next chapter, external applicants often, but certainly not always, apply for lower-level jobs that they know they can do in order to gain access to the new company. In such circumstances, external applicants may have a track record of success in a higher-level job. When this is the case, selectors may find themselves assessing more fit-related than skill-related issues. The question might be whether this person can perform as well in the recruiting organisation.

A third difference between internal and external candidates, and one highlighted in Nicola's story, is the responsibility of the organisation to the different types of candidate. After working there for many years, does the organisation have a responsibility to Ann? Should it recognise and reward her commitment and service? Should it help her gain promotion? Should it protect her from situations where she might get hurt? Briony, on the other hand, has no relationship with the organisation, although Nicola tells us that she was recommended by the previous incumbent. The organisation should be grateful she applied and needs to treat her professionally and with respect; but is there any other responsibility? From a purely pragmatic point of view (and this is something I shall return to Chapter 7), if rejected, Briony leaves the organisation and continues with her current employment, if employed, or job search, if not. Ann, in contrast, returns to work and continues her ongoing relationship with the company.

Returning to the details of Nicola's story, I find myself thinking about the reasons Briony was offered the job. She 'was very alert and answered all of the questions promptly and with confidence'. In contrast, Ann 'seemed to lack confidence and answered most of the questions in monosyllables'. Putting aside the poverty of a selection process that relies on interviews as the sole measure of assessment for a secretarial role, Nicola's highlighting of the issue of confidence seems strange to me. My own reading of this short story suggests that confidence was used as a surrogate for ability: if someone was confident it meant they could do the job. But this sort of logic is truly horrid. What would make someone confident? You might be confident because you fail to understand or underestimate the complexities of a situation. You might be confident because you are naïve. You might be confident when the costs of failure are low, for example because you have a job in another company to go back to. What would make applicants convey the impression that they are lacking in confidence? What if they truly appreciated the challenges in the new role? What if they know that their failure to get the job will be known to their colleagues? What if they are nervous because they have been waiting for years for this kind of opportunity to come up? Confidence, to my eyes, will often be a negative indicator rather than a positive one.

Stories such as Nicola's appeared time and time again in my sample. It seems that both selectors and applicants know that a level playing field is impossible to create. Selectors realise the impracticality and foolishness of denying themselves valuable information about candidates. Internal applicants believe it is unfair for their work records to be excluded from the selection process, and external applicants believe they are at a disadvantage to internal candidates regardless. While these concerns might be dismissed as merely perceptual differences, they appear to have practical ramifications: the selector who ignores interview performance and relies on their own subjective assessment of someone at work, or vice versa; the internal applicant who leaves the company; and the external applicant who loses respect for a major supplier. These stories seem to suggest that the people on the receiving end of recruitment and selection believe it is impossible to treat every applicant in the same way. More than this, though, the impression is formed that these people do not think it is right to treat every applicant in the same way.

THINKING ON

1. Under what circumstances are external applicants favoured over internal ones?

2. Under what circumstances are internal applicants favoured over external ones?

3. Is it possible to create a 'level playing field' that is equally fair to internal and external applicants? Is a level playing field ethically sound?

4. Is it right for selection panel members to deprive themselves of information (such as performance appraisals, and disciplinary, attendance and sickness records) regarding internal applicants so that they have the same sort of information for all candidates?

5. Does an organisation (through their selection panels) 'owe' anything to people who have worked for them for a considerable period of time?

6. How would you react to a two-stage recruitment and selection process that first sees whether there are any suitable internal applicants before opening out to external applicants if none of the internal candidates is up to the mark?

7. How would you react to the use of different selection techniques for internal and external candidates?

8. Is it more important to understand each applicant as fully as possible against the selection criteria or to treat all applicants similarly?

READING ON

Most recruitment and selection textbooks work from the premise that selection is conducted by the organisation among external candidates (e.g. Cook, 2004; Cooper & Robertson, 1995; Gatewood & Feild, 2000). While these authors recognise that there are important differences between internal and external applicants, most suggest that internal candidates should be treated as if they were external applicants. For example, in the introduction to their textbook, Gatewood and Feild (1994) assert that, as there are usually more applicants than positions available, the assessment of internal applicants is conceptually the same as for external applicants.

> *Therefore, it is necessary to collect information about the job-related skills of the applicants and identify those individuals with the best skills. Logically, the accuracy of internal movement decisions will increase if more information is collected.*
>
> *(Gatewood & Feild, 1994, pp. 4–5)*

These authors argue that it is detrimental to the organisation not to treat internal candidates in a similar way to applicants applying for their initial job with the organisation; that is, external candidates. Further, they contend that basing promotion and transfer decisions on factors such as 'seniority, non-systematic opinions of others in the organisation, and ill-defined reputations' is selection without any evaluation of the applicant's job-related qualifications.

In contrast, Heneman and Judge (2005) have separate chapters for internal recruitment, external recruitment, internal selection and external selection. They note that internal recruitment has additional considerations over external recruitment. These include the different approaches of open, closed and targeted recruitment, the use of job posting and nominations, and issues of succession planning. Selection methods that are more usually suited to internal rather than external applicants include peer assessments, self-assessments, job knowledge tests, managerial sponsorship, and informal discussions and recommendations. Much less is known about the validity and reliability of these methods than those used for external selection (Heneman & Judge, 2005), and little is known about their prevalence. Heneman and Judge do not explain how a selector might combine the recruitment and selection methods when there is a mix of internal and external applicants. This is an important omission, because organisations are increasingly 'externally benchmarking' internal appointments. This is particularly the case for not-for-profit and public organisations that see external benchmarking as a way of giving legitimacy to appointments and checking the quality of staff (Harris, 2000).

The combination of internal and external applicants can create dilemmas for the selector. For example, Harris (2000, p. 40) reports on the recruitment and selection processes used in a British city council. She reports that the work records of internal applicants were not taken into account when final selection decisions were made. Although such an approach is designed to maximise procedural justice, the internal candidates found it most unfair. 'Such prior knowledge was held to be disadvantaging external candidates so the final decision rested entirely upon interview performance to ensure uniformity of treatment, a principle that clearly rankled with the internal candidates.'

REFERENCES

Cook, M. (2004) *Personnel Selection: Adding Value Through People,* 4th edn, Chichester: John Wiley & Sons Ltd.

Cooper, D. & Robertson, I. T. (1995) *The Psychology of Personnel Selection,* London: Routledge.

Gatewood, R. D. & Feild, H. S. (1994) *Human Resource Selection,* 4th edn, Fort Worth, TX: Dryden.

Gatewood, R. D. & Feild, H. S. (2000) *Human Resource Selection,* 6th edn, Fort Worth, TX: Dryden.

Harris, L. M. (2000) 'Issues of fairness in recruitment processes: A case study of local government practice', *Local Government Studies,* 26: 31–46.

Heneman, H. G. III & Judge, T. A. (2005) *Staffing Organizations,* 5th edn, Mendota House, WI: Irwin McGraw-Hill.

CHAPTER 6

Salvation

Another piece of quantitative data I was able to retrieve from these stories was the reasons for applicants applying for jobs. I had naturally assumed that most people apply for reasons for promotion or advancement or because they are out of work. However, as I read the stories I became aware of differences in the reasons for application between internal and external people. So I read through the applicants' stories specifically looking for the primary reasons they applied. These data are contained in Table 6.1.

The data in this table suggest a fundamental difference between the reasons for application between internal and external applicants. By and large, internal applicants apply for reasons of promotion, advancement and development. External applicants apply for very different reasons. Many apply because they have no job. For others, a new job is an escape from an unhappy work situation. Others have to move due to relocation or reorganisation. Although there are a few moving for 'positive' reasons, the main reason for someone applying for a job from outside the company is for reasons of salvation. Given the dislocation, disruption and uncertainty associated with changing employers, this should not come as a surprise. The decision to move companies is rarely taken lightly. In these stories, applicants were able to describe their 'real' motivations. Whether these are the ones presented to selection panels is another matter entirely.

Due to people's natural human tendency to want what they cannot have, this difference in the reasons for application between internal and external candidates results in a terrible irony: the greater someone's desperation for work, the less likely they are to get it. Someone in employment who is apparently valued by their existing employer will usually be seen as more attractive than someone who is apparently unappreciated by organisations. Making matters

Table 6.1 Primary reasons given for application

	Occurrence	Percentage
Internal applicants		
Promotion	26	72%
Desire to relocate	3	8%
Wanted permanent work	2	6%
Development	1	3%
Relocation of partner	1	3%
Invited to apply	1	3%
Merger – applied for own job	1	3%
Couldn't say/doesn't say	1	3%
External applicants		
First job	12	26%
Dissatisfaction/frustration with employer	9	20%
Redundant/unemployed	7	15%
Headhunted/approached	4	9%
Wanted different type of work	4	9%
Promotion/advancement	3	7%
Relocation	2	4%
Reorganisation meant job disappeared	2	4%
Wanted permanent work	1	2%
Return from maternity leave	1	2%
Break back into management	1	2%
Couldn't say/didn't say	18	39%

worse is the difference in confidence levels between the 'advancers' and those looking for salvation. The advancers are likely to be more confident. What have they got to lose? If their application fails, they have a job to go back to. Whereas if someone seeking salvation fails, they return to their dire situation. Naturally, a hint of desperation may creep into their behaviour and, if it does, they will again appear less attractive to selectors.

BRIAN'S STORY: FINDING SALVATION

I was made redundant from my job as a store manager for a large British retail chain. Within two weeks I attended outplacement sessions and compiled my CV. I researched the retail industry and sent my CV off to a number of recruitment agencies, high-street retailers and supermarket chains. I received positive replies from the majority and started on the interview trail with a number of retailers. Very soon, I received a phone call from a recruitment agent who described a role at a major furniture store that was rapidly expanding in the UK. I said that it sounded like the type of role I would like to take on and I was invited to an interview at the company.

On arrival, I was directed to the visitor and staff entrance where a very friendly receptionist greeted me and engaged me in pleasant conversation. Within minutes, the person with whom I was to have the interview appeared. He introduced himself and we conversed as we walked across the store to the interview room. Once there, I was offered refreshments and told that I could take my jacket off if I liked. The interviewer introduced himself again, this time by his first name.

He discussed my school days, my working life, my social interests and hobbies before moving on to discuss the vacant role and the company. The interviewer kept eye contact and listened attentively to me. It was clear that he had prepared well. At the end of the interview, he went over the selection process, thanked me for coming for the interview, and wished me a safe journey home. He then walked me back to the visitor entrance where I signed out and then drove home.

My thoughts after the interview were that the staff seemed friendly and they smiled at me, everyone seemed calm and laid back. Everyone appeared eager to put me at my ease and to make me feel welcome. It seemed they all enjoyed what they were doing. I was pleased the interviewer was well prepared and that the interview was not rushed. Also, I was pleased that I had been able to put myself across in a fully rounded way as a professional retail manager. I must admit that I was slightly nervous. I was anxious that I should be on time, presentable, calm and collected. These thoughts and emotions were caused through fear of the unknown and a slight lack of confidence in myself having been made redundant. Generally I was the one who interviewed other people for jobs; this time the tables had been turned.

As soon as he was made redundant, Brian set about the task of finding another job. He rapidly got himself organised and 'trained' for the job of finding a job. To all intents and purposes, he was still an employed person; it was just that his job had changed. Despite this, Brian admits to anxiety, fear and lack of confidence in going for an interview when unemployed. For him, the stakes were very high. His nervousness was probably heightened by the pleasant demeanour of everyone he met and the professionalism of the selection process. This would have made the job and the company even more attractive and, as a result, may have increased his level of anxiety. Imagine how these states would have been exacerbated if he had been unemployed for a longer period of time and had suffered many knock-backs.

Brian's story illustrates another difference between internal and external applicants that I saw in many stories. To gain salvation, Brian was prepared to do a lower-level job than his previous one. He had been the store manager in one of the largest high-street retailers. He was prepared, and happy, to take a more junior role at another retailer. Brian does not explain why this particular role was attractive to him, other than his mention of the friendliness and professionalism pervading the place. In other stories, applicants openly discussed their willingness to take jobs for which they were over-qualified. Many people were just desperate to find work and would have been prepared to accept anything to which they were remotely suited. Others rationalised accepting a junior role to themselves in the following way: I will soon prove myself and rise to the level my skills and experience warrant. Sadly, many of these people were deluding themselves and found themselves under-valued and under-appreciated, as the following story illustrates.

PAUL'S STORY: THE STEPPING STONE

Recently, I attended an interview with a Rugby-based engineering company. The agency that had set up the interview had only supplied the name of the person I was due to meet; I did not know his title or function. The person I was scheduled to meet, I eventually discovered, was the senior mechanical engineer. This came as a bit of a shock as his position was about three levels below my last position in South Africa.

He explained that the first interview would be with the personnel officer and when this was completed he would have a technical chat with me. He also explained that, due to the Christmas break, I may be called back again in the New Year for a second interview with the general manager and/or the operations director, both of whom were on leave at this specific time. I assumed that, as I was being interviewed by the senior mechanical engineer, he was the highest-ranking technical member of staff available to talk to me about my technical ability and relevant experience.

My first interview was with the personnel officer, who attempted to explain what the company did and failed miserably due to his self-admitted lack of engineering knowledge. He actually stated that he did not know exactly what the company designed and engineered. He explained that he knew the company supplied equipment to the oil and gas sector and that was about it.

If I had not known my industry, I would not have understood what the company's core business was based on his explanation. He had obviously read the company profile, but the technical jargon (his words) meant nothing to him. I asked him why he needed to interview me. He explained that he had to assess whether he felt I would 'fit in'. When I asked how he was supposed to work out if I would 'fit in' from such a short meeting without assessing the level of my engineering or technical ability, he simply said 'with this' and handed me a sheet full of questions. It was the first psychometric test I had ever done and I had been in the engineering industry for over 20 years at this time.

I completed the psychometric test and handed it to the personnel officer. He compared my answers to his checking sheet while I sat in front of him. He eventually calculated a shape from my answers and produced what appeared to be some form of an elongated tick. He then informed me, in what seemed an animated and positive fashion, that he had only seen this pattern once before and that had been the result of a test he carried out on the managing director at his last firm. I assumed this was a good thing as he seemed quite happy with the results, but he didn't offer any other information about what it actually meant or what he thought he had discovered.

After this interview with the personnel officer, I was taken to the office of the senior mechanical engineer. My interviewer explained that he had read my CV and that I was known to two of his staff who had both spoken highly of me and that he believed my background covered the company's requirements. I asked him questions about what the company was involved in. He told me about the type of equipment that it designed, engineered and manufactured. He explained that the overall organisational control came from the American owners of the company and he outlined the organisation's foreseeable problems. He painted a very rosy picture about how busy the company was and outlined a couple of projects for which the company expected to receive orders that were in excess of £20 million. It was because of these projects that the company was interested in bringing me on board.

When the interview finished we walked around the project engineering office and I was re-introduced to the two engineers who had worked for me overseas. We then concluded with a tour of the fabrication facility and workshops. At no stage during this second interview did we discuss the prospective job title or its requirements or salary details, though the relocation package was mentioned and I was told it was very generous. On reflection I realised that a carrot was being dangled! The interviewer knew that I was returning from South Africa and the relocation package would definitely relieve my financial burden.

In the New Year, I was contacted by the organisation and asked to return to its offices to attend a third interview, this time with the general manager. At the conclusion of this interview I was offered the position of lead mechanical engineer. I was taken aback when I realised that I would be answerable to the senior mechanical engineer. In the discussion I had with him at the first interview stage, he admitted that he personally lacked the large project management experience to control major projects and hinted that I would be offered a job to handle these projects. The salary that was offered, though good for the position, was still less than what I would have expected if I was being employed as project manager or head of projects.

I felt that I had completely wasted my time. From the first round of interviews, I felt sure I would be offered a position and salary that would reflect my background, experience and knowledge of the project engineering industry. I had been employed as a lead mechanical engineer some 10 years previously and had continued to rise successfully up the career ladder since then. I was being offered a position at least four levels below my last position in South Africa; a job that provided excellent references from my previous employer and from four of their clients and consultants.

I felt somewhat deflated and I was rather annoyed because I had been offered an interview as a project manager with a company on the south coast subsequent to attending the first interviews with this company. I had turned down the offer to attend the interview as a result of the positive feedback (and the details of the relocation package). It was primarily the relocation package, coupled with a location close to friends and family, that eventually led me to accept the job that was offered.

The short-term impact of this was that I accepted a position that suited my personal needs at the time but not my professional career needs. I had found a solution to the financial aspect of moving from one country to another and had sorted out short-term accommodation and transport requirements. The cash that was forthcoming and what I saved in shipping fees and estate agents' fees combined was enough to purchase a house without its costing me anything.

I knew that I had accepted a position I didn't believe I would be happy in, but I was content with the fact that my domestic situation was comfortable. I also believed that once the company realised my project management ability and my experience in managing large projects recognition would follow, either in promotion, salary reviews, bonuses or a combination of all three.

The long-term impact of this was that I was in a position that was not demanding enough of me. The organisation had informed me at interview stage that it was my broad project experience in the oil and gas sector that they valued in me. After a couple of months it became apparent that this was not being utilised. I was not being used in a project management capacity, which is where I had spent 12 of my 20 years in engineering. My salary and promotional prospects were never discussed. The result was that I left the company after working there for only 10 months.

Paul's story illustrates the plight of people who *need* work. Even though they may have skills and abilities far and above the requirements of the job and know that such a junior job (comparative to their experience) will be dull and demoralising, they may accept it. In Paul's case, the lure of a generous relocation package mitigated his concerns. But accepting a job four levels below the 'right' level will always cause problems. Paul must have known that this job was simply a stepping stone from one country to another. Could he really believe that the company would recognise his project management talents and make amends? In most organisations, once someone enters they take a place on a pay, rewards and seniority 'ladder'. Once on a ladder, it is very difficult to 'overtake' someone else, let alone rise four levels. As a result, people who accept jobs at lower levels than they feel they deserve in order to get work usually find themselves disappointed. In Paul's case, he left after just 10 months, glad that this company had paid for his international relocation.

Paul's story reveals the different intensity that applicants and selectors give to the recruitment process. He hangs on every word and nuance. Such is his confidence in the positive feedback and glitter of the relocation package that he prematurely terminated his application to another organisation. To be honest, this is usually not a very good thing to do. Until applicants receive acceptable offers in writing, they should not do anything that jeopardises their current employment or other prospects. Interviewers know that everything an interviewee says *might* be untrue. Similarly, applicants should realise that everything a representative of an organisation says also *might* be untrue. If it is not a deliberate lie it may be an exaggeration, or, more likely, events may simply change to nullify earlier statements. *Caveat emptor.*

EDWARD'S STORY: SEEKING SALVATION

A few years ago, I applied for the job of project officer with a homelessness charity run by a local church in London. I applied for the job because, as a committed Christian, I was interested in working in a Christian project. I was shortlisted and appointed. This was probably because I was the churchwarden of another church in the same district, which provided good support to the project, and because my vicar almost certainly gave me a good reference.

In retrospect, I can say I had strong reservations about the job after the interview. But I accepted it because my wife was due to give birth to our second child and I needed an income to support my family. As it turned out, the job bore little relation to the job description. In particular, it had not been made clear that a major part of the job was secretarial, and since I have dyslexia this proved a real problem. Also, the job bore little relation to the jobs of project officers working for similar projects elsewhere in the capital. It involved little or no contact with the people it was supposed to be helping. I also discovered that I was the fourth person in the role in the past two years.

Despite being run by a local church, there was almost no spiritual input into the project. I was almost left with the feeling at times that it did not matter if people went to Hell, as long as they had a full belly each evening! Needless to say, we soon parted company.

Edward accepted this job because he needed work. With a second child on the way, he needed the money to support his family. He knew the job was likely to be unsuitable and frustrating, but he had to earn a living. In such circumstances, applicants cannot make decisions based on their fit, their ambitions or their self-esteem. Instead they have to attend to baser needs of food, warmth and security. As long as the job is tolerable, it will be accepted.

The experiences of Paul and Edward contrast sharply with those of internal applicants who almost always apply for jobs at a higher level to their current one, as the following story illustrates.

VERONICA'S STORY: WOMAN ON THE VERGE OF A NERVOUS BREAKDOWN

One morning I was called into an empty conference room by Neil and asked if I had 'heard anything on the grapevine'. I hadn't. Thinking that I must be there for a disciplinary reason, I replied nervously, 'No. Why? Should I have done?' He explained how Kath had been offered a golden opportunity to further her career by transferring to another account. He asked how I felt about replacing her in her current role and taking over as the manager of our Finance department.

My initial reaction was one of numb shock, quickly followed by blind panic coupled with vague excitement. I realised that this was the only way I would be promoted considering my lack of qualifications and the current downsizing that was taking place. I said something like, 'Well, I'd be mad to say no really, wouldn't I?' Neil replied 'Yes!' and laughed. He was very encouraging, but I was well aware that I wouldn't get any technical support from him, as he knew nothing about the finance process. We discussed whether we could cope with the remaining three of us and how I had a five-day handover period to pick up relevant training from Kath. Neil told me he had negotiated a pay rise of double the normal rate for promotion without a board.

I didn't know whether to laugh or cry when I emerged, shaken, after no more than 15 minutes. On the one hand I was faced with the prospect of promotion without having to sit a board, but on the other I was painfully aware of my shortcomings. Part of me wanted to go with Kath, which would have been a safe option: to continue to be her deputy with no real responsibility. Worse news was yet to come. Kath was to leave at the end of that week and Jennifer, my colleague who had critical knowledge, wanted to go with her. Our team was to be halved and the majority of the management accounting skills were to be transferred to the new account.

The short-term impact of these decisions left me feeling shocked and the team in disarray. None of us knew how we would cope. I immediately re-allocated tasks and arranged on-the-job training for Colin and me. I had approximately three days' basic training on critical tasks that I knew nothing about. The second-quarter forecast was overdue by two weeks and I was expected to have that done by the end of the following week. No one was available to help me. I was unlikely to produce accurate or timely work, having no training and no time to plan or prepare. I heard one manager remark, 'Why the hell did they give her the job? She doesn't know enough to run that department.' Although true, it was a severe blow to my confidence and dented the confidence that others had in me.

The long-term impact on me was ill health. The constant pressure and severe demands on my time, coupled with the fact that I actually knew a lot less than others realised, led to me working unrealistically long hours. I was determined to produce the reports and tables required. I was struggling to make sense of data I had never seen before and refused to give in. In effect, I was trying too hard to prove myself. The result was that within four months I lost nearly two stones in weight and was suffering symptoms of extreme stress. The day I burst into tears in the office over a triviality was the day I was told by friends to slow down before I had a nervous breakdown.

The effect of this has actually been positive in the long run. I developed personal discipline in order to survive. I have found strengths I never knew existed and have become ambitious. I felt that if I could survive what one friend described as 'being thrown to the sharks with a millstone round your neck', then I could do anything I put my mind to.

For most people in the early and middle stages of their careers, promotion is not just attractive, but it is a powerful driving force. With it comes more money, better perks, more power and influence, more autonomy and greater respect; or so the thinking goes. The reality is often very different: more responsibility, less security, less control over your future, more pressure, more stress, more anxiety, less role clarity and longer hours. This is certainly the reality that Veronica experienced; so much so that she ended up unwell.

Being offered promotion is flattering. It shows that your manager believes you are excelling in your job and ready for fresh and more demanding challenges. It tells you that you are doing a good job and people are noticing. It tells you that you are trusted and part of the team. How do you turn it down? Even if you have concerns, the allure is just too strong. This is the situation in which Veronica found herself. She did not seek promotion: she was approached. When she was, she did not know 'whether to laugh or cry'. She had the advantage of not having to prove herself through the usual promotion board (or formal panel interview), but this increases the risks. How does she, or anyone else, know that she is competent to do the job? She says, 'I was painfully aware of my shortcomings.' To her credit, she worked incredibly hard to keep her head above water and in the long run this appears to have paid off. If it had not, Veronica may have become another victim of the Peter Principle: the idea that people get promoted to their level of incompetence. This occurs when people are promoted due to excellence in their current jobs, only to find themselves unable to perform effectively in their higher-level jobs. Neil's approach to promotion increased the possibility of this happening by sidestepping the usual promotion board. It is to Veronica's credit that she worked her socks off to survive and eventually thrive in the role.

Veronica says: 'within four months I had lost nearly two stones in weight and was suffering symptoms of extreme stress. . . I burst into tears in the office over a triviality.' Such things are not trivial. Being on the verge of a nervous breakdown is a serious matter and one requiring action. But where was the managerial support? Apparently, they were bad-mouthing her, making matters worse. Had Veronica not had friends to help her, I wonder what the outcome would have been. If she had succumbed to the intense stress and folded, who would be to blame? I can just hear the manager who criticised her saying something like, 'she brought it on herself. . . we're well shot of her.' Will the paucity of her selection be remembered? Will the stripping of skills from the department be appreciated? Probably not. It will be Veronica who is to blame. The company, after all, gave her an opportunity. It is her problem if she was unable to take advantage of it.

This kind of thinking is a natural human process. As mentioned in Chapter 1, we tend to attribute causality for our own behaviour to external factors (i.e. the things influencing us), especially when things go awry, and attribute causality for other people's behaviour to internal factors (i.e. their personality). We tend to under-appreciate the factors influencing people. Hence, people will forget the dire circumstances surrounding Veronica's promotion and instead will tend to blame her for her failure. Fortunately, this is all speculation, as Veronica fought through the problems and came out stronger from the ordeal: she is the heroine in this drama. Her ambition is not dented. In fact, she tells us that she is more ambitious than before. Such is the allure of promotion that not even suffering like hers can diminish it.

THINKING ON

1. Why does the atmosphere of a selection process have such a large impact on the attractiveness or otherwise of organisations?

2. Is finding a job a 'job' in itself?

3. Under what circumstances would you accept a job that you knew to be at a lower level to what you are used to? How would this make you feel?

4. Why might representatives of organisations say things to applicants that later turn out to be untrue or incorrect?

5. Under what circumstances would you *not* accept a promotion?

6. What responsibilities does the organisation have to the people it promotes?

READING ON

Strangely, very little is known about why people apply for jobs. The careers literature mainly focuses on the description of vocations and on aligning people with the sort of work they want. In the economic geography literature, Steinnes (1982) asked whether people follow jobs or whether jobs follow people, and showed that in the manufacturing industry 'jobs follow people'. As mentioned earlier, researchers who consider applicants' reactions tend to focus on issues of fairness and the acceptability of recruitment and selection techniques. When reading the recruitment and selection textbooks, little attention is paid to the reasons for people applying for jobs. There seems to be an acceptance that people apply for jobs either because they need work or because they are keen to improve their situation, or because they seek advancement.

We do know a little about what applicants look for in jobs, with the type of work, pay, security and advancement usually emerging as the key reasons (Jurgensen, 1987; Lacy, Bokemeier & Shepard, 1983). An alternative perspective is taken by Schneider (1987), who suggests that people apply to organisations where they believe they will be similar to other employees. Barber (1998) offers a thorough review of the decision-making process that applicants go through, with a specific focus on their reactions to organisations' promotional literature.

In comparison to the enormous focus on external applicants in the recruitment and selection literature, there has been very little consideration given to internal applicants and virtually no attention at all to occasions when internal and external applicants compete against each other. This is important because, as pointed out by Heneman and Judge (2005), very different selection methods are possible with the two types of applicants. One notable exception is Chan (1996), who uses economic theory, in particular game theory, to argue that due to the moral hazards and potentially disruptive office politics, internal applicants should be given a competitive advantage over external applicants, who should only be appointed if they are 'significantly superior to the internal contestants' (Chan, 1996, p. 555).

REFERENCES

Barber, A. E. (1998) *Recruiting Employees: Individual and Organizational Perspectives*, Thousand Oaks, CA: Sage.

Chan, W. (1996) 'External recruitment versus internal promotion', *Journal of Labor Economics*, 14(4): 555–70.

Heneman, H. G. III & Judge, T. A. (2005) *Staffing Organizations,* 5th edn, Mendota House, WI: Irwin McGraw-Hill.

Jurgensen, C. E. (1987) 'Job preferences (What makes a job good or bad?)', *Journal of Applied Psychology*, 63: 267–76.

Lacy, W. B., Bokemeier, J. L. & Shepard, J. M. (1983) 'Job attribute preferences and work commitment of men and women in the United States,' *Personnel Psychology*, 36: 315–29.

Schneider, B. (1987) 'The people make the place', *Personnel Psychology*, 40: 437–53.

Steinnes, D. N. (1982) 'Do "people follow jobs" or do "jobs follow people"? A causality issue in urban economics', *Urban Studies*, 19(2): 187–92.

CHAPTER 7

Failure

Several of the stories in previous chapters have involved internal applicants going for jobs and failing. The costs of these failures are often considerable. Fatima left the organisation, Malcolm was angry and Ann felt that she had been treated unfairly. Clearly, internal applicants put themselves at risk when they apply for a promotion: they put their heads above the parapet. If they are unsuccessful, they return to work dispirited with, in all likelihood, their colleagues knowing that they 'failed'.

I did not feel that the person who had been given the position had the same amount of experience as me and I felt cheated out of the position. On returning to my job, I did not see the point in doing any extra activities. Doing all the extra hours did not get me anywhere.

Worse still, they may have to work with, or under, the newly appointed person.

I found out that one of my colleagues had the job. She was very happy and everyone was congratulating her. I was sitting there in silence. It was not my colleague's fault. She had every right to be happy on her success. I was thinking if the management wanted to appoint her, why did they have to go through the pressure of job advertising, shortlisting and interviewing?

Rather than simply relate more stories demonstrating the impact of failure on internal candidates, I have chosen to expand my gaze and look at the impact of failure on other parties: managers, selectors and colleagues. It is not just internal applicants who suffer when their dreams are not realised.

ANDY'S STORY: RESTRUCTURING

The organisation I work for made the decision to restructure its produc-tion management. Prior to restructuring, the production management team consisted of four shift supervisors and a senior supervisor, who also shared the role of quality manager. The role of the quality manager had grown to the point that he was unable to perform adequately in the senior supervisor role. As a result, the decision was taken to replace the senior supervisor role with a production manager who would manage the day-to-day running of the factory.

The workload for the shift supervisors had grown considerably over the past year, due to expansions in the production department, which increased the shift labour force by approximately 90%. The job had become increasingly difficult for some of the supervisors, to the point that many had found it difficult to cope. The factory manager made the decision to replace the supervisors with shift managers. The shift managers' roles would be similar to the supervisors', but with increased responsibilities. They would be directly answerable to the production manager.

The positions of production manager and shift managers were advertised in a national newspaper, an industry-wide weekly publication, and internally on the internal job vacancy notice board. The job descriptions were very vague and left much to interpretation. All applications for these positions were to be made to an executive recruitment consultant in Leeds, approximately 180 miles from the manufacturing site and not through the Human Resources department. This was not normal practice for the company, as all positions had been dealt with solely by the Human Resources department.

Two supervisors, of whom I was one, were encouraged by the factory manager to apply for the production manager's position. We were informed that we fitted the requirements of that job. We were given 24 hours' notice to travel down to the recruitment agency for intelligence and psychometric evaluation and an in-depth interview with a consultant. We requested a copy of the production manager's job description to study before the interview, only to be told by the human resources manager that one 'had not been formulated yet' and the factory manager had still to discuss this with her.

We had to arrive at the consultants for 10 a.m., which required an early start in order to arrive in time for the evaluation. Chatting after the tests, we both felt that we had done well in the intelligence and psychometric testing, but that the questions we were being asked at the interview were directed more at the shift managers' positions. The interviewer did not have a job description to work from and the interview was made up of questions involving the then management system: 'What were the problems involved on shift?' or 'How did the supervisors carry out the work?' The question 'What would you do if you were unsuccessful in attaining the production manager's position?' was asked on more than one occasion during the interview. We came to the conclusion that we were not being interviewed for the position we had applied for.

On our return to work, we began to feel a certain resentment towards the company. Why did it have to go through this assessment when other recent managerial posts had been filled through the normal recruitment procedures it had in place? If the company was unsure of our abilities, why had we been encouraged to apply for this job? Approximately six weeks later, we were given a copy of our performance from the consultants. We were both recommended for the positions of shift managers without any mention of the production manager's job.

We confronted the factory manager about why we had not been considered for the production manager's position. He did not initially give us a satisfactory answer to this question, but intimated that he did not want to upset the present structure too much and that he wanted us to carry on running shifts, with two external candidates filling the other two positions. The production manager's position would also be filled externally.

The factory manager eventually admitted that the reason we were sent to the consultant was to provide a benchmark for the external candidates and that he had already made the decision that we would be given the jobs of shift managers. To appease us, he gave us considerable increases in salary, with the promise of 'more to come' when we took up our new posts. I felt that we had wasted our time going through the assessment. I also felt partly let down by my manager and also lost faith in the organisation.

The final outcome was that both of us applied for senior management positions outside the organisation. We were both shortlisted and I was successful. My colleague is actively pursuing employment elsewhere. Neither of us would have considered employment outside the organisation prior to the 'restructure'.

The company was not very successful in filling the shift managers' positions with external candidates. All but one of the people the consultant recommended for the positions decided that they did not wish to accept. The supervisors who had been discouraged from applying for the shift managers' positions were told that they were not suitable and would be offered 'suitable other employment' within the company. Unfortunately this was announced to them before the shift managers' positions had been filled. The supervisors were then told that they had to carry on with their duties until the shift managers were employed.

The sort of management behaviour experienced by Andy is commonplace in today's business environment. Many senior executives seem keen to 'restructure' their organisations as a means of coping with change. The irony in this case is that the 'restructure' is deemed necessary to cope with success:

managers and supervisors are having to deal with more work and increased numbers of staff. Rather than build on success, the factory manager seems intent on wreaking destruction in his organisation. Why not nurture people? Why not train and develop them? Why not reward their successes? Why not believe in your staff? Why not make them feel good about their successes? Instead, he makes people apply for their own jobs, which not only causes tremendous disruption, but also angers staff who start to look elsewhere for work. Of course, it is the best employees who are most able to find work with other employers.

Being forced to apply for your own job is an increasingly popular way of managing change in business. It seems to happen in organisations where the senior management are detached from day-to-day work, where they have little attachment to the workforce, where they feel their role is to take decisions, and where they rely more on the advice of external consultants than the judgement of people inside the organisation. Usually this happens when an organisation is facing a crisis and needs to contract, but the procedure is increasingly being used to 'restructure' companies to cope with relatively minor changes in the business environment. Andy's story is a case in point. This 'restructure' was a result of a factory manager having to reorganise a few duties due to the increase in work. What the factory manager failed to realise was the impact that this competition for jobs would have on the workforce. The workers feel like commodities who are not appreciated by the company. More than this, the fact that external consultants have to be brought in to assess them creates the impression in the workers' minds that the organisation knows little about them and is keen to keep the bonds between managers and workers weak. It reinforces the 'them and us' syndrome and is likely to result in a more militant workforce. 'If managers treat us like commodities, then we will get the maximum price for the minimum effort', the thinking might go. Staff who care about the way they are treated will take more drastic action, like Andy, and leave.

AL'S STORY: IN AT THE DEEP END

We were trying to recruit a road foreman. Four candidates were interviewed. Three were external and the fourth was one of my own machine operators. The interviews were conducted under Civil Service guidelines. The panel consisted of my boss as chairman, a lady from Personnel and me. My role on the board was to probe for technical knowledge and experience, explain what duties were to be performed and answer questions from the candidates. Each candidate was asked the same questions from each board member and the scores were systematically recorded.

Of the candidates, one had no machine operation experience and was discounted. Another had potential but lived a considerable distance away and was unwilling to move closer without assistance to relocate. The internal employee was given an equal chance, but, as expected, he did not outperform the final external candidate, whose scores were well above all the others. I remember my boss's comment when we were making our assessment of the successful candidate. On his first meeting with him, he said, 'This man has presence.' My impression of him was similar. He was smartly dressed, the smartest of the four. He answered the questions put to him reasonably well, without 'flannelling', and if he could not answer he said so.

When he arrived on his first day, I took him into the forest to introduce him to the workforce and show him the current job. All seemed to have gone well during the day.

Later that night, I received a phone call from our new 'start' to tell me he had thought better of a career as a road foreman and would not be returning! He felt having met the men, he would be unable to manage and achieve anything with them. We had some problems within the 'squad' and my boss and I felt a new supervisor would resolve some, if not all, of these. This appointment was the first external recruitment for some time. Vacancies were usually filled from internal rearrangement. It had been a chance to get a good people manager to improve efficiency and resolve some long-standing problems. I had been optimistic.

But instead, the short-term impact was 'loss of face'. I felt embarrassed and let down. The long-term effect was a weakening of my position in my managerial role. I had placed confidence and trust in him and was 'dumped on'. The internal candidate was also 'huffed' at not being selected and this added to the poor relationship with me in the longer term.

Failure is not limited to occasions when someone did not get a job. Sometimes, being offered a job can be a failure in itself. The first day is always a bit nerve-wracking. Much of the time though, 'first days' are pretty tame affairs. Lots of waiting around, lots of form filling, lots of introductions, lots of forgetting people's names, lots of questions and the next thing you know, it's going-home time. The second day is usually the big test, because people often assume you know what you are doing and can get on with the work. They forget that everything is new to you and you often feel more awkward asking questions. But the successful candidate in Al's story did not make it to day two. One day in the forest in charge of a squad of men with 'some problems' was sufficient for him to flee. Al does not say whether this is the usual induction procedure at the organisation or whether much thought was given to the newcomer's orientation, but he does appear to have been dropped in at the deep end. Being sent into the depths of a forest to manage a squad of men with 'some problems' is not a gentle start.

Walking away from a job like this takes some bottle. Most people are simply unable to do this. Their previous employer may have hired a replacement or may feel let down by the employee's exit, making a return almost impossible. Most people need work and so are willing to tolerate a bad situation until they can find something better. Finding a job while in work is, for most people, a lot easier than finding one when you are unemployed, as we saw earlier. Leaving so abruptly is likely to be a tremendous wrench for the individual.

Another side to this decision to walk away is that accepting a new job is, for most people, a large psychological investment. It means cutting ties with a previous employer, throwing away all your organisational knowledge, and casting aside work-based friends, colleagues and networks. It may mean moving house, which may disrupt non-work friendships. Children may have to move schools. People do not do these things lightly. So giving up a job so precipitately will probably have dire consequences and is not usually entered into lightly.

Al feels the early exit personally. He had high expectations of the newcomer and had set a lot of store by him: he was going to sort out this 'problem' squad. Clearly he feels 'let down', but what is causing the 'loss of face' and 'embarrassment'? He says that he had placed confidence and trust in the man, but this would not seem sufficient to cause this extreme reaction and the long-term weakening of his managerial position; so we are left to speculate. One possible explanation involves his relationship with the team, which seems to include the failed internal applicant. Such a person may react quite aggressively or fractiously and cause all sorts of irritation.

DERMOT'S STORY: RATIONALISATION

One positive incident I experienced occurred about a year ago when we had to recruit a permanent technician. Our workforce consists of a 40/60 mix of company staff and contractor staff. On rationalisation two candidates were to be interviewed: one was a current contractor with us and the other an external applicant. The contractor, Trevor, had worked for the company for three years.

Although I was on the interview panel, I did not take the final selection decision. I regarded Trevor as a good all-round technician and I was naturally biased towards him. What surprised and disappointed me was that the external candidate was employed and Trevor was retained as a contract technician.

I could not understand why Trevor did not get the job. Were the selectors blind to the fact that the other supervisory staff and I all agreed he was an ideal person in most respects? I naturally felt disappointed for him and also myself. I was also embarrassed, as I think I may have led him to believe he would get the job. I also felt anger towards the decision. I felt the company had let itself down in not obtaining his skills. The short-term impact of this decision was my resentment towards the company, Trevor's ill feeling and low morale, and a strained working relationship between us.

Fortunately the new recruit, Eion, turned out to be an excellent employee: dedicated and exhibiting very positive behaviour coupled with fresh ideas and a natural progressive flair. Because of Eion's personality and commitment, Trevor accepted him very quickly and they have subsequently formed a very good working relationship; both production and morale are back up to their former standard.

Dermot's story brings some balance to this discussion. Sometimes recruitment and selection do go right and employees' morale increases. Eion's appointment is interesting on several levels. First, it shows how 'risky' decision making by managers is rewarded when the risks play out in their favour. Employing Eion, when the alternative candidate is highly regarded by other employees including a member of the panel, is a brave decision. But if the panel members trust their judgement and the weight of evidence, then it can work out well. In this case, Eion turned out to be an excellent, dedicated and positive employee with fresh ideas. His manner helped win over the failed 'internal' applicant who witnesses the strengths of the newcomer at first hand. This justifies the decision and repairs the damage done by disappointing the internal candidate.

The second point of interest in this story is the impact on Dermot himself. He found himself in a difficult position as the future manager of the newcomer, the manager of one of the applicants, and a member of the selection panel with little say in the final selection decision. His predicament is easy to imagine. What does a manager say to an internal applicant who seeks out your opinion on whether to apply for a promotion? If you believe in their qualities and their suitability for the role, should you say so? If you do not, you might risk undermining your existing relationship. If you do, you raise expectations and risk the person being disappointed. If you prevaricate, you risk looking indecisive, unsure of yourself and weak.

Thirdly, I find it interesting that someone is on a selection panel but has little or no say in the decision the panel makes. This is most unusual and I can't think what the rationale might have been. Was Dermot not trusted? Was he just an observer? Perhaps, his phrase 'I did not take the final selection decision' simply means that he did not agree with the decision that was made. His presence on the panel demonstrates the difficulty panels have when they have a pool of applicants some of whom they know. Earlier we saw how a panel's prior knowledge of candidates raised issues of how even-handedly they can assess applicants from different sources. Dermot's comment raises another dimension: How can the selectors ignore what they may have said to applicants? Is it possible for Dermot to be objective on this panel given his comments to one of the applicants and his 'loss of face' if the panel contradicts what he has said to Trevor?

THINKING ON

1. How would you react to news of your company's restructure, which means you have to apply for your own job in competition with other people? How would others react? What is the cause of this reaction?

2. In what circumstances is it sound for an organisation to 'restructure' its workforce?

3. What do you give up when you accept a job at another company? What upheavals does a change of job bring?

4. What sort of induction do you expect when you join a new employer? How long does it take to become effective?

5. Al felt a loss of face because the newcomer did not come back for a second day. Should he have? How would you view a manager whose new recruit does not come back for a second day? If you feel negatively towards such a manager, what is it that you are reacting to?

6. Should selection panels include people if they know any of the candidates? Should colleagues assess each other? Should a manager be on the panel for someone they will manage if that person is not appointed?

7. How should a manager react if a member of their staff asks whether or not they should apply for an internal promotion? How should the manager respond to questions about suitability for the post?

READING ON

The developing applicant-reaction literature is giving us some insight into the ways in which recruitment and selection affect external applicants (Barber, 1998), but we have very little data on the ways in which recruitment and selection affect internal applicants. Heneman and Judge (2005, p. 280) describe this as a 'glaring omission'. Intuitively, the impact of recruitment and selection practices on internal candidates seems especially important, as those who fail are usually still employed by the organisation and they will take any altered attitudes or behaviours to work with them. They get to see the performance of the people who were selected instead of them. And when procedural justice has been high, internal applicants have the discouragement of knowing that it is their own failings that have caused them to be unsuccessful (Brockner, 2001).

In addition to Brockner, the leading writers in the organisational justice literature who refer to recruitment and selection include Gilliland (1993), Arvey (Arvey & Faley, 1988) and Folger and Cropanzano (1998). The last is an excellent book on organisational justice, which contains a chapter on perceptions of fairness in recruitment and selection. There the authors explore some of the justice dilemmas that recruiters face: the more rigorous the selection, the less likely the applicant is to accept the job; the better selection tests are, the more likely they are to disadvantage protected groups; the better the test, the more likely applicants are to attribute their failure to themselves; and the more rigorous and valid selection tests are, the easier it is for failed applicants to make a legal claim. The authors also look at what makes selection fair and use Gilliland's (1993) framework for improving applicants' perceptions of fairness.

REFERENCES

Arvey, R. D. & Faley, R. H. (1988) *Fairness in Selecting Employees*, 2nd edn, Reading MA: Addison-Wesley.

Barber, A. E. (1998) *Recruiting Employees: Individual and Organizational Perspectives*, Thousand Oaks, CA: Sage.

Brockner, J. (2001) 'The pain and pleasure of high procedural justice', paper presented at the annual meeting of the Academy of Management, Washington, DC, August.

Folger, R. & Cropanzano, R. (1998) *Organizational Justice and Human Resource Management*, Thousand Oaks, CA: Sage.

Gilliland, S. W. (1993) 'The perceived fairness of selection systems: An organizational justice perspective', *Academy of Management Review*, 18: 694–734.

Heneman, H. G. III & Judge, T. A. (2005) *Staffing Organizations,* 5th edn, Mendota House, WI: Irwin McGraw-Hill.

CHAPTER 8

Disrespect

The most common theme in the stories I received was applicants being on the receiving end of interviews. I have already included a few examples (and there are more to come later in the book), but in this chapter I have selected some examples that demonstrate the impact of bad interviewing on applicants' subsequent behaviour. Specifically, the stories in this chapter demonstrate how interviewees' perceptions of being disrespected cause them to abandon their applications.

One of the surprises for me is how applicants' good manners prevent them reacting to the abuses they suffer. Why do they not tell interviewers just how rude and disrespectful they have been? Too often, interviewees allow themselves to be putty in the hands of selectors, who seem to get away with murder because they have something the applicants are desperate for. But there are limits and the stories in this chapter transgress these.

GORDON'S STORY: THE WOMAN WHO ENJOYS MAKING MEN CRY

I applied for the position of food and beverage manager at a four-star hotel on the south coast. It was advertised in a local newspaper by an agency. The advert mentioned the job title, the name of the employer, the salary and the qualities that candidates would be expected to possess. Following the instructions in the advert, I telephoned the agency and arranged a time and date for the interview to take place. I stressed that I had another interview in London and would be travelling on to Scotland on the same day. I said that I would very much appreciate the hotel keeping to the agreed time. At the time,

I was actively seeking full-time employment having just returned to the UK after working in South Africa for four years.

I arrived at the hotel with 10 minutes to spare and informed the reception desk of my arrival. I was asked to take a seat and told that 'someone' would be with me shortly. Ten minutes after the agreed start time of the interview, a secretary approached me and offered me a coffee, which was served shortly after it was offered. Twenty minutes after the agreed start time, the secretary approached me again and said, 'The area manager is running late as he is a rather busy man, you know.' I mentioned to her that I had other appointments in London that day, and I would appreciate seeing him soon. Thirty minutes after the start time of the interview I was informed that he would be with me 'shortly'. Forty-five minutes after the start time, the area manager sent for me so that the interview could take place.

The highlights of the interview included:

- *Being asked if I would like to work for a woman who 'enjoys making men cry'.*

- *Being told that the current holder of the position is not aware that a replacement is being sought.*

- *Derisory remarks being made about my previous country of residence.*

- *When I tried to clarify the salary, the area manager quoted me $4,000 less than the agency had stated in its advert and said that the agency had got it wrong,*

- *At this stage the area manager also laughed when I asked if there were any other benefits. He said that there weren't any as they were not in the habit of 'mollycoddling' staff. He said that if employees wanted pensions and things like that they should pay for them themselves.*

- *The person who interviewed me was not the person I would have worked for because she 'does not enjoy this sort of thing; anyway, she is too busy'.*

I terminated the interview approximately 20 minutes after it started. I was running late for my afternoon's appointments and getting rather angry.

My thoughts at the time of the interview ranged from confusion about proceedings: What was this person trying to find out about me? Am I going through this or is this a bad dream? I remember feeling angry that this was going on and that having stressed the importance of keeping to time, the person who was carrying out the interview did not appear to have considered this to be of any importance. My thoughts now that I look back on the incident are still those of anger that I had been treated in this way by someone who should, in my opinion, have been trying to show me that this was an organisation I would have wanted to work for. No consideration had been given to my previous experience and the area manager was reading my CV as he was conducting the interview, giving me the impression that he had not bothered to prepare.

The short-term impact of this incident was that I did not wish to work for this hotel or the company concerned if this was the way the area manager behaved. I told the agency about my experience and will not use it again.

Gordon's experience has made him very angry. He feels he was treated with contempt by an organisation that kept him waiting. Gordon's description of the interview reveals another unpleasant side of the organisation, with an in-joke about a female manager that the applicant cannot understand (does she really enjoy making men cry?); insults about the applicant's background; confusion over the salary level, leading to a suspicion that, at the very least, the interviewer is playing games with the applicants; laughter at the thought that the company should pay for employees' pensions; and managers who are 'too busy' to attend to staff management matters. All in all, this company sends out a very clear message that it has little respect for people regardless of whether they are applicants or employees. I find myself wondering how it treats customers.

This story reveals some of the abuses that interviewers think they can get away with. I get an image of an interviewer who is completely unaware of how he comes across and the impact his comments have the applicants. To give him his due, he does convey a vivid portrayal of what working for this employer is likely to be like. I get the sense that this interview is a realistic preview of what working life will be like in this hotel. But it is not an image that many will find appealing. Who would want to work in a place that condones behaviour like this? Certainly not Gordon.

Gordon did something few people do when faced with situations like this. Despite being desperate for work, he terminated the interview and walked out. This is quite unusual, as people's natural politeness and aversion to conflict means that they stick it out to the end; you never know, things may get better. But Gordon had pressing engagements elsewhere and was not prepared to waste his time in this fashion. He had decided this was not a company he wanted to work for: Why drag the interview out?

DEREK'S STORY: MEN IN BLACK

I had just finished six years' army service, and was keen to find work in civilian life. I noticed an advertisement in the local newspaper that interested me and seemed relevant to my experience. The company installed and monitored alarm systems and communications controller was the advertised job.

I arrived half an hour early. I was told there was a form and a short 'test' to be completed, and that I could start them now. I filled in the details, on my knee, and started the test sheet. I was about halfway through, when a man from the opposite room jerked the door open, barked a few orders at the receptionist, and turned to me and said, 'Interview?' I looked at him for a second then replied, 'Yes, I was given this form.' He stopped me in mid-sentence by saying, 'Oh, that's just to see if you are dyslexic!' He took the papers off me, glanced at the test, said, 'That's fine,' and put it on the reception desk. He retained the personal details form and suggested I follow him. The receptionist, who looked a little flustered, shrugged at me as I complied.

The interviewer's room was evidently his office and was extremely untidy. Books and folders were stacked in unsteady piles, the telephone cable was strewn across the desk and a half-glass panel wall behind him allowed people to glance in as they passed. He asked my name and invited me to sit down. He pulled my application form and attached CV from a small pile and immediately began asking questions. His first question was, 'Right then, why have you applied for this job?' This caught me off guard a little and I paused, for what seemed like an age, then replied, 'I thought my experience would be suited to the job.' He stopped me mid-sentence by saying, 'Ah, yes, you have considerable accounts experience.' This was true because my final year-and-a-half of service was in the stores accounts section of the technical stores accounts department.

The remainder of the interview consisted of constant reference to my accounts experience by the interviewer. One of my referees was the technical stores officer and was therefore heavily biased towards this area of expertise. I attempted to relate some of my other experience to the interviewer, but I got the impression he was not really listening. The questions he asked seemed to leave me no choice but to answer them in a way that was not particularly in my favour. He said, 'If you get this job, do you not think you will miss out on your accounts experience?' I said no and he immediately said, 'How would you cope if one of my operatives said to you, on the radio, "Do you know what the **** hell you are doing?"' This question really unsettled me, *because of the language more than the content, and he continued before I could answer.*

The rest of the interview seemed to be a barrage of questions aimed specifically at my accounts experience, and I had the feeling he had made his mind up that, if he gave me the job, I would leave within a short period of time to pursue 'my accounts career'. He finally said, 'That's it then,' and walked towards me. He continued, 'If you are not successful, then I wish you every success with your accounts career.' This convinced me that I had little chance. I thanked him for his time and left.

Derek does not say whether or not he would have accepted this job if it were offered to him; I suspect not. He seems quite appalled by the boorish manner of this interviewer. Derek highlights three different episodes: the literacy test, the interviewer's fixation on his accounting experience, and the swearing. The subterfuge of dressing-up a literacy test as something grander irritates Derek. I suspect that the source of irritation is not about being asked to prove his literacy skills, but that the extra work required in the test was taken for nought. It was merely discarded without a second glance.

In highlighting the interviewer's fixation with his accounts experience, Derek illustrates a common mistake that people make when assessing other people: namely, the tendency to simplify the decision by stereotyping. In Derek's case, he was stereotyped as an accountant. Although stereotypes can be useful in helping people confront new and challenging situations, they can act like blinkers and prevent people seeing the wider and more complex picture, which is exactly what the interviewer needs to do. Derek's exasperation at not being able to shake the interviewer from an obsession about his supposed accounts bias is palpable. I get a sense that he regrets ever mentioning it and would prefer to start the process all over again with a new CV. The fixation of this interviewer on Derek's accounts experience illustrates how interviewers tend to make decisions early on in interviews and then do not budge from them.

The swearing in the question about the incumbent's competence came as quite a shock to Derek. This question was probably asked to reveal how applicants will react to the culture of the organisation. If people in the organisation are rude and unpleasant to each other and if the successful applicant will be the hub of communications between them, the selector needs to discover how they will react to that culture. That it comes as a shock to Derek probably indicates that he is not the right person for the job. Earlier, Anne was let down by her interviewer who portrayed the organisation as more attractive than it proved to be. Does this mean that recruiters have a responsibility to portray the organisation accurately even if this means showing its darker side? If so, does this excuse the interviewer's foul language?

PETER'S STORY: A COMPLETE WASTE OF TIME

As I stepped on to the Glasgow train at Edinburgh Haymarket station, I was glad to be at last making some concrete progress in my search for a new job. I found a seat and took the letter from the London-based recruitment agency out of my jacket pocket and laid it on the table in front of me. I double-checked the time of the interview to make sure I had plenty of time to get there and looked over the map that had been included to make sure that I knew where I was going. The train arrived on time at Queen Street station and, map in hand, I headed towards the company offices, which were thankfully fairly close to the station.

I reached the entrance to the building exactly on time and went directly to reception to let them know I had arrived. They asked me to take a seat while they informed someone that I was waiting. I took a large leather seat in a comfortable waiting area and looked around at what was quite an impressive entrance hall to a modern office block. Within a few minutes a smiling, clipboard-wielding woman came down the stairs to greet me. She introduced herself as Jill from HR and asked me to accompany her upstairs to the main offices.

Jill led me through the offices, which looked very busy but slightly disorganised, to a small meeting room with a large window overlooking the Clyde river. She indicated for me to sit on the other side of the table while she took the chair opposite. Jill then described the structure the interview would take. First of all she would handle the HR area, then I would speak to the project manager and he would explain the project on which the vacancy had arisen, and finally I would speak to two of the senior programmers currently working on the project. She then dealt with the HR issues and sorted out my travelling expenses. Jill then left, saying that she would tell the project manager I was ready to see him.

After a few minutes he arrived and, following a few pleasantries, he introduced himself as Jim and said that he was the man in charge of the project. Jim went into some detail about the project and that they need to employ someone else as one of their programmers was leaving. After quite a pleasant and informative chat he let me ask a few questions and before leaving said that he would let Max know he had finished.

At this point in the interview I was still quite nervous, but quite impressed by the company so far and the people I had met. I thought that things were going quite well. After about five minutes wait the next two interviewers appeared, a man and a woman. They asked me if my journey had been okay and I said that it had been fine and that the Edinburgh–Glasgow trains were normally pretty good.

They both sat down opposite me and put a handful of papers, including my CV, onto the table in front of them. The woman began. She said, 'We are looking to replace our database guru, Max,' indicating that Max was the man who had come in with her. At this sentence I thought that things were taking a turn for the worse, as I was definitely not a database guru and had never said I was. The next question confirmed my fears. 'Database design,' she continued, 'is the major skill required for this job. How much have you done?' My heart sank. 'Not much,' I said. 'Working on such a large project I haven't had the opportunity.' As I said this I could see the look of disappointment on their faces and I knew that this was the end of the interview. They went through the motions for the rest of the interview and after asking me if I had any questions, thanked me for my time and I left.

I was furious. Nowhere on my CV did I say that I knew anything about database design; I had wasted a whole morning on an interview for a job I wasn't even qualified to do. After a short bout of retail therapy in a music store, I headed back to Edinburgh with a slightly bad taste in my mouth.

The first two stories in this chapter dealt with disrespect through of acts of commission. Peter's story is different as it illustrates how selectors can be disrespectful to applicants through acts of omission. In this case, an organisation that appears very professional in its approach to recruitment and selection fails to ensure that the people it asks to attend an interview have the fundamental prerequisites to be credible candidates. In this story, the organisation failed to check that Peter had the required database design skills they sought. The result was half a day wasted for all concerned. In addition, both the selectors and Peter have had their expectations raised only to be dashed when the incompatibility is identified. Everyone concerned must feel a combination of annoyance, embarrassment and disappointment.

In this story the problem has arisen at the junction of employer and agent. Both might be at fault. The company may not have been explicit about database design skills to the agent. The agent may not have been as rigorous in assessing these skills as it should have been. The recruiting organisation still had opportunities to rectify the mistake when it agreed to the shortlist, but did not.

Selection panels can be quite cavalier with applicants' time. Usually though, it is done for the best intentions. They want to give people a 'chance'. Sometimes they cannot decide between a few applicants. But when these clearly weak applicants are shortlisted, they have to compete against applicants who have the required skills and they fail. The key KSAOs assert themselves and the people who were already known to be deficient on these are rejected. Their 'chance' was an illusion. Worse still, their 'chance' comes with a cost to all concerned, as Peter's story illustrates.

THINKING ON

1. At what point would you walk out of an interview? What do you regard as the limits of acceptable behaviour?

2. Gordon is told that his potential future manager is 'too busy' to attend his selection interview. Should he expect his future manager to attend his interview? If he were appointed, what issues would the manager's non-attendance have on their working relationship?

3. What can interviewees do if interviewers receive incorrect or slanted impressions of them?

4. To what extent should interviewers reflect the culture of their organisation? Should interviewers ever use swear words during interviews?

5. How would you feel if you were invited to attend an interview for a job for which you were obviously unqualified? Would you see this as an opportunity to impress or a waste of your time?

6. Under what circumstances should you invite someone for an interview or further tests? Do organisational selectors have a responsibility towards applicants' time?

READING ON

Many of the themes contained in this chapter (e.g. fairness perceptions, applicant reactions, applicant decision making, selection as a social process and interviewing) have been discussed on earlier Reading On sections. Instead, I would refer you to the growing literature that explores the relationship, or lack of it, between employees and employers. The changing nature of the employment contract has been well described in the literature (e.g. Bolsover, 2005; Bunting, 2004; Gabriel, 2005; Herriot & Pemberton, 1995; Storey, 2005), with transactions between the parties replacing relationships, and with disengaged managers, increased separation between management and staff, the commoditisation of employees and a worsened work/life balance. This changing organisational context not only has an impact on the working environment that employees join, it shapes the 'culture' or atmosphere of the recruitment and selection process.

REFERENCES

Bolsover, D. (2005) *The Living Dead: Switched Off, Zoned Out – The Shocking Truth about Office Life*, Chichester: Capstone.

Bunting, M. (2004) *Willing Slaves: How the Overwork Culture Is Ruling Our Lives*, London: HarperCollins.

Gabriel, Y. (2005) 'Glass cages and glass palaces: Images of organization in image conscious times', *Organization*, 12(1): 9–27.

Herriot, P. & Pemberton, C. (1995) *Competitive Advantage through Diversity: Organizational Learning from Difference*, London: Sage.

Storey, J. (2005) 'New organizational forms and their links with HR', in J. G. Salaman, J. Storey & J. Billsberry (eds), *Strategic Human Resource Management: Theory and Practice*, 2nd edn, London: Sage, pp. 189–207.

CHAPTER 9

Fairness

Fairness is an issue that runs through this book. At the culmination of many of the stories, there is a sense that the storytellers felt they were treated unfairly. Some selectors felt they were put in an unfair situation. Some applicants felt they were discriminated against. Some storytellers felt their organisations were treated unfairly.

Fairness is a complex and multi-faceted emotion that captures the feeling that someone has been discriminated against in an unreasonable or unlawful way. One approach to fairness is to view it from the perspective of people who believe they are victims of an injustice. In this sense, unfairness does not have to be grounded in reality. It can arise from misunderstandings, misinterpretations and simply having a decision go against you. This approach to fairness is a state of mind, a perception that you have been prejudiced against. When viewed from this perspective, 'being fair' is impossible to do with any certainty, as the 'victim' may have unreasonable requirements of organisations and their selectors. Indeed, you might have already identified some storytellers in this book who seem to have unrealistic expectations of recruiting organisations.

Given the importance of recruitment and selection to people's lives, there is a large body of law relating to the appointment of people. In Britain this law, particularly that relating to discrimination, is written to protect people who have historically had difficulty gaining access to work. It protects people from discrimination based on the fact that they are married, or because of their gender, race or disability. New and emerging legislation protects people based on their age, sexual orientation and faith. The law lays down what selectors should not do. It says they may not discriminate against people based on these qualities. In this sense, it is limiting legislation. It allows selectors to do anything they wish to do regardless of whether or not it would generally be thought to be unfair. So, for example, selectors are allowed to discriminate against people who wear brown shoes, even when such a factor would have absolutely no bearing on their ability to do the job and would be a stupid way to make a selection decision. As the list of protected groups gets larger and larger, I find myself wondering how long it will be before legislators overhaul the law and opt for a positive rather than a negative approach to discrimination. Would it not be easier for everyone if the legislation outlined what selectors should do rather than what they should not do?[1]

Fairness is another of the paradoxes of recruitment and selection. It is a discriminatory process in which one of the main goals of the selectors is to discriminate between applicants to discover who satisfies the selection criteria and who does not. It must discriminate between the applicants, but should do so in a 'fair' way. The stories in this chapter reflect this discriminatory paradox and contain examples of the different ways in which unfairness manifests itself. In particular, the collection of stories in this chapter illustrates the discrimination that female applicants face and the difficulty they have in seeking a legal remedy. The issues illustrated by these stories apply equally to other forms of discrimination. I chose to focus on discrimination against women simply because the stories I received gave me the opportunity to focus on this form of discrimination in detail and to show the multi-faceted nature of unfairness; it was not because I want to single out this particular form of discrimination or because I see it as any more nasty or worthy than any other form.

DEBRA'S STORY: EYE CONTACT

I was put forward for an interview by a recruitment agency for the position of personal assistant (PA) with a London-based public relations (PR) agency. Not having any previous knowledge of PR, I decided to invest in a small book on the subject in an attempt to equip myself with some information about the industry before my interview. As coincidence would have it, an article in the book was written by a senior manager at the agency by which I was to be interviewed.

---

[1] While the legislation in the UK is limiting, various bodies (e.g. the Chartered Institute of Personnel and Development and the Equal Opportunities Commission) have set out positive guidelines on how recruitment and selection should be conducted. Although these guidelines do not have statutory authority, industrial tribunals see them as best practice and any organisation differing from them is likely to have a very difficult time defending its case.

At the appointed date and time of the interview, I turned up punctually at the agency's offices. Unfortunately, as is customary, I waited 15 to 20 minutes in the reception area before a woman approached me and introduced herself as a member of the interviewing team. After shaking her hand and introducing myself, she led me to a meeting room, which was just off the reception area. Once seated, she asked if I would like any refreshment; I answered yes. She then informed me that the other interviewer would be with us shortly.

Refreshment in hand, and still no sign of the other interviewer, the woman decided to commence the interview. She started by asking me a couple of basic questions: What was my last position? Where was I working now? She then informed me that they had already interviewed quite a number of applicants and that they still had quite a few to see. I remember thinking that this wasn't a very good sign as it showed that they did not have a clear picture of what they were looking for in a prospective employee. It also became apparent that she wasn't very adept at interviewing: she didn't have a list of questions in front of her and therefore it wasn't long before the questions dried up.

Approximately 15 minutes after this wonderful and moving interviewing experience began, the interviewer appeared at the door. On entering, he seemed to be momentarily 'immobilised' by the door as his eyes stumbled on me. My immediate interpretation of the look in his eyes – which I must stress I have, thankfully, never experienced before or since – was that I was not a tall, blonde, attractive female with shapely legs. I'm 5' 3" with short brown hair and medium build! He was obviously disappointed with my physical features. Regaining his composure, he walked over to the table and sat down beside his team member opposite me. He introduced himself but did not proffer his hand to me. I knew instantly from that look that there wasn't a 'chance in hell' of me being seriously considered for the position, which was confirmed by the manner in which the interviewer conducted the rest of the interview.

He commenced the interview by asking (or more precisely mumbling) the exact same questions as his team member had asked, all the while avoiding eye contact with me. He too clearly had no set list of questions to ask me and the conversation again soon dried up. I remember sitting there thinking I can't believe he works in public relations, where the ability to communicate effectively is of paramount importance. I then found myself in the alien position of having to drive the interview, as they both seemed to have given up asking me questions. My next thought was that although I knew I wasn't going to be offered the position, which I wouldn't have taken anyway, I was 'damned' if I was going to leave the interview without mentioning the book I'd purchased. At that stage I was already driving the interview, so manoeuvring the conversation around to the subject was not terribly difficult. At the end of the interview, which lasted half an hour in total, they reiterated that they still had a large number of candidates to see and that they couldn't give me any clear indication as to when I would receive a response to their decision.

Standing outside their offices afterwards, my emotion was total disbelief at how thoroughly unprofessional they were in their handling of the situation and at their ineptness at interviewing. This was the worst experience of being an interviewee that I have ever encountered. Looking back at the incident now, my feeling is still disbelief at how unprofessional the interviewer had been, in that I was judged solely on my physical appearance and not on my ability to do the job.

Debra's story could have fitted comfortably in a number of other chapters. She was shown little respect and was subject to some appalling interviewing. But it is the perception of discrimination she encountered that is of interest here. In many ways, I believe that the discrimination Debra encountered is probably the commonest form. In involves someone deciding that an applicant is not worthy based on some personal dislike. In this case, it was physical appearance. It might equally have been colour, race, religion, a disability, or a million and one other personal prejudices. But the issue is never raised. It is unspoken discrimination that is manifested in inaction. There are no physical remnants. There is nothing the person on the receiving end can pinpoint to illustrate the discrimination other than interpretations of body language. As such, it cannot be challenged without being impolite and starting an unpleasant slanging match, which is rarely advantageous to the applicant. If challenged, interviewers can simply refer to other ways in which they believe the applicant is inappropriate to justify the selection decision; and, of course, there will be occasions when the person on the receiving end misreads these non-verbal signs and misjudges the interviewer.

On a personal level, I really feel for Debra. It must be horrendous to receive the sort of glance she was given. Not only does it objectify her with all the attendant psychological feelings of worthlessness, frustration and anger, it also reinforces power structures. She is reminded that she is the powerless person in this relationship: powerless both because she wants something this interviewer has the power to grant and because she does not conform to particular archetypes. One glance 'damned' her application and unleashed negative emotions that she was unable to confront.

An interesting aspect of this exchange concerns the way in which behaviour during recruitment and selection signals the nature of work in the organisation. We have already seen how organisations tend to be on their best behaviour when recruiting staff and how sometimes this conveys a false impression of future work. Debra's story shows the opposite side of the equation: it signals the unpleasantness either of work in this organisation or of one rogue employee. If there is an upside to this story, it is that she found out about this organisation and this individual before taking the massive step of joining them. Nevertheless, this is a very small benefit and this sort of behaviour cannot be condoned.

However, this story raises the issue of the connectivity of pre- and post-entry behaviour. Should behaviour during recruitment and selection mirror the behaviour of people in the organisation? Most people accept that applicants should receive a realistic preview of what working in the recruiting organisation will be like. But if the organisation is awash with discriminatory beliefs, behaviours and practices, recruitment behaviour that mirrored this would prevent people who might challenge these prejudices joining the company. It would reinforce the bad behaviours and it block the discriminated from opportunity.

BILLIE'S STORY: THE COAL MINER'S DAUGHTER

The interview I am going to recall took place between me and the personnel director and regional manager of a construction company. This was my second interview for the position of marketing manager for the South Wales region.

As soon as I entered the interview room I felt uncomfortable: the personnel director and the regional manager were sharing a joke. They had been looking at my application form, which included a photograph, and the personnel director started the meeting by commenting that they both felt that my looks were more suited to the cover of Vogue *than a construction site. Although this was not the way I would have ideally liked the meeting to begin, I thought perhaps it was better to clear up any misconceptions that my sex would mean I would have difficulties doing the job in question. It became clear at this stage that they had great difficulty with the idea of employing a woman in the construction industry. They felt that I would need 'looking after' and that clients and consultants would be frightened to accept any invitations to lunch I might give them 'in case their wives found out'.*

While I was trying to explain that I had never had any difficulties with either my colleagues or business associates, the personnel director changed the subject. This time I was asked what my father's occupation was. I explained that my father's family had originally been coal miners. This is not unusual in Wales, since most people can trace their families back to the coal mining industry, and I usually found it helped me when I was marketing in the region.

Unfortunately such a background did not help me in this particular interview; the personnel director explained that they were looking for people from a 'higher class'.

Before I had the opportunity to explain that my father was a director before he died, the personnel director had picked up on the fact that I was studying Social Sciences with the Open University. I was relieved that we had at least begun to start to concentrate on topics other than gender and class, and explained that the course included politics and economics and that it was very interesting. It had improved my writing and analytical skills. Unfortunately, once again, the personnel director was not impressed. I was labelled a socialist and not someone who could comfortably work in 'a capitalist society'.

While I was trying to come to terms with what the personnel director was saying, the conversation refocused on the subject of honesty: did I think that this was an important trait in business? I explained that it was difficult to give an 'honest' answer without being given more details of the situation but, in general, I felt that honesty between colleagues was important since this engendered trust and a 'team spirit'. With regard to clients, I commented that good relationships often meant good references, repeat orders, increased opportunities and the chance to negotiate work, and it would be difficult to maintain these relationships if clients found that a company had been deliberately dishonest. The personnel director then described a particular occasion when he had deliberately lied to a client and made the company a 'very handsome profit'. After telling this tale the personnel director commented that obviously 'you wouldn't be happy with this situation' and used my answer to illustrate his earlier finding: 'your socialist principles would get in the way of good business practice'.

Now, if you are anything like me you will not be sure at this stage whether to laugh or cry. I felt that either of these options would just reinforce their view that women had no right to be in business, so I decided to try to be professional and get through this interview with as much dignity as I could. To do this I tried to bring the regional manager into the conversation to see if I could get him on my side. Unfortunately, it soon became apparent that the regional manager wasn't being very honest with his head office with regard to forthcoming work opportunities in South Wales and the contacts he had with clients. This made the conversation regarding the construction industry in South Wales a little difficult.

The interview ended by the personnel director saying, 'Thank you. I think you can go on for some time trying to convince us of your capabilities for this particular job. but I think we have heard enough to make an assessment.' Thankfully, a secretary gave me the opportunity to freshen up before I made my journey back. I declined a cup of tea because I just wanted to get out of the office, but I was very grateful for a few minutes to 'pull myself together' before I got into the car.

After initially feeling upset about the incident, I began to feel cross with myself for letting people talk to me in that manner. Meanwhile, having failed to find a suitable candidate through advertising, the company appointed a specialist recruitment firm to find a marketing manager. Although the firm has now appointed a marketing manager, three members of their senior management team, including the chief executive, have commented that they wished I was working for them.

You can't win, can you? Whereas Debra was damned for not being 'a tall, blonde, attractive female with shapely legs', Billie was condemned for having the looks of a model. The context clearly matters, but the key issue here is that bigoted individuals make unfair judgements on matters that have little to do with success in the role. In Billie's case the discrimination is spoken – but where is the independent witness to corroborate her side of the story? Worse still, the justification for this prejudice is the weakness of others: 'clients and consultants would be frightened to accept any invitations to lunch I might give them "in case their wives found out"'. This is clearly unlawful behaviour, as this criterion would not be relevant to male applicants. But it is also a ridiculous consideration that would not withstand serious scrutiny. This personnel director seems to have a very poor opinion of clients and consultants; I wonder how he regards his staff.

Perhaps the most pernicious aspect of this story is the way the unacceptable behaviour causes the person at whom it is directed to recoil and question herself. Billie has done nothing wrong. She has applied in good faith, tried to answer the interviewers' questions openly and honestly, and refused to be provoked by their unreasonable comments. As she says, 'I decided to try to be professional and get through this interview with as much dignity as I could.' So why should she feel angry at herself? Why should she be the one who is hurt?

MARJORIE'S STORY: LESBIANS AND HOMOSEXUALS

It was a warm July morning. My husband drove me from our home for the 9.30 interview. I was apprehensive about being interviewed for a job in a prison by a board of three people I knew nothing about. I was already an established civil servant working in the Department of Health and Social Security, where we were a predominantly female staff. The only information I had about the board members was that they were all men.

I arrived with about 10 minutes to spare and reported to the reception area at the prison gate. It was a shabby, dark space and the staff seemed very remote behind the glass screen. I was collected by a member of the Personnel department and escorted to the interview room.

The board chairman sat in the middle of his two colleagues behind a large table. The previous board I had sat was much less formal, so this was some-thing I had not expected, considering that it was still within the Civil Service. They introduced themselves and it soon became apparent that they were all governors of various grades, aged between 45 and 55. I was 28 and felt very young and inexperienced in comparison to them.

The questions they asked were broadly based on the information I had provided on my application form. They were interested in my educational qualifications, my experience of working with people from all kinds of back-grounds, and my previous jobs as a bank clerk and barmaid before becoming a benefits clerk. They asked me what my expectations of the job were. I said that I was looking for a new career that would utilise my 'people' skills, develop me and be a secure source of employment.

Everything was going quite well and I was relaxing into the interview when the line of questions changed tack to a more personal level. I was asked what my 'child-care arrangements were likely to be' if I were selected. My children at that time were aged 6 and 8 years and were being cared for by my husband, who worked from home, and a child-minder on the rare occasions that neither one of us was available. This question seemed rather irrelevant to me, as I had been in full-time employment for two years at that time and there had been no problems highlighted by my employers.

The next question was, 'You are quite petite, aren't you? How do you think you would be able to deal with an aggressive prisoner who was threatening you?' I am 5' 4" tall, but I explained that I regularly cleared a public house at closing time, by myself, and if I could reason with a load of drunk men nearly twice my size, I didn't think I would have too much difficulty dealing with men who were sober. I pointed out that women could have a more calming influence in potentially violent situations than men, who could sometimes escalate the problem.

The 'pièce de résistance' was their final multiple question: 'We note from your application form that you are married. Are you happy? Could you tell us what you think about lesbians and homosexuals?' As you may well imagine, I was rather embarrassed by these questions. I took quite a while to answer. I said that I didn't much care what people did in the privacy of their own homes

as long as they didn't try to get me involved, and yes, I was happily married!
They then went on to say that they recognised that the prison service had a
problem within the female estate, with a large number of lesbian women in
positions of authority who were abusing their powers when it came to man-
aging their subordinates. They added that were actively recruiting straight,
married women into the service to try to break the cycle.

My initial reaction was one of relief that we seemed to have come to the end
of the interview, but during the drive home I became increasingly unsettled
by their closing statements. I was apprehensive about what pressures may be
placed on me if I were deployed to a female establishment. I was also intrigued
by the thought of the reaction they would have received if they had asked the
same questions of a male candidate.

In many respects, Marjorie's interview is similar to those related by Debra and
Billie. Like them, she was questioned in an intimidating fashion by men about
personal issues, her physical appearance and her attitudes. And yet there is
something different about this story. Although there are clear indications that
she was unhappy with the treatment she received (e.g. the phrases 'This question seemed rather irrelevant to me' and 'pièce de résistance' both suggest indignation), her reaction seems more centred on her shock and embarrassment
at being asked questions on these matters rather than their inappropriateness
or unfair nature. There are several factors influencing this shift of focus. First,
the manner in which the questions were asked appears to have been much
more considered and set against a context of rigorous interviewing. Secondly,
when the potentially contentious questions were asked, they were qualified
in such a way that their relevance was demonstrated. Examples of this are
the confrontation with an aggressive prisoner and the culture change initiative. Thirdly, they appear to be genuine issues that the job holder needs to
understand. Set in these circumstances, difficult and potentially contentious
questions can be asked.

It is one thing to justify the use of these questions to the interviewee; it
is another to prove that they are lawful. Three of the questions are particularly troublesome: the child-care, size and marriage questions. The child-care
question is likely to be answered differently by men and women given social
convention. The size question will clearly have a bias against women. Normally, both of these questions would be seen as unlawful by tribunals, who
would deem that they discriminate against women. However, in this circumstance (and this is one of the very few organisations where this is likely to be
the case), the members of the selection panel are probably on safe ground (although the child-care question still seems inappropriate). The reason for this
is that there are some exemptions against the sex discrimination legislation

when the job holder will be caring for people living in single-sex residential establishments. In such circumstances, the employer is entitled to employ only people of the gender of the people under their care.

The question about Marjorie's marital status is troublesome. The law prevents discrimination against married people and is not concerned with discrimination against single people. Interestingly, this may change in the near future, with the likelihood of new legislation protecting people from discrimination on the basis of their sexual orientation. This question is problematic, because it raises the issue of applicants' marital status. Who can say how the responses will be used? They may not be used to discriminate against married people, but on the other hand they may be.

ANG'S STORY: THE VOLUPTUOUS CANDIDATE

We had a vacancy in our Accounts department for an accounts clerk. The person needed to be able to use a computer. The job involved processing basic accounting data into the accounting software package, installed in the company's mainframe computer. The managing director and I, as the head of the accounts department, had agreed that we should ask a recommended recruitment agency to send us a shortlist of candidates.

Our organisation was small to medium in size and it was agreed that the MD and I would conduct the interview, since there was no Personnel department. To our delight, three women were introduced by the agency. Perhaps it just happened that no suitable males were available at that time. Of the three interviewed, two were middle-aged married women who were experienced, but unfortunately their personality and appearance did not appeal to us.

Julia, our third candidate, was in her mid-30s. After the MD had given a brief description of the company, I began to explore her experience. Some of the dialogue went like this:

Me: Do you know how to do a bank reconciliation? I ask because you mentioned that your previous job was keeping books for a bar and you might only have kept a record of the bar takings.

Julia: Yes I do, and there should be no problems for I have worked as a bookkeeper in a company prior to that.

Me: When sums of money are received on a daily basis, how do you categorise those funds? Which should be allocated to the Debtors Control

Account (Accounts Receivable Account), and which should go else-where?

Julia: *I am not totally sure what you mean exactly, but I am sure when you show me, I will understand and should be able to deal with it.*

Me: *I see. Have you dealt with Value Added Tax (VAT) accounting before?*

Julia: *Yes, I have.*

Me: *Our company is VAT registered. Would you know the difference in the methods of recording VAT on a cash basis compared to that on an accruals basis? Do you also know how to prepare and reconcile a VAT control account?*

Julia: *I cannot explain the difference, but I was shown how to do a VAT control account before.*

Further questioning revealed that she was not very familiar with our account-ing package, but would like to learn. I was not fully at ease with her work experience.

The MD decided to offer Julia the post, even though I had opposed the idea. There was no doubt that he was enthralled by her voluptuous appearance. Julia knows the art of winning approval from the male sex more than how to keep proper books of accounts. She was a vision in her green and black plaid skirt and white blouse, with little flecks of clay dusted across her glasses. Her blonde hair was in a ponytail. She had been attracted to this job because of a higher salary.

In the short term, I was displeased with the way Julia was recruited. I felt the MD had done something unacceptable. The consequence was that the new recruit required constant supervision to obtain reliable and accurately processed information. In the long term, her quality of work did improve. With the pay increment and her eagerness to learn new techniques, together with occasional support from me, her work could be acceptable.

Although I find Ang's story deplorable in the way in which a poorly qualified candidate is appointed simply on her 'voluptuous' looks at the expense of two other people, there is a refreshing honesty to it. He knows that they made a poor decision based on sexual magnetism. He knew they made a bad decision at the time and that it would mean a lot of extra work for him. The extract from the interview demonstrates that the candidate is 'winging' it and has little of the required knowledge. But, as Ang says, 'Julia knows the art of winning approval from the male sex more than how to keep proper books of accounts.' Assuming Ang is right and Julia did knowingly engage in this activity, how should we judge her? Is her behaviour appropriate? We have already deplored a sexual predator when that person is the interviewer. Is it different for applicants?

This is an ethical issue that is not simply resolved and much will depend on your moral stance. To be honest, I am not sure where I stand on this question. Clearly applicants must not misrepresent themselves, but they should be able to 'manage' the image they present to put themselves in the best light possible. Generally, organisations design selection processes and determine what selection tests to deploy. At times, applicants must feel like guinea pigs in a tester's laboratory. Just to get a job, they can be subjected to assessments of their intelligence, personality, knowledge, skills, behaviour and even blood. In such a climate, applicants are likely to feel alienated from the invasive organisation and will deploy their own counter measures. Given the power imbalances that usually occur in recruitment and selection and the all-or-nothing hurdle to clear, who are we to deny salvation-seeking people the use of all the weapons in their armoury?

On a more practical level, I worry about the long-term effects of recruiting such unqualified people. This might turn out to be a poisoned chalice for Julia. How much respect will people have for her? Will she just be the MD's trophy? By raising the sexual stakes (if indeed she has), will there be a time for payback? Shifting attention to the selectors: if they are stupid enough to be suckered into offering jobs to unqualified people because of their 'voluptuous' appearance, what will it do to their reputation? How will they be perceived when it becomes apparent that she cannot do the job?

One way of looking at recruitment and selection is through the lens of love and relationships. Recruitment involves the bonding of two parties: the employer and the employee. They must meet, fall in love and then live together. The relationship sometimes goes through tough times, divorces or affairs, and other times things are much happier. Recruitment and selection involve the discovery of each other, the courtship and the consummation. And just like the formation of a loving relationship, it is a highly charged moment that potentially changes people's lives for ever. Viewing Ang's story through this lens highlights the fundamental nature of the forces at work. Perhaps we are just being naïve when we try to make recruitment and selection a sterile, emotion-free environment focused on cold, rational and scientific assessment.

An interesting aspect of this story is how the law applies to it. I have shown this story to three employment lawyers and they agree that the interviewers have not breached the sex discrimination laws. The logic appears to be that as they were presented with three women to choose between, they did not favour one gender over another. Hence, there cannot be any sexual discrimination. However, the lawyers had a different opinion with regard to other legislation. They thought that there might be a case to answer on age discrimination grounds, depending on what Ang means by the term 'middle-aged'. And they agreed that there was certainly a case to answer for discrimination against married people.

MARGARET'S STORY: THE SHOWER SCENE

I went for an internal interview at the company for which I was then working. I had seen the job advertised on the staff notice board. It gave a brief job description that was not dissimilar to what I was already doing, but it was on another site much nearer to home and at a grade higher. I felt really excited: I had the experience and qualifications that the post required. It would also cut my travelling time to work by half. I applied.

I was invited to see the personnel officer dealing with the vacancy. I had a brief interview. I was then offered a second interview with the manager of the department at the other site. I arrived feeling nervous, but fairly confident. I was hopeful of obtaining the position.

During the course of the interview I discovered the interviewer was not the person who would be my line manager. Instead, he was a senior technician in the area who had been asked to carry out the interview by the manager. This only became apparent as he explained the nature of the position; I felt misled and confused. He made himself out to be much more important than he was. Moreover, he gave no explanation why there had been a change of interviewer.

I was taken to the area and given a tour of the unit, which included an office (which was a mess!) and changing facilities (a shower is normally part of daily routine, but as the area was not fully open I did not have to do this).

The work was explained in detail and I was interested and motivated by what I heard. One slight concern was that only two people normally worked in the area: the interviewer and the person who would fill the vacancy. I had been used to a large working group. We returned to the office, where I was asked more work-related questions. Unfortunately a lot of the questions were repeated, as we had covered a lot during the tour. I was given little chance to ask questions of my own. Nor was I asked if I had any concerns.

I was asked, 'Do you want the position?' I was given no time to consider and being slightly confused and a little flustered I said, 'Yes.' 'Great! I will inform Personnel and you can start in a month. You will need to let your current manager know that you are leaving tomorrow.' This caused me to panic inside: what had I agreed to? I had said yes, but under pressure and had not really thought it through.

The interview turned to more general topics such as hobbies. He then told me that it was 'common to go for a drink after work: did I mind?' Well, I had just told him I would take the job, so what else could I say except, 'No, I do not mind.' By this time I was anxious: there was something in the way he kept referring to socialising and I felt very uncomfortable. His parting remark was banter about there only being one shower and we would be sharing!

It may have been a joke – I will never know – but it scared the hell out of me. I worried about it all the way home. I discussed the interview with my husband. I would have liked the job, but could not work for that man. We decided I would stay where I was. I phoned Personnel the next day to say I had changed my mind and was no longer interested in the job.

Looking back, I think the man was being friendly and was joking. I suppose I will never know. I ended up having some contact with him, but I always had a certain impression of him and I never did change it. I now realise that the company is also being 'interviewed' and his style reflected badly on the company. Now it would be classed as sexual harassment.

Margaret is right: this behaviour could be interpreted as sexual harassment or something a lot more serious. This sort of behaviour is completely unacceptable and against the law. Even if the interviewer had completely innocent intentions, such behaviour is inappropriate. Interviewers are gatekeepers who have considerable power – they must realise the power they have. This interviewer's comments can easily be construed as a sexual proposition and blackmail: if you want this job. . . I would like to think that this interviewer made an innocent mistake and that such occurrences are uncommon. But I fear they may not be. Some industries – the film industry springs to mind – are notorious and have their own sexual innuendo for recruitment and selection – the 'casting couch'. This interviewer's behaviour may have led to such a situation.

Margaret was able to walk away from this job offer. In material I have not included, she reveals that she was quickly promoted in the organisation and this incident did not cause her any problems. She occasionally had to liaise with the interviewer. Although she had a very low opinion of him, it did not become an obstacle.

WAYNE'S STORY: ON THE BUSES

The incident occurred while I was employed as the human resources manager of a large local bus company. The company was seeking to make an internal appointment for a relief driving instructor. The individual would come out of the ranks of bus drivers and carry out the role of driving instructor on an 'as and when required' basis. When not required in the training capacity, the individual would revert to normal duties as a local bus driver. We already had one excellent driving instructor and were seeking to fill the relief position with a person of similar calibre. I had appointed the existing instructor and felt quite confident about setting out to repeat the process.

The position was discussed at the monthly management meeting and we decided to make it an internal appointment. We wanted to involve the driving standards officer in the selection process, as his expertise would be essential for the driving aptitude aspect. He and I had previously combined as an interview panel, so I felt very positive when we set out to plan the selection process. We posted an internal vacancy announcement on all company notice boards inviting applications from positive, committed employees with an unblemished driving record, a good attendance at work record and an exemplary standard of customer care. We received five applications; four male and one female, and decided to shortlist all of them.

The selection process had four stages. First, applicants were asked to give a short presentation on a topic of their choice. This was followed by an assessment of their driving, a formal interview and finally, a test of their ability to instruct others.

Four out of the five candidates were impressive at the presentation stage, and of these four candidates three, including the female, scored highly in the driving assessment. All the candidates were invited to a formal interview. References were then sought from the relevant personnel managers and the personnel files were perused to review attendance, quality reports, customer complaints and customer testimonials. These assessment activities resulted in two male candidates being shortlisted. Both candidates were 'neck and neck', so it was decided to put them through the instruction test. We felt it was unnecessary to subject the other candidates to this final test, because it would prolong the process and good scores on this test would not sufficiently compensate for their lower scores in other tests. The two shortlisted candidates were given the task of instructing a non-PCV-licensed manager to drive a double-decker bus around the depot yard.

Following the announcement of the successful candidate, there was an amazing adverse reaction from the female candidate. I invited her to my office to review her application and to give her constructive feedback that might aid in a future application. She appeared satisfied with the review, but within 24 hours she lodged a grievance citing that the selection had been unfair.

It appears that during the selection process she had been advised by the driving standards officer that she had been placed second in the driving assessment section. She had interpreted this as warranting selection to the shortlist. She also felt that, as the only female in the frame, she should have automatically been shortlisted.

Because I was a member of the senior management team, the grievance had to be taken by one of the directors. He thoroughly reviewed the whole process and the relevant paperwork and felt that the selection was fair. The female candidate appealed against his decision and this appeal went to the managing director, who upheld the decision. I was then advised that the case was being referred to a female official in the trade union as an example of sex discrimination.

Up to this point in time I had felt quite confident that the process had been fair and, even though my colleagues and the MD had rejected the grievance, I became unnerved: I expected something untoward 'to jump out of the woodwork and hit me over the head'. My MD felt that I was overreacting because he was quite satisfied about the process and outcome. While I was totally convinced that we had selected the right person for the position, I found these accusations most unpleasant.

This incident received unprecedented attention, even in far-flung departments of the company. This was strongly fuelled by the vociferous and vehement style of the rejected female candidate, who was happy to discuss the situation with all and sundry; this was an endorsement that she would have been unsuitable for the position. Although I was fully conscious of the company grapevine and the canteen culture, her accusations felt like a vicious personal attack.

I was extremely concerned about the impact on the successful candidate, particularly on his motivation and confidence, especially as he came from the same depot as the female applicant and would have to continue working with her. Fortunately, his response was very measured and he was able to calmly wait for the furore to die down. The outcome could have been very different!

Wayne found himself in an awkward position. Being accused of discriminatory behaviour is very unpleasant. If you believe yourself to be innocent, it is easy to become a victim yourself and to feel that the world is against you. You imagine that people are thinking 'there's no smoke without fire' and you are forced onto the defensive. It feels most unfair, you feel vulnerable, helpless, abused. You begin questioning everything you did and expect things 'to jump out of the woodwork' even though you are sure you did everything correctly. It is very nasty situation to be in and the effects can last a long time; misperceptions can stick.

But how else can it be? Applicants need channels through which they can make complaints. They need a process to highlight and challenge unlawful behaviour and it is much more difficult for them to make and then prove a complaint. The failed candidate is more likely than not to put a bad incident 'down to experience' and walk away. To launch a complaint is likely to be seen as futile or counterproductive: 'I don't want to work there anyway.' Making a complaint involves confrontation, conflict and reengagement with the unpleasant organisation. How many people know how to go about making a complaint? Then, if a complaint is made, what sort of evidence can be mustered to support it? We have already seen how much unlawful behaviour is not recorded and easily hidden. The interviewee is 'in the room alone', while the interviewers may have a whole team to support them. Psychologically, therefore, making a complaint is an extraordinarily difficult thing to do and this is particularly the case when the complainant is outside the company.

Perhaps the trauma that Wayne experienced is inevitable if candidates are to be encouraged to make their complaints about unfair treatment. And complain they must, because it is only when people complain about the shoddy treatment they receive that things will change for the better.

THINKING ON

1. Should interviewers change their behaviour during recruitment and selection? Should they try to behave as they do at work so that applicants can judge what work will be like in the organisation?

2. Are there any occasions when someone's physical appearance is relevant during recruitment and selection?

3. Are there occasions when someone's command of English or accent is relevant during recruitment and selection?

4. Should applicants secretly tape their selection interviews? Should interviewers? What impact would the taping (covertly and openly) of interviews have on the conduct of the interview? How would people's behaviour change if they knew the interview was being taped?

5. Imagine the situation where a female interviewer used her 'voluptuous' appearance to flirt with a male applicant. What is your reaction? Is it any different to a male interviewer making sexual innuendos to female applicants?

6. To what extent should applicants 'sell' themselves? What are the limits of impression management? When does managing the image you present become lying?

7. What sort of evidence would be necessary to convince a tribunal that you have been unlawfully discriminated against? What sort of evidence could an applicant muster?

8. 'No smoke without fire', or so the saying goes. What is the impact of bringing accusations of unlawful discrimination against people?

9. Conversely, what are the implications of not saying something when you have experienced unlawful discrimination?

10. The focus of this chapter has been on two aspects of discrimination: unlawful discrimination and perceptions of unfairness. Is one of these more important than the other?

READING ON

For all the social process advocates' exhortations that selection is not about hurdles to jump but about the start or continuance of a relationship, there is no escaping the truth that recruitment and selection processes are gateways into the organisation for external applicants and an obstacle that internal applicants have to clear for promotion. In this way, if we view recruitment and selection processes through capitalist spectacles, they are a major influence on people's access to opportunity, advancement, power, influence, higher salaries, privilege and a better lifestyle. They can also serve a more sinister role in maintaining the status quo and protecting the privilege of the advantaged. As a result, most countries have developed laws and codes of best practice to ensure fairness. Interestingly, though, the laws of most countries are reactive as they tend to protect particular groups (e.g. genders, races, faith, disabilities) rather than adopting a more active stance by enforcing particular positive approaches. As mentioned earlier, there is one terrible dilemma at the heart of assessments of fairness in recruitment and selection: if the process is as fair and as even-handed as it can be, those who already have privileged places in society are advantaged in the recruitment and selection process.

The seminal text on fairness in recruitment and selection is Arvey and Faley's (1988) *Fairness in Selecting Employees.* Although a little out of date now, this is an excellent exposition of the field. To find more up-to-date material, you should refer to any good recruitment and selection textbook. All have sections, usually whole chapters, on the subject. One word of warning, though: make sure you get a text written for your country, as laws and guidelines vary greatly. In addition to recruitment and selection textbooks, there are many books available on employment law, but as the law is changing all the time you should look for a text written or updated in the past year or two.

Impression management is a topic that has attracted a great deal of attention in recent years. There are now a number of different ways of approaching the subject. One way is to look at how language has been hijacked by management. The books by Watson (2003) and Wheen (2004) are particularly good on this. Then there are the books focusing directly on impression management. A classic is Goffman's (1990) *The Presentation of Self in Everyday Life.* A more recent book that focuses on impression management at work is by Rosenfeld, Giacalone and Riordan (2002), who provide an excellent overview of the research and much good advice. The authors draw a clear distinction between impression management and ingratiation, look at ways to repair a damaged reputation and consider different impression management strategies.

REFERENCES

Arvey, R. D. & Faley, R. H. (1988) *Fairness in Selecting Employees*, 2nd edn, Reading MA: Addison-Wesley.

Goffman, E. (1990) *The Presentation of Self in Everyday Life*, London: Penguin.

Rosenfeld, P., Giacalone, R. A. & Riordan, C. A. (2002) *Impression Management: Building and Enhancing Reputations at Work*, 2nd revd edn, London: Thomson.

Watson, D. (2003) *Gobbledygook*, London: Atlantic.

Wheen, F. (2004) *How Mumbo-Jumbo Conquered the World: A Short History of Modern Delusions*, London: Harper Perennial.

PART III

Multiple Perspectives

One of the greatest failings of the recruitment and selection literature is that it rarely considers both sides of the event. Studies of new selection tools, for example, tend to use employee performance data (usually through supervisor ratings) to assess their predictive validity. It is very rare for a study to include outcomes such as applicants' reactions to the test, although the emergence of this domain may encourage more researchers to do so. Conversely, within the applicant reactions literature, very few organisational measures are included, making them equally one-sided.

One area where it is impossible to separate the two constituencies is the emerging field of person–organisation fit. Researchers taking this approach only consider that a 'fit' has been achieved if the appointment turns out to be in the best interests of both parties. The inescapable consequence of such a position is that the researcher has to capture outcomes for both the recruiter and the appointee to calculate the degree of success. However, even in this domain, most researchers opt for quite a limited interpretation of fit, such as the alignment of values between the two parties. One major problem with assessing the fit between people and organisations is that there are so many variables to take account of. Which ones are salient and which ones are not?

Getting away from selection tools, there are other aspects of recruitment and selection that benefit from being considered from both sides of the encounter simultaneously. One of these is the issue of market forces. When I read the recruitment and selection literature, I notice that very little regard, if any at all, is given by researchers to the way in which laws of supply and demand influence recruitment and selection outcomes. It is almost as if recruitment and selection research is conducted in what economists call a 'perfect market', which operates efficiently. In the real world, I see something else and this is reflected in these stories: applicants who will accept any job such is their desperation; or interviewers who turn the interview into a selling pitch in order to recruit someone; or applicants who make exorbitant demands knowing that they are the preferred candidate; or recruiters who turn shortlisting into a lucky dip as a way of coping with a mountain of applications. In all of these cases, market forces alter the way in which participants interact.

Another aspect of recruitment and selection that is often forgotten is the influence of political forces. I am not referring to government intervention or legal issues, but the sort of internal politics that interfere with effective recruitment and selection. Already, we have read stories in this book that show people being cast adrift by their colleagues and dropped in at the deep end. Others have hinted at power relationships in making selection decisions. For example, a chair of a selection panel riding roughshod over his panel, or a managing director's decision of which applicant to appoint despite the finance manager's insistence that the person does not have the required skills. The stories in Chapter 12 on 'Politics' explore the subject of political interference in more depth.

The final chapter in this section is different to the others as it focuses on one particular selection process, the Prison Service's Assessment Centre. As I mentioned earlier, when these stories were being written, the Prison Service was sending a large number of students to the Open University. This coincided with its roll-out of a new assessment centre for assessing staff for promotion. This assessment centre was particularly thorough and represents many aspects of good selection. However, it was not without its flaws and was subject to some of the paradoxes of recruitment and selection. For example, the more rigorous the assessment, the more people feel aggrieved by it. Because we were receiving so many students from the Prison Service at this time, I received a lot of stories about this assessment centre. Importantly, people wrote about the assessment centre from many different perspectives and this helps us draw insights about the process that might not otherwise be possible.

CHAPTER 10

Fit

Researchers have long known that selectors in organisations are looking for people with three qualities. The first is having the KSAOs (knowledge, skills, abilities and other attributes) to perform well in the job, or the ability to learn the KSAOs quickly. The second is having the motivation to perform well in the role. It is not sufficient for people to have the skills: they must also have the inclination or drive to use their skills effectively. Thirdly, they must 'fit in'; that is, get on with other people in the environment. Selectors have a huge armoury of tools and techniques to assess KSAOs. They have a smaller stock of tools for assessing motivation. But virtually nothing to help them assess applicants' fit.

Despite not having any tools to assess fit, it is a central part of most selection processes. Selectors want to assess how new recruits will fit in and new recruits want to assess whether or not they will be happy in the new organisation. Perhaps the most 'modern' way for selectors to assess fit is letting applicants determine their fit for themselves. This was the approach taken by the MD in Emma's story in the first chapter, which proved successful. With such an approach, the recruiting organisation must create ample opportunities for applicants to explore and discover the 'true' nature of the organisation for themselves. The alternative, and much less successful, approach that selectors adopt is to try to assess new recruits' fit for them. But as selectors have no tools to assess fit, they have to rely on untried and unscientific methods to assess fit, which are often based on nothing more than someone's gut feeling. And because recruitment and selection form an artificial environment, where all the parties 'manage' their image, these gut feelings are often wrong.

The stories in this chapter do two things. First, they show the various ways in which people assess fit during recruitment and selection. Second, they show the consequences of fit and misfit on those recruited. The first story relates a very professional approach to the assessment of applicants' fit that typifies the way in which fit is assessed in many recruitment and selection episodes.

PHILIP'S STORY: CLASSIC CARS

I was recruited to set up a new business under a group umbrella. As the position within the organisation was at a senior level, three simultaneous methods were used to recruit: a headhunter was briefed with the profile of the type of person envisaged, several specialist placement agencies were contacted, and an advert was placed in the trade press. As a new position was being created and a new business being set up (which were both sensitive to existing suppliers and to competitors), the advert asked for responses to go to a box number and did not state the company name (all very mysterious to the candidate!).

I responded to the advert. After replying with my CV and a covering letter, a reply confirming receipt was received within three to four days, and a further letter asking me to make contact followed a few days later. I telephoned the next day and was asked a few basic questions and told a little more about the role. Was I still interested? Yes, then a date was set for an initial meeting.

The first interview was held at the office that had been put aside for the new venture and in the evening so that I could attend after work from my current employment. I was greeted at the door, offered a drink and led to a quiet office. This initial interview was held by the person who is now my business partner. It was conducted on a one-to-one basis and covered a broad range of topics. The interview actually started very gradually, as we informally chatted for quite some time about our common interest in classic cars (I had arrived at the interview in my MG) and the conversation gradually turned to more formal business. I was shown the company portfolio, which demonstrated its experience. I, in turn, showed the interviewer my portfolio, which demonstrated my experience and style of working. I was given a job description, a tour of the building, a company brochure and a very clear picture of the role and its potential. This meeting lasted over two hours, which was a very positive outcome from an initial meeting. I felt extremely positive about the company and the venture it was embarking on. I thought it had a great deal of potential.

A week or so later, a further meeting was arranged by letter as I had made it through to the shortlist of three. I was greeted at the door by a different person, offered a drink and led to a meeting room. This second meeting was very different, starting with a proof-reading test of a recruitment advertisement (which contained deliberate mistakes). The conversation then turned into a very detailed discussion about the profile of the business, potential clients, suppliers and equipment. Following this, each of the key department managers in other areas of the business that I would be dealing with were invited to have a chat with me, on a one-to-one basis. During these discussions much wider issues were covered, such as my interests, how I relax, where I see the new venture going and how quickly; and of course this was my chance to ask a few questions to managers working for the boss who was setting up the new company. I got reassuringly honest answers! This session ended with another tour; but because this visit was during the work day there were actually people at their desks when we wandered round, and we chatted to each person as we did so. Finally, anyone who wanted to was asked if they would like to join us for a drink at the pub for a more informal chat, which several people did.

It was a few days later that I took a call from the man who conducted the first interview. He let me know I had the job and he asked me to think about my decision overnight or a couple of nights and call him back with an answer. I gave him an answer straight away, as I was confident that I wanted to accept the offer and said I would confirm this in writing. A reply confirming my position, salary, starting date and job title followed a few days later.

I have now seen this approach to recruitment from the inside (when the company was recruiting after I had joined) as well as being a candidate. Unusually, every member of staff is allowed to have their say about a prospective employee, so it is important that as many people as possible meet that person before the final decision is taken. Ensuring that a different person meets and greets the candidate and that senior members of staff have the opportunity to talk to the candidates on the shortlist makes sure that all members of staff are comfortable with recruits, even before they come on board. It also ensures that candidates get the chance to see different staff members' points of view of the company, and get a feeling for the type of people they will be working with, the office environment and the organisation's culture. Thus over the longer term, this policy has involved everyone and given them confidence and experience of the recruitment process, and has encouraged a culture of openness and the ability to express opinions with colleagues.

I have noticed that over a period of time (I have now been part of this organisation for five years), often when asked whether we can work with such and such a candidate, someone is just as likely to ask 'Are they an Omega[1] person?' or 'Would you invite that person to the pub on Friday evening?' The recruitment process we go through to get the right people is not an analytical process, although they may be asked to perform certain

---

[1] Omega is a pseudonym for the company.

basic procedures and have certain predefined requirements (such as distance travelled, qualifications, enthusiasm and ambition), but also a subjective, social process to ensure that people fit in and that social capital is built between each team member.

Philip's story relates one of the three main ways in which recruiters currently assess fit. In Emma's story, we saw the use of a realistic job preview and a job trial. Another approach is to have the candidates attend so many selection tests on so many occasions that only the keen survive and they enter fully aware of what the company will be like. The third method is to have applicants meet as many people as possible. This is the approach taken at Omega. Its underlying principles are different from the two other methods. In the first two, applicants are able to experience the work and the organisation and to decide for themselves, based on prolonged and relatively deep contact, whether or not the recruiting organisation will be one they will enjoy working in. In effect, the recruiting organisation gives the applicants the opportunity to discover for themselves whether they will fit. In the process, the organisation discovers whether the person has the required KSAOs through simulated and analogous tests and actual work.

The third approach is based on very different assumptions towards fit. Instead of basing this on assessment and prolonged contact, it is about interpersonal contact and multiple short interactions. The interpersonal contact is conducted under the auspices of recruitment and selection, which is an important distinction from realistic job previews as the participants are all aware of the 'unreal' nature of these interactions. Applicants are on their guard and may be manipulating the impression they convey. As I have said before, organisations are on their best behaviour and trying to show themselves in the best light. Consequently, these are interactions of actors. Both parties may be inquisitive, but they are confronting manipulated and managed faces.

Omega's approach has other weaknesses, some of which are quite worrying. Philip openly admits that this is a subjective social process. While subjectivity is a complex term that may not always be bad, as I argued earlier, Philip uses subjectivity in its common usage to signify a decision based on 'gut feeling' or intuition. His firm's approach is an emotional, non-systematic, non-scientific or irrational method of making a selection decision; only the proof-reading test provides any objective counterbalance, but that merely seems to play a minor role. Worse still, it does this in an environment of managed images. Who will get a job at Omega? Who will thrive in this speed-dating assessment process? Presumably, someone with an 'everyman' quality, someone who can form instant friendships, someone whom no one dislikes, someone with charm, someone who makes other people feel good about themselves, someone who conforms to the archetype of an organisational employee, someone who shares your passion for classic cars. If you were recruiting a politician this might be an admirable set of qualities that form part of the selection criteria, but for most jobs these characteristics are just one aspect of being successful and fitting in.

Another worrying aspect of this approach to selecting for fit is its impact on equal opportunities. It is well known that, contrary to the adage that opposites attract, similarity attracts. People like to be with people like themselves. Omega's selection process is likely to reinforce the existing profile of employees and recruit 'similar types'. In such environments, it is notoriously difficult for people who are 'different' to the organisational norm to enter. Omega's process is particularly bad as it hints at a 'black-balling' ethos, the process where one naysayer can eliminate a candidate from the running. One bigot could unreasonably, unfairly and irrationally block people for no other reason than personal dislike.

This approach is not just disadvantageous and potentially discriminatory to candidates, many question whether it is beneficial to the recruiting organisation. While 'right types' might be recruited who don't rock the boat, the danger is what Schneider (1987, p. 446) has described as organisational 'dry rot'. This is the destruction of the company based on employing a workforce that has similar experiences, interests, personalities and ideas. He argues that in such circumstances, the organisation occupies an increasingly narrow ecological niche.

Finally, I find myself worrying about the balance of Omega's recruitment and selection process. The company has gone so far down the interpersonal fit route that it seems to have forgotten the importance of assessing applicants' ability to do the job. There is a strange disjuncture between the large amount of time and effort it puts into its recruitment and selection process and the paucity of its assessment of applicants' KSAOs.

Overall, Omega's approach to recruitment and selection, although very typical, demonstrates many of the mistakes that organisations wishing to 'select for fit' make. The process is open to abuse, probably disadvantages many people, might be detrimental to the organisation over time, relies on intuition, and does little to assess the KSAOs of applicants. Despite the professional and thorough appearance of this approach, it is not one that can be recommended.

JENNY'S STORY: 'DON'T COME HERE, YOU'LL HATE IT'

I attended an interview at a large regional hospital for a place on its registered midwife training course for nurses who had already completed their

Registered General Nursing training. I had completed my training in London and decided that I wanted to specialise in midwifery. I had family living nearby and knew the city was a good place to live. It was a big decision to leave London, but I felt it was the right time to go.

Before the interview I was sent a comprehensive pack of information, including directions to the hospital and some details about the midwifery school and the course. On arrival at the hospital I was shown to a waiting room with the four other candidates who were to be interviewed that day. They were all local women who had done their nurse training locally. They were surprised to learn that I was from London and couldn't understand why I wanted to live in the provinces.

We had access to refreshments and toilet facilities before we were taken for a tour of the obstetrics and midwifery department. We saw all the facilities and had a chance to speak to both qualified midwives and some that were still under training. On this tour I met a student midwife who had trained at the same hospital as me. She took me to one side and told me that I should not do my training at the hospital. She said, 'I hate it here. They hate the fact I'm from "Big London" and every time I make a suggestion or show some initiative they tell me not to show off my "fancy London ways". Don't come here, you'll hate it.'

Whereas Philip's story demonstrated how one big happy family built social capital through their personal interactions, Jenny's story suggests that this does not always happen. During her walk around a large public-sector hospital she inevitably bumped into some disaffected staff. 'Don't come here, you'll hate it.' As I read this, I found myself bracketing this encounter with Philip's story of Omega. Do selection panels know what employees say to applicants? Do selection panels manage what employees say to applicants? Do selectors choose which employees they invite applicants to speak to? The inbreeding that Omega's recruitment and selection policy has produced probably means that Philip has few concerns about what people will say. The selectors in the regional hospital may have mixed feelings. They will be pleased that an applicant was able to discover that she would probably not be happy working there, but concerned that good applicants are being scared off.

This is the double-edged sword of effective recruiting for fit. It opens up the possibility that excellent candidates who satisfy all the KSAOs discover, rightly or wrongly, that they will not fit in. It is quite frustrating for companies to find good people only to have them reject job offers because the panel has given them opportunities to find out more about the organisation than they otherwise would have done. This might be the right thing to do, but it comes at a cost and it is better than taking someone on only to find out a little later that they are a poor fit.

PETRA'S STORY: ADVERTISING SPACE

I was dismissed from a job after 10 days because the company felt that I could not learn the job fast enough. I had graduated from secretarial college in Germany and this was my first permanent job. The company is based in London and sells advertising space in German magazines to British advertising agencies.

The company used an employment agency to fill the position. It wanted to hire a college leaver, who would take over the job as PA when the current PA went on maternity leave in six months' time. The variety of skills and tasks it itemised in the advertisement (using languages, supporting the entire team, getting an opportunity to familiarise myself with everybody's tasks since the company counted only six people) attracted me. I also felt a strong draw to the profession: I was interested in advertising and work of the media in general and thought that this would provide me with a good stepping-stone.

During the interview, the company tested our mental abilities using a work simulation: I was asked to draft a letter on a given subject. In feedback, I was told, 'You have shown almost too much imagination. This is more than we expected.' I felt very comfortable during the process and was delighted to accept the job when it was offered to me.

After I had joined the organisation, I received training by staff members and was invited to attend meetings. I found it difficult to understand how their business actually works: I was confused by the jigsaw of advertising agencies, magazine publishers and the administration holding them all together. Also, I found myself struggling with the jargon. The general attitude towards me changed when I asked people to explain the nature of the business and the industry.

A few days later I was dismissed. I quote the manager, she said, 'We did not know what we were looking for, actually, we thought a college leaver could do the job. We have the feeling you have too many gaps in your experience and general knowledge and we do not feel that you can learn the job within six months. It might be too demanding for you.' She also added that she felt I am not suited for office work and that I should change careers entirely, possibly towards a more artistic field.

My thoughts and emotions at the time of the incident were of utter dejection. I could not understand how they could take me on without knowing what they were looking for in a candidate and then decide that after only ten days I could not learn the job in six months. Also, I could not understand the sudden change of attitude towards me as soon as I started asking questions and told them where my problems were. Looking back at the incident, I realise now that I should not be blinded by nice people. After recovering from the disappointment, which I put down to experience, I feel the company should have been either more tolerant towards my weaknesses or not taken me on in the first place.

The callous disregard this company showed towards Petra is shocking. To take someone on only to kick them out two weeks later demonstrates brazenness towards applicants and a 'hire 'em, fire 'em' attitude towards people. When a company offers someone a job, it takes on a responsibility. The reason for this is that when applicants accept jobs, they may have to give up a lot. They may already have a good job, they may have to move house, many friendships with colleagues may end and so on. To give all this up, successful applicants should expect some sense of commitment from their new employers. But this is another of those recruitment and selection paradoxes, because the law offers least protection to employees in the first months of employment, precisely when they are most vulnerable.

Petra seems to have responded stoically to these events and has decided to learn from the experience rather than get angry. Perhaps the fact that this was her first job and she was relatively naïve about the world of work led her to think that this was how organisations treated their employees. Or perhaps she had other opportunities to fall back on. But it has left her with a cynicism about organisational life: 'I realise now that I should not be blinded by nice people.' How sad is this? Petra appears to be an enthusiastic, bright individual straight out of college who was open about her weaknesses and who was keen to learn this job. Two weeks later she has developed a world weariness usually reserved for grumpy old men.

As I read Petra's story I find myself unconvinced by the reasons offered by this organisation for her early departure. Someone cannot learn a job they have already been trained for in six months? This seems most suspicious. I wonder if she did not fit in. Petra's questions, her lack of familiarity with the jargon, the comment about her unsuitability for office work, the comment about her working in a more artistic field, coupled with her naïvety about work all suggest to me that the real reason for her dismissal was the organisation's categorisation of her as a misfit. This highlights one of the real practical difficulties in selecting for fit: at the moment there are simply no tools available to selectors to help them assess applicants' fit. Give someone a couple of weeks in the role and it becomes a lot more apparent.

So far in this chapter, the stories have focused on the difficulties that external applicants have had in understanding their potential employer and those of selection panels trying to assess the potential fit of people they know little about. The assessment of fit becomes a very different matter when the applicants are internal, as the following story illustrates.

TREVOR'S STORY: KNOWING YOU, KNOWING ME

The position we were interviewing for was deputy team leader in the com-pany's executive support team. This four-person team provides secretarial support to the various senior management groups in the firm: organising meetings, ensuring that papers are written and circulated in advance, taking the notes, preparing the minutes and so on. The team doubles in size and takes on a very high profile during the five-yearly periodic reviews, when the director resets the company's strategy.

The three selection panel members had received all relevant papers on the five internal candidates from Human Resources (HR) four or five days before the interviews. Included in the papers was the document called 'Notes for Board Members'. A covering memo from HR made it clear that we were required to read and understand the rules and principles therein.

We met for a preliminary discussion at 9.30 a.m., half an hour before the first interview. This session was used to coordinate our thoughts on which candidate looked best on paper, to confirm the structure of the interview and our individual areas of responsibility. In line with standard company policy, the panel consisted of a chairperson from HR, the relevant line manager and a third person (me) unconnected with either. As usual, the chair asked questions arising from the application form (education, previous jobs and so on), the line manager asked questions connected to the specific role, and I asked general questions connected with our policies and culture.

The third candidate in was Belinda who, for three years, had been deputy personal assistant in the director's private office. She had returned from ma-ternity leave three or four months earlier and had made it clear that she wanted to move on. She is well known in the company for being charmless, aggressive, a malicious gossip and dismissive of junior colleagues. When dealing with middle or senior management, she behaves as though she is the director and expects everyone else to respect the aura of his personal authority.

We expected a fairly torrid time. What we got was a near-perfect inter-view. The person specification had identified team working, flexibility and diplomatic skills as essential criteria for the job. About half of the interview consisted of open questions being used to explore Belinda's aptitude against these skills. She related examples of how she had used them in her previous and present jobs.

The only problem was that she was talking to an audience who knew her. All three panel members had first-hand experience of Belinda and how she actually worked. We knew how abrasive she could be and what she was really like at supporting and helping colleagues. At the end of Belinda's interview,

the prospective line manager and I looked across at each other and said at
the same time something like, 'That wasn't the Belinda we know and love.'
But if she had been an external candidate, we would not have learnt that just
from the interview, and would almost certainly have offered her the post.

For me, Trevor's story is one of the most interesting in the book. This appeal is not due to it being particularly dramatic, funny or heart warming, but because of the fundamental question it asks of those who advocate the level-playing-field approach to recruitment and selection. To recap, this approach to recruitment and selection advocates the isolation of the process from other organisational processes so that all applicants are treated the same. Prior knowledge of candidates is forgotten by selectors and only information introduced by applicants during the recruitment and selection process is used to make the selection decision. In this way, internal and external candidates are treated even-handedly and selectors have a similar array of information on each candidate.

There are both conceptual and practical problems with the approach. It fails to appreciate the information asymmetries of selectors: selectors will always have different types and amounts of information on applicants. Human nature will always drive selectors to use this information. The approach raises the issue of the abstractness of the selection environment. Is information gathered during recruitment and selection better, different or inferior to information gathered elsewhere? Undoubtedly, the process favours those people who can 'put on a show' during the assessment. As a department personnel officer explained to Harris (2000, p. 41), 'The good bullshitters who know the system tend to do best.' There are also moral dilemmas. Internal applicants believe that their employer is ignoring all of the commitment they have given to the organisation. Moreover, they feel that they are being treated as commodities rather than as people who have a relationship with the employer. Nevertheless, it is a popular approach that is commonly used in public-sector organisations.

Although all his applicants were internal, Trevor's story illustrates the issue of information asymmetry very well. He and his panel members find it impossible to ignore their prior knowledge of Belinda. 'That wasn't the Belinda we know and love.' Should they ignore this prior knowledge and force themselves to use just the information introduced during the selection process? Should they make a selection decision they know to be wrong? Perhaps the problem is not with the level playing field they are trying to create, but with their questions. Perhaps the reason there is a disconnect between the information they gathered about Belinda during the interview and the knowledge they have about her from observing her at work is simply down to poor interviewing.

Perhaps they should have asked her about occasions they have observed when she was less than diplomatic; this would have given her a chance to confront their prejudices about her. But this is another problem with the level-playing-field approach: it prevents interviewers forming questions based on their prior knowledge of applicants. So the approach forces Trevor and his colleagues to ignore his prior knowledge in making selection decisions and in formulating questions.[2] They found it impossible to do the first of these and consequently did not offer Belinda the post.

This story highlights a crucial, rather obvious, but commonly ignored difference between internal and external applicants. Selectors have, or have access to, information on how well internal candidates 'fit' the organisation. They should know if people in this category thrive in the organisation and whether their behaviours are appropriate. They can assess actual behaviour and performance in the workplace. However, the opportunities for doing this with external applicants are far fewer. In most selection processes, external applicants are a complete mystery to selectors when they walk through the door; all the information they glean about them is gathered in the highly charged, surreal and egotistical environment of selection.

SIMON'S STORY: THE PATH OF LEAST RESISTANCE

My company is part of a large organisation. Market forces, mainly driven by our customers, have forced us to look at our costs and subsequently to go through a change programme. As a result we have reduced the size of the workforce from 1,000 to 700 people. This was achieved through non-voluntary redundancies. Concurrently, 200 people were transferred to a satellite office outside London. The personnel who did not wish to relocate were made redundant and other people were selected for the transfer. Due to the size of the task this was done in stages. We were the first division to be downsized.

Approximately one month after we had gone through this process, a member of my group resigned. As we had already been cut to the bare minimum to service our clients, a request for a replacement was put to the directors. This was approved with certain provisos. I had to go through an internal staff recruitment procedure. And I had to target the other divisions, specifically looking for people made redundant due to their unwillingness to relocate.

---

[2] I find myself thinking that this selection process would have been greatly strengthened by some form of in-tray exercise, a group activity, probing behavioural questions and references.

Internal recruitment is done through a bulletin board on our intranet. The vacancy went out and I had 16 replies from a wide variety of people: van drivers to adjusters. I was pressurised to interview all of them even though it was obvious that most would be inappropriate. I justified interviewing them all by the thought that as I was unlikely to find someone with the skill level or experience, I should try to find someone with positive personal attributes such as enthusiasm, good attitude and willingness to learn, and develop them as an adjuster.

The interviews were a disaster. I spent days going through people who just weren't suitable. Some looked wrong, others had a poor attitude and others were unable to answer the most basic questions. Also, some were so embittered by the company that they would have been a negative influence on the section. Others incorrectly thought that they had to go for internal interviews or they wouldn't get their redundancies. I was torn between telling them why they were not suitable and just wishing to get the whole thing over with.

I managed to whittle down the list to three. I was not convinced about any of them. I decided to consult with my staff, as they knew the three individuals involved and their reputations. This proved to be another mistake, as they could not agree and had now created the situation that whichever one I hired would upset some of them. With this in mind I took the path of least resistance and hired the one I felt would have the least disruptive influence (and he had a law degree, which may have been useful).

The whole way through this process I wasn't convinced he was the right person for the job, but I felt he could be trained to be. The main reasons he didn't fit were as follows:

- *Lack of outward enthusiasm. Maybe just quiet and needed to be motivated.*

- *Badly dressed. I felt I could explain to him that as a marketing division, presentation is important.*

- *Too quiet. Adjusters need to communicate effectively to brokers, Lloyd's syndicates and other adjusters. I felt this may come with training and confidence in his role.*

Things did not work out. He did not seem to respond to any encouragement. During this time the salary reviews came up. He received no consideration and I explained why. He felt the company was persecuting him, as he had the same last year in his old division. I explained his unwillingness to adapt was the problem; he did not agree. From this point on, he became unruly and was affecting other members of the group. They were baffled by his behaviour and his inability to learn from his mistakes. I had to inform him that his whole behaviour was unacceptable. He stated he would leave at the earliest opportunity and he has since taken a role in another division. I spoke to his new manager and he is pleased with his progress. It is now apparent to me that he just wasn't suited to the role.

Simon found himself in a very awkward situation. Faced with the need to recruit an insurance broker with specialist skills, he was forced to recruit from a general pool of workers who were being made redundant. These workers had a different range of skills and would need training to become effective as insurance brokers. Simon is clearly upset by having to adopt this approach when he knows it is most unlikely that he would find someone suitable, but bowing to the organisational reality, he decides to make the most of the opportunity and 'find someone with positive personal attributes such as enthusiasm, good attitude and willingness to learn and develop as an adjuster'.

Simon expected to find an unsuitable set of applicants and was not disappointed. He says of the three shortlisted candidates, 'I was not convinced about any of them' and he 'hired the one I felt would have the least disruptive influence'. This is not a good approach to recruitment and selection and it seems to have been forced on Simon because he would lose the opportunity to recruit if he did not find someone in this applicant pool. Despite this, it seems a 'bit rich' to complain that the person he thought would be the 'least disruptive influence' turns out to be 'too quiet'.

Throughout this story, I found myself thinking about the nature of Simon's own behaviour and whether this might have caused some of the problems he encountered. He expected to find unsuitable applicants: he found them. He wanted someone who would not disrupt his department: he found someone very quiet. Given the combination of Simon's negativity all the way through this encounter coupled with the imminent threat of redundancy, is it surprising that the new recruit did not respond to Simon's encouragement? This is reinforced during the salary reviews when the new recruit received no consideration, which was accompanied by Simon's explanation that the 'problem' was the new recruit's unwillingness to adapt. Once in a new division away from Simon, the new recruit became an effective worker. To me, this is a relationship that got off on the wrong foot and never recovered. The tone was set during recruitment ('I wasn't convinced he was the right person for the job') and this created a managerial mindset that the new employee was unsuitable. That the 'least disruptive influence' became 'unruly' simply indicates the degree of alienation between the parties.

I spotted three other ways in which Simon's story relates to the process of recruiting for fit. First, it illustrates the proposition that people leave organisations when they do not fit. In this case, the new recruit found employment in another division when it was clear that he did not fit in Simon's division. Second, the story demonstrates the complexity of fit and how it is influenced by all manner of things, large and small, known and unknown. Third, it shows how difficult it is to assess fit during selection. Simon's criteria revolved around enthusiasm, a good attitude (whatever that means) and a willingness to learn and develop. These attitudes are very general and come from the selector's perspective. There is no consideration of what would make a good fit for the new recruit. This is a one-sided approach to selecting for fit that completely fails to appreciate the needs of the applicant, and therefore it can be no surprise that there was no fit from the moment the person was recruited.

THINKING ON

1. What can selectors do to discover the 'real person' and not just the image that is projected? What can applicants do to find out what working in the organisation will 'really' be like?

2. At what point does an informal chat with someone during a walkabout become part of the selection process?

3. Put yourself in the shoes of applicants being given the opportunity to meet people in the organisation during a recruitment process. You are told that your meetings are informal and not part of the selection process. Do you believe this?

4. Again, put yourself in the shoes of applicants. You will receive lots of differing information about the recruiting organisation: the way people talk and listen to you, the administrative handling of the process, the guided tours and so forth. What types of information do you give most credence to?

5. To what extent should selectors 'select' the people applicants will meet when they visit the recruiting organisation?

6. Should the law skew protection towards workers who have longer service with a company? Should all workers have the same protection regardless of their tenure?

7. Do you accept the view that selection is a highly charged, surreal and egotistical environment? If yes, what sort of information gathered in such an environment can selectors trust? Also, if yes, what sort of information gathered in such an environment can applicants trust?

8. Imagine yourself as an external candidate. How can you prove to selectors that you will 'fit' the organisation?

9. Imagine yourself as an internal candidate. How can you make the panel aware of your history of high performance, commitment to the firm and good fit?

10. Should internal and external candidates be treated the same?

11. Think about your own fit at work. What factors influence your sense of fit? What sort of things would make you think about leaving?

12. Can a selector ever know what is in the best interests of an applicant?

READING ON

Fit is a little bit peculiar because it is a term that has many different meanings. Frequently, I find myself talking to someone about fit only to find that we are talking about very different things. These definitional problems with the term are well explained in a chapter by Schneider *et al.* (1997). Among other things, this chapter explains how fit is concerned with predicting the behaviour of individuals and how this is thought to stem from the interaction of people (internal) and environmental (external) factors. Within the organisational environment, researchers have broken down the external factors into various components. These include people's fit to their jobs, vocations, employers' cultures and values and work/life balance. My colleagues and I have discovered 16 facets to people's sense of fit at work (Billsberry *et al.*, 2006).

When talking about fit in a recruitment and selection context, most people are interested in the notion of whether a potential new recruit will 'fit in'. Three strands of the fit literature focus on this definition. The first is work that has been conducted into person–organisation fit. This is usually conceptualised in terms of people's fit to their employer's values, goals or mission, or in the similarity of people in the organisation. The best introductions into this field are Chatman (1989), Kristof (1996) and Kristof-Brown, Zimmerman and

Johnson (2005). One of the main findings of the PO fit literature is that fit is associated with increased levels of job satisfaction, organisational commitment and tenure. However, there has been a noticeable scarcity of work looking at the crucial questions of how higher levels of fit relate to performance (both individual and organisational) and creativity.

The second strand of research focuses on Schneider's (1987) Attraction–Selection–Attrition (ASA) framework. This framework contains the idea that organisations are increasingly occupied by similar types of people because of the processes of attraction, selection and retention. Based on the idea that similarity leads to attraction, he argues that these processes cause people who are similar to other employees to enter and stay with the employer, and causes misfits to leave. Despite the oft-cited nature of this essay, relatively little research has tested the propositions. We know that 'fits' stay with organisations and that misfits leave, and that over time organisations do increasingly become occupied with people with similar personalities, although the effects are very slight (Schneider et al., 1998). However, we know much less about the attraction and selection phases.

The third strand of this literature focuses on practical attempts by organisations to recruit or select for fit. The seminal work was conducted by Bowen, Ledford and Nathan (1991). They looked at how three large organisations recruited for fit. These organisations were looking for 'whole people' who would grow and develop with the organisations. By and large, these organisations rejected the notion that people should be recruited to a static and non-changing set of KSAOs. However, they were somewhat at a loss to know how to select for fit. They bombarded applicants with almost every selection device known and required them to visit the organisation many times, but ultimately handed over the fit decision to the applicants. Sadly, since the publication of this work, there has been a scarcity of follow-up work exploring the different ways in which organisations recruit and select for fit.

The level-playing-field approach to recruitment and selection is well described in Webb (1997). Harris (2000) draws on this definition and relates a case study from a British council to show its impact on internal applicants.

REFERENCES

Billsberry, J., Van Meurs, N., Coldwell, D. A. & Marsh, P. J. G. (2006) 'The dynamic dual interest model of fit: A metatheory for understanding the complexity of fit', paper presented at the Academy of Management, Atlanta.

Bowen, D. E., Ledford, G. E. & Nathan, B. R. (1991) 'Hiring for the organization, not the job', *Academy of Management Executive*, 5: 35–50.

Chatman, J. (1989) 'Improving interactional organizational research: A model of person–organization fit', *Academy of Management Review*, 14: 333–49.

Harris, L. M. (2000) 'Issues of fairness in recruitment processes: A case study of local government practice', *Local Government Studies,* 26: 31–46.

Kristof, A. L. (1996) 'Person–organization fit: An integrative review of its conceptualizations, measurement, and implications', *Personnel Psychology*, 49: 1–49.

Kristof-Brown, A. L., Zimmerman, R. D. & Johnson, E. C. (2005) 'Consequences of individuals' fit at work: A meta-analysis of person–job, person–organization, person–group, and person–supervisor fit', *Personnel Psychology*, 58: 281–342.

Schneider, B. (1987) 'The people make the place', *Personnel Psychology*, 40: 437–53.

Schneider, B., Kristof-Brown, A., Goldstein, H. W. & Smith, D. B. (1997) 'What is this thing called fit?', in N. Anderson & P. Herriot (eds), *International Handbook of Selection and Assessment*, Chichester: John Wiley & Sons Ltd, pp. 393–412.

Schneider, B., Smith, D. B., Taylor, S. & Fleenor, J. (1998) 'Personality and organizations: A test of the homogeneity of personality hypothesis', *Journal of Applied Psychology*, 83: 462–70.

Webb, J. (1997) 'The politics of equal opportunity', *Gender, Work and Organization*, 4: 159–69.

CHAPTER 11

Market Forces

One of the most amusing and thought-provoking essays on recruitment and selection was written some 50 years ago by C. Northcote Parkinson (1985[1957]). In his book, which is famous for Parkinson's Law (i.e. works expands to fill the time available[1]), he includes a chapter on recruitment and selection in which he argues that the greatest problem with personnel selection is that there are simply too many applicants. Tom's story in Chapter 1 illustrates this problem very succinctly. With his tongue firmly in his cheek, Parkinson suggests that the perfect advertisement will only produce one applicant and that applicant will be 'from the right man'[2] (1985, p. 34). Parkinson says that the advertisement should balance inducements against risks so finely that only one person will apply.

Although Parkinson was lampooning modern methods of management, there is a lot of truth in his words. When organisations advertise themselves as much as the vacancy, as is increasingly the case, they should not be surprised when they are deluged with applications. In such circumstances, seeking out

[1] The recruitment and selection version of this law is that the time, money and effort spent on recruitment and selection increase in direct proportion to the seniority of the vacancy to be filled (but without any evident increase in the quality of the decision making).
[2] I have retained and chosen to highlight Parkinson's 'right man' terminology even though such language is unacceptable today. I have done this because one of the charms of Parkinson's writing is that his old-school language is part of the parody of 'modern management'.

the better candidates is well nigh impossible and shortlisting becomes a haphazard affair.[3]

Ironically, Parkinson's suggestion that the perfect advertisement should only receive one application and that 'from the right man', is flawed in twenty-first-century Britain because most vacancies are not so different from others that there is a clearly defined 'right man'. Nowadays, small applicant fields can be a major problem for selectors when they cannot find people with the right KSAOs.

An issue that intertwines itself with the size of applicant pools is the way it alters the perceptions and bargaining positions on the various parties. When applicant pools are large, selectors can become complacent or haughty. Tom did very well to avoid this trap and it brought out his humble side. But others are less successful and adopt a superior air with applicants. In these periods of feast for organisations, applicants have little bargaining power (until they become the chosen candidate, when their position can be transformed because they have shown their eminence in a competitive situation and the large field has been jettisoned by the recruiters) and have to do what the recruiting organisation requires of them if they want the job and the salvation or advancement that it brings.

However, when applicant pools are small and organisations are desperate for someone, the balance changes. In these times of famine for organisations, recruiters can become salespeople and may feel that they are unable to use the selection tests they would like to. Applicants, on the other hand, are well aware of their power in the process and may well be able to veto particular selection tests as well being able to dictate their terms and conditions.

RACHEL'S STORY: PROMISES, PROMISES

I was talking informally at a networking event to a colleague who had recently been appointed as the chief executive of a county council. She advised me that she was finding her new role challenging due to the limitations of

---

[3] Parkinson humorously notes that the common practice in such circumstances is to 'Reject everyone over 50 or under 20 plus everyone who is Irish' (p. 34). I should note that this practice is now unlawful as well as being both unwise and reprehensible. But Parkinson's dig at the sort of rules of thumb to which selectors have to resort is important because it highlights the randomness of shortlisting when there are a large number of applicants.

her senior management team and that she would shortly be making radical changes.

A few days later she rang to ask if I would consider going to work for her, as she thought I was just the person she needed to help her get the organisation sorted out. She outlined the changes she was planning. I advised that I had not thought about moving, but after a long conversation I said that for the right offer – that is, a more challenging role and the right financial package – I may consider a move. She asked what my current salary package was and what I would be looking for. She advised that she would need to 'do some work on her board' to get them to agree to a management post at that salary level as it was above their usual scale. In her opinion, this was part of the reason the existing management team was of such a poor quality. She said that if she could persuade the board to agree a post at that level she would be in touch.

Two weeks later she rang to say that she had three vacancies on the management team and she had persuaded the board to accept a salary level that would be appropriate for me. The post in question was head of lifelong learning. She advised that although she knew this was not my preferred area of operation, it was the only one for which she could persuade the board to pay an appropriate salary. She asked me to put in an application, and said we could make changes to the role once I was in post. She advised that 'it had to be seen to be an open recruitment process' and therefore all three posts would be advertised in the national press. I had reservations about applying as the job was not really what I wanted, but eventually I was persuaded to apply for the post.

The final interviews for the senior management team posts of head of lifelong learning and head of policy and planning took place on the same day. At the interview, they said that they would be making job offers to successful candidates the next day. Frankly, by this stage I was almost hoping that I had been unsuccessful and could forget all about it and get on with my current job, where I was quite happy.

However, the chief executive called me at home that evening. She asked how I thought the interview had gone. I said it had been hard to judge, as the panel seemed very reserved and had not asked as many questions as I had expected them to. She said that I had 'knocked their socks off' and added, 'You were brilliant; you didn't put a foot wrong. At one stage I was worried for my own job, particularly when one of the board commented what an attractive girl you were.' She went on to say that they wanted to offer me a job, but not the job that I had applied for. She said that the board were so impressed that they had brought forward development plans that they had for one to two years down the line and had spent the last hour revamping the head of policy and planning role to encompass the additional elements that they wanted me to undertake. On that basis they were prepared to offer me the kind of package that we had talked about. She went on to say that she had only given the board a commitment to stay for two years when she joined them and they felt that I would make an ideal successor for her when she moved on, which is why they were keen to get me on board. She said that they would be looking to appoint me as deputy chief executive as soon as possible, but for the present did not wish to go public on this as it would cause problems with another member of the management team who was expecting to get the post. I was of course extremely flattered by this, as the job was more in line with what I wanted to do and the package on offer was above what I had expected. I rang her back later that evening to accept.

At that point my feelings returned to being extremely positive, despite the fact that they had swung from positive to negative throughout the process. I think the cause of the emotional changes was the apparent contradictions. In effect they had approached me and almost pressurised me into applying by making a lot of promises and flattering me along the way. They had implied that the job was mine if I wanted it and they had constructed both the package and the job specification to favour my application. But they had introduced a rigorous selection process that seemed to make it as difficult as possible with the introduction of psychometric testing. It resulted in very mixed feelings. Sometimes I felt very confident and flattered that they wanted me to join them, at other times I felt unsure of myself and I began to doubt their intentions.

Reflecting on the impact of these events, I fear that the company may feel it has attracted the right candidate for the job, but there is a danger that it may have exaggerated expectations of what I do; it may be disappointed if I do not live up to their expectations. It has also proved an expensive exercise for the company. It could probably have attracted a head of lifelong learning for less than they advertised the post for when it was aiming to attract me. And they have the additional expense of the upgraded package they have offered me.

From my perspective, although I have accepted the job, I feel that I have been unduly pressured and I still do not feel sure that I have made the right choice. I have also been made a lot of promises and a consequence of this may be that if the job does not live up to my expectations I may want to move on again.

Rachel's story illustrates the power that the preferred candidate has. Such a person can shape the terms and conditions, the nature of the job and the promotional prospects. This is a power normally associated with more 'glamorous' professions such as footballers, actors and writers, who have agents to negotiate on their behalf. The fact that Rachel could exert such influence is due to several factors. She possesses a rare combination of skills and experience. She was not only able to demonstrate these to the selection panel, but did so in a way that made her appear to be better than many existing senior managers. She had an 'agent' of her own in the current chief executive, who was able to lobby the selection panel from the inside. But perhaps her trump card was the fact that she had been approached. As she was happy where she was currently working, she could stand back and say 'make me an offer I can't refuse', which is precisely what they did.

The strange thing about this story is Rachel's unease with the whole situation. Her writing betrays an anxiety about accepting this job: 'I still do not feel sure that I have made the right choice.' Is this anything more than a sense of loss for her previous position? I think it might be. In indulging in this bargaining and power politics, Rachel has changed the rules of the game. She is following the money and the status; she has become a 'wage tart' who will move on to the next job as soon as she believes that the promises made to her have not been fulfilled or when someone offers her a better deal. She is using this organisation as much it is using her. No longer is her job a relationship between two mutually dependent parties; this is now a transaction of two independent parties who come together for transient convenience.

In such transactions, both parties utilise whatever ammunition they can muster to win in the negotiations. Rachel used her inside contacts, her comfort in her current job and her rare skills and experience to get what she wanted: money and prospects. The council wanted to prise her away from her current employer. They turned her greed and ambition on herself and wrapped up the package with some ego stroking. In today's society, these are powerful emotions to play to and very difficult for people to resist. She may feel 'unduly pressured', but this is a negotiation she entered into of her own free will and it is a bit rich to complain of being pressured when you are pressuring the other party.

JASON'S STORY: 'I'M NOT WHAT YOU'RE LOOKING FOR'

A capital equipment manufacturer was recruiting field service engineers. The personnel director, Rob, based himself in a hotel for several days in the town of the company's main rival. Advertisements were placed in the local paper for drop-in, informal interviews. The interviews were for 'electrical and electronic engineers with knowledge of a second European language'.

Being unemployed and having these skills, I applied. I was asked to attend a preliminary interview with the personnel director. The interview began with Rob describing the company, who owned it, how it was run and what the product was. At some stage in describing the product, I felt completely overwhelmed by the level of technical detail that he was giving. I felt out of my depth and was afraid that I was going to be asked a question I didn't understand. I interrupted him and said, 'I don't understand what you are talking about' and mumbled, 'Maybe I'm not what you're looking for.' I recognise that this is not usually considered to be good interview technique. Far from winding up the interview, Rob took time to ask me about my skills and experience. I said that I spoke French and that I had spent the previous two years working in Africa. His attitude changed dramatically and he seemed to be trying to persuade me to make an application. He actually helped me to fill in the application form that he had given me, probing me for information and advising me on the best way to write this on the form.

Amazingly, I was called to a second interview about two months later. This time Rob was joined by another manager. Their approach was relaxed, smiling and even joking. The questions were not complicated or particularly relevant to my ability to do the job. Many were trivial. For example: 'Do you smoke?' They did talk honestly about the job, including some of the negative sides such as time away from home. They asked about my personal life: 'Are you married?' 'Are you in a long-term relationship?' I do not know if they checked my references, but I suspect not. Basically they appeared to have already decided that I had the job. My new manager said that he could see me going far. After joining the company I described my experience to a colleague who had joined just before me. He said that his interview had been very different and that he had had a difficult technical grilling.

At the time, I thought that I had been given a chance. I was amazed that the decision to offer me a job was based on so little personal information. Now I am still grateful that the company took a chance in employing me, as it opened doors to a whole new career. I did feel that the company had taken a risk in employing me and I worked harder than I otherwise might have done to prove my worth.

In retrospect, though, I don't believe that the company employed very good recruitment practices. My face happened to fit, but would it have been the same if I was not a young able-bodied, white male (the company employed some 30 field engineers and none was either female or black)?

Market forces appear to be influencing this organisation's recruitment and selection policy. Ensconcing the personnel director in a hotel in another town seems pretty desperate, a form of do-it-yourself headhunting. This impression is reinforced by the absence of rigorous selection, although Jason's colleague suggests that previously it had been in place. There are different explanations for this loosening of procedures. The most natural one was that the organisation was more desperate to find suitable people and was afraid of scaring them off. Jason offers a less generous explanation with his comments about his face fitting. Whatever the explanation, I suspect it is not that unusual to welcome someone into the company with virtually no examination of their suitability.

This organisation was fortunate: Jason reacted to his good fortune by working harder. He wanted to prove his worth. Not everyone would have reacted so positively. This organisation's approach differs to the council in Rachel's story. The council took the 'risk' of asking the applicant it wanted to appoint to sit some psychometric tests. In that story, the council wanted to assure itself that the commodity it was paying over the odds for was the genuine article. In Jason's story, the organisation appeared terrified of finding out anything that might cause them to reject applicants: 'Do you smoke?' 'Are you married?' 'Are you in a long-term relationship?' It is as if they closed their eyes and relied on luck.

BEN'S STORY: ONE FLEW INTO THE CUCKOO'S NEST

We had to recruit 20 nurses (E grade) to work in the health-care centre of a regional prison. Unfortunately, none of the management team had been involved with staff recruitment before. My manager, the principal officer (PO), called a meeting of his line managers and the two senior nurses. The PO told us he would advertise in the local newspaper for the nurses. The criteria would be easy to set and it would be easy to interview because 'An E grade nurse is an E grade nurse'. How wrong this statement by the PO proved to be.

I had only been at the prison for a month. I had arrived as a promotion and had no management experience. I can remember thinking at the time, 'I'm so glad I have a manager who knows what he is doing.'

The advert was placed in a local newspaper. It invited applications from people who wanted to work within the health-care services at the prison. The salary was comparable to NHS rates and had a £1500 environmental allowance on top. All other employment benefits were comparable. Fifteen applications were received and all were called for interview.

The interviews were arranged one month in advance, but had to be cancelled as the PO needed to take sick leave. The rescheduled interviews clashed with the holidays of several candidates and were scheduled for a third time. Eventually the interviews did take place, but only eight candidates turned up. All eight were successful, due chiefly to the fact that we were now desperate for staff.

Alas, disaster struck yet again, and the personnel coordinator went on sick leave before the letters of notification were completed, causing further delay. By the time the candidates received their letters, six months had passed since the closing date for applications. This, unfortunately, was not the end of the matter. It stated in the letters that appointments would not be confirmed until security clearance had been confirmed, which could be between six and eight weeks.

When, finally, the successful applicants started at the prison, there were just three left. In the meantime several staff had been transferred due to promotions and other things and we were actually worse off than before the review.

Initially, when the review gave the go-ahead for extra staff, our staff were pleased at the thought of no more staff shortages. In this period, they came up with many new initiatives for better health-care provision and their whole attitude to work had altered for the better. As time dragged on and the ultimate reality of the recruitment became known, their interest and motivation fell until they were just going through the motions. Sickness levels were at an all-time high and commitment was non-existent. They felt the management was incompetent in not getting the new people, as many of the applicants were known as suitable candidates to staff. Staff felt that management was paying lip service to the problems and no solutions were forthcoming. One person even said the money being saved was another reason why the positions weren't being filled. I felt personally responsible and embarrassed, as I had been talking about the light at the end of the tunnel, and how much better it would be when we were fully staffed.

Of the three new nurses we recruited, two left within three months after finding it impossible to 'nurse within such a restrictive environment'. After a lot of time, trouble and expense, we had just one new member of staff. What a disaster!

Later in his assignment, Ben mentioned how other workers in the prison began to refer to the health centre as 'the place where no one wants to work'. This must have been soul destroying for all concerned and Ben notes the impact on staff, with higher sickness rates and lower commitment. The irony is that as these problems get worse, the more difficult it becomes to recruit people to break the cycle. Ben resorts to offering jobs to all eight interviewees, but only three people join and only one of them lasts more than three months. In the meantime, other members of staff have left.

Ben's plight is made worse by his inability to use market forces. One solution would be to offer higher salaries, better terms and conditions, or inducements to attract people into the unit. However, Ben is restricted by his organisation's set pay and reward structures and finds himself hamstrung. What is he to do? I fear that his reaction will be to leave and find a more pleasant environment in which to work.

THINKING ON

1. In what circumstances do applicants obtain the power to negotiate aggressively with potential employers?

2. Conversely, in what circumstances do employers obtain the power to negotiate aggressively with potential employees?

3. What impact (positive and negative) do protracted or confrontational negotiations have on the future employment relationship between new employees and employers?

4. What are the advantages and disadvantages associated with the removal of rigorous selection procedures? Will it always help the organisation look attractive to applicants?

5. Put yourself in the role of an applicant. How would you react to being offered a job when the organisation has failed to discover your strengths and weaknesses?

6. How would you recruit staff to a department that no one wanted to work in?

READING ON

Parkinson's Law states that 'work expands to fill the time available for its completion' (Parkinson, 1985, p. 14). So starts one of the most amusing and profound books ever written on the topic of management. To the uninformed eye, Parkinson reads as an amusing set of essays with an 'old-school' or patrician tone to them. On closer inspection, these essays are parodies of management and the tone of voice a satire on the privileged classes who run many organisations. Parkinson's Law about work and time can be employed as a base for further parodies of recruitment and selection: The cost of the recruitment and selection process increases in line with the seniority of the post.

In his book, Parkinson includes an essay on recruitment and selection. In this essay he talks about the difficulty caused to the recruiter by too many applicants, subjective interviewing, bias, shortlisting, interview panel politics, recruitment advertisements and the benefits package. In many ways, this is an essay about the changing nature of work expectations associated with a changing society. It was written in 1957, when education, class systems, lifestyles and work expectations were all changing. The mass workforces of the first half of the twentieth century were now expecting increased opportunity in the workplace. So rather than there being one or two candidates from 'the right families' applying for managerial jobs, there were many thousands. During this transitional period, recruitment and selection changed greatly and Parkinson's essay captures it beautifully. Looking at Parkinson's essay more than 50 years after it was written, I find myself witnessing the same challenges that Parkinson lamented: too many applicants, ineffective selection techniques, weak job advertising, poor shortlisting, and assessors making decisions on personality rather than competence.

There is a large literature on negotiation and bargaining, which is often linked to conflict resolution, managing change or industrial relations. Comparatively, there is very little on the subject in the recruitment and selection domain and most studies (e.g. Lindquist, 1992; Rynes & Boudreau, 1985) have been conducted with college graduates. The practical recruitment and selection books (e.g. Roberts, 2005) offer advice on how to form offer letters and the like, but few talk about the negotiation or bargaining. One of the better books on negotiated skills is Cohen's (2002) *Negotiating Skills for Managers*. In this book, the author argues that negotiators must be aware of both their bottom line (the point beyond which they will not go) and their BATNA (best alternative to a negotiated agreement), which is a measure of the balance of power between the parties.

Market forces are strangely absent from the recruitment and selection literature. Although some textbooks mention them in passing (e.g. Heneman & Judge, 2005), few empirical studies factor market forces, issues of supply and demand or workforce dynamics into their studies. In fact, there is a preponderance of studies using graduates as research participants. The characteristics of this group of people are very unlike the applicant pools in 'normal' recruitment and selection processes. There is a considerable body of work showing that graduates are largely unaware of the world of work, are naïve about working practices and have multiple applications and offers to consider. The stories in this book demonstrate how different this profile is to the mid-career applicant who applies to single-vacancy openings. In addition, these stories have demonstrated how labour market imbalances have a profound effect on the way in which recruitment and selection are conducted. Instead, many empirical studies of recruitment and selection completely ignore market forces in a manner reminiscent of perfect-market theories in economics.

REFERENCES

Cohen, S. P. (2002) *Negotiating Skills for Managers*, New York: McGraw-Hill.

Heneman, H. G. III & Judge, T. A. (2005) *Staffing Organizations,* 5th edn, Mendota House, WI: Irwin McGraw-Hill.

Lindquist, V. R. (1992) *Trends in the Employment of College and University Graduates in Business and Industry*, Evanston IL: Northwestern University Placement Center.

Parkinson, C. N. (1985[1957]) *Parkinson's Law or the Pursuit of Progress*, London: Penguin.

Roberts, G. (2005) *Recruitment and Selection*, 2nd edn, London: Chartered Institute of Personnel and Development.

Rynes, S. L. & Boudreau, J. W. (1985) 'College recruiting in large organizations: Practice, evaluation and research implications', *Personnel Psychology*, 39: 729–57.

CHAPTER 12

Politics

When thinking about recruitment and selection, it is too easy to focus on the interaction of applicants and the recruiter. We worry about how applicants are assessed and how they respond to selection tools. We worry about how applicants are attracted. We worry about fairness issues. And we worry about how applicants are inducted into the organisation. All of these areas are important and thoroughly deserving of the attention they receive. However, it is all too easy to forget that recruitment and selection form an episode in a bigger story: the running of an organisation or the living of someone's life. It is a small episode with much wider consequences. And because it is a small but influential episode in a much bigger story, it is often subject to influences other than the pressure to recruit someone who satisfies the selection criteria.

JULIAN'S STORY: OLIVER'S ARMY

The incident was the internal recruitment of a chemist into my group. At the time I was the section head of a new area of the company. My role was to build a team of suitable personnel, equipment and chemistry.

The position was advertised internally and received a reasonable amount of attention. The instructions in the advert asked interested people to discuss the position with my boss, a director (Frank), after informing their manager. About 12 people showed interest; I cannot be sure of the exact number as Frank did not involve me in the discussions, which I found highly frustrating.

Three people formally applied for the position: Gillian, who had joined us nine months previously after completing an MSc; Oliver, an employee of 10 years with no qualifications; and Keith, who had 18 months' work experience after completing a degree. Gillian and Oliver had relevant chemical expertise, but both worked in an unrelated technology. Keith had direct technological expertise, although his chemical knowledge was unrelated. My initial view was that nobody perfectly matched the mental picture I had of a suitable candidate.

The interviews were conducted by me and a colleague from Personnel. Oliver was glum, uninspiring and showed little interest. At one point he commented that he would be unsuitable for the role because he didn't like working very hard and the job seemed too busy for him. It appeared he had been pushed into applying.

Keith interviewed well. His overall lack of industrial experience came across and although he had relevant product development experience, a lot of training in technology and chemistry would be required to help him become an effective performer. Keith gave every indication that he would work hard to do whatever was necessary to succeed.

Gillian appeared keen to gain the position. She had relevant chemical and industrial experience, but would need training in technology relevant to the product. It came out in the interview that Frank had tried to put her off applying.

After completing the interviews, there was a follow-up meeting with Personnel to discuss the applicants. Based on the relative performances, the choice was between Keith and Gillian. It was agreed that, on balance, Gillian appeared to offer the greater potential and had more relevant skills than Keith.

Later, Frank called me into his office to discuss the interviews. He was not pleased that Gillian was likely to be offered the position, suggesting Oliver would be better a proposition as moving Gillian or Keith gave him a resourcing headache in already understaffed areas. I fed back Oliver's comments from the interview and gave a structured argument as to why Gillian was most suitable, but this fell on deaf ears. I deduced that Frank's motivation was that Oliver was 'due' the position because he had been with the company the longest of the three applicants.

I was given the impression that he had let the interviews occur, but had no intention of allowing an impartial process. But, as Personnel had independently stated that Gillian was the most suitable candidate for the position, Frank's arguments were immaterial. I was angry with the attempted manipulation and I felt Frank's view should have been unbiased. It clearly wasn't.

Frank informed Gillian and Oliver's manager, Roger, of the situation. Roger also called me into his office and tried to persuade me to employ Oliver, stating he was more suitable 'because he had been with the company longer'. I repeated my arguments as to why Gillian had been selected. Roger saw this as irrelevant and lost his temper. He revealed he did not want to let Gillian go *because she was highly talented. A start date of three months' time was offered, the maximum period permissible for an internal move. I found Roger's bloody-mindedness unpalatable and felt that both he and Frank were attempting to force me to employ someone unsuitable, regardless of my findings.*

Within an hour, Roger bluntly informed the rest of his group of Gillian's new role. They were highly unimpressed and ignored Gillian, telling her that, once she had moved, she should not use any of their laboratories or equip-ment. A request was placed with Roger that she be expelled from the group immediately.

Responding to their views, Roger came to see me and, in front of a number of people, told me Gillian would be joining in two days, rather than in three months' time. I informed Gillian of the situation. Though we were both pleased she was joining my team sooner than anticipated, the situation was very unfortunate.

Julian found himself in a terrible dilemma. On the one hand, he had done what his training had taught him and come to a considered decision about who to recruit based on suitability in the role. But, as a practical and astute manager, he understands the importance of showing respect to his superiors. When these are in direct opposition, he has a problem. He was fortunate in this case that his hand was forced. The presence of a representative from Personnel on the selection panel meant that it was most unlikely the panel's decision could be overturned. Julian's job in the aftermath was to reduce the fall-out. But Roger's blunt public declaration pre-empted that and set up potential future problems for Julian.

This story captures the rise of the professional manager in modern busi-ness. Both Julian and the representative from Personnel set about recruitment and selection in the right way. It is clear from the way Julian talks about the three candidates that the panel was able to perform thorough assessments of their suitability for the role: assessments that he is able to explain and justify. This professional approach clashes with Frank and Roger's old-school style of management. They want to use their positions to confer patronage on their charge: 'because he had been with the company longer'. These days, relatively few organisations operate with this feudal style of management. The increase of management training, the rise of Human Resources and the increased like-lihood of legal recourse have combined to bring about changes to the way that organisations manage their staff. If anything, the pendulum may have swung too far the other way, with people having to apply for their own jobs during restructuring and psychometric tests being used to determine who gets made redundant. The old-style managers like Frank and Roger may huff and puff and make everyone's life miserable, but ultimately they do not have a leg to stand on and have to acquiesce to newer, more professional ways of managing.

GERRY'S STORY: JUNGLE WARFARE

When I was a sergeant in the constabulary, I was involved in the selection process for police constables. The process adopted for final selection at that time involved a mini-assessment centre, which required the candidates to perform various listening, report-writing and communication tasks on the first day. That was followed by attending an evening meal with the selection panel, where behavioural and interpersonal skills were further observed. On the following day, the final part of the process was for each candidate to be interviewed by the selection panel for approximately half an hour. I was one of three members of the selection panel, the others being the civilian head of human resources and a chief superintendent. I was completely untrained and was given the task at short notice due to the trained members of the selection team being on sick and annual leave.

Of the eight prospective candidates, one male failed to appear. The other seven consisted of two females and five males. Subsequently one female and three males were accepted. It is the circumstances surrounding the interview of the female who wasn't selected that concerned me most. It was quite clear that the head of human resources had preconceived ideas, and prior to the applicant being interviewed she commented that she didn't consider her suitable due to her 'limited educational qualifications'. She had stated this prior to the candidate coming in for interview. Both the chief superintendent and I pointed out to her that the candidate had passed the standard police entrance examination, otherwise she would not have been shortlisted. Any additional qualifications may be desirable, but were not essential. The head of human resources was reluctant to accept this view and had quite clearly made up her mind.

During discussion it became apparent that the chief superintendent was very determined to recruit this female. As far as I could gather, his main reason was an adverse comment made in a recent report on the constabulary about the low percentage of female officers serving with us. It was also apparent that my colleagues on this selection panel disliked each other.

I noted another problem relating to this particular candidate, in that the background papers indicated that she had not passed the police medical and fitness tests, primarily because she was overweight. For this reason alone, this candidate should not have been shortlisted. However, she was interviewed but was not accepted for medical reasons at that time. (She subsequently passed the medical and fitness tests and has joined the Special Constabulary. She has not yet reapplied to join the regular force, but intends to do so in the future.)

During this experience, for which I was ill prepared, I felt very uncomfortable and under pressure. The situation was made worse by the unprofessional behaviour of the other members of the selection panel. As a result of incidents like this, a training programme has been implemented. Also, the force now prevents any untrained personnel from being involved in recruitment and selection procedures and administrative procedures have been tightened up to ensure that all shortlisted candidates fit the criteria.

Arguments between members of an interviewing team are not uncommon. Sometimes they appear because the panel members see different sides of a candidate. Sometimes they interpret the selection criteria differently. Sometimes they draw different conclusions about a candidate's suitability. In these sorts of disagreement, discussion can often iron out the differences and allow those that disagree to reach a consensual decision. However, when the disagreement is based on a prejudice, the protagonists may find it impossible to compromise. The discussion may turn into an argument and positions may become polarised as the parties are backed into corners. As the differences are not based on reason, there is no common ground on which to hold a sensible debate. Often the most senior person will 'win' the argument by dint of their position. On other occasions, a stalemate will be reached that results in no one being appointed. However, on this occasion Gerry was able to find some neutral territory on which the two protagonists could consider the applicant rationally, allowing them to save face and reach an agreed decision: the applicant should not have been shortlisted because she failed the physical. This solution has 'parked' the disagreement between the warring parties, but it seems certain to reappear soon.

Gerry's story also highlights the difficult position of the untrained or inexperienced member of a selection panel. How does the 'voice' of such a person make itself heard? How do they participate fully in the selection decision? Throughout this book, I have referred to selection panels as if they are a group of people who form the same opinions on people when presented with the same data. I have also tended to assume that all members of a selection panel have an equally strong say in selection decisions. Gerry's story demonstrates that there are powerful dynamics running through selection panels and that the episodic nature of selection may itself cause conflicts and disagreements to surface. Rather like the skirmishes in Africa and Asia during the Cold War, these contained situations allow the factions to fight without risking nuclear war and its mutually assured destruction.

GLYN'S STORY: HAIR

We were looking to recruit a vehicle service engineer. We advertised the job in the local press and received 114 applications, all of whom were male. We shortlisted six candidates.

I chaired the interview. The other interviewers were the human resources and training manager and the senior transport engineer. We verbally agreed what was required of the candidate beforehand. We also agreed among ourselves the share of the questioning and the topic we wanted to cover. During the interview, each interviewer completed an interview record and assessment form.

I collected Dylan from reception and introduced him to the rest of the interview group. Our first impression of him was his very long hair. As the interview progressed, Dylan answered the questions very well, and it became apparent that he was confident, articulate, honest, motivated and very adaptable to change.

At the end of the interview came the 'crunch decision' whether or not Dylan was suitable for the job. The information gathered and recorded on the assessment form during the interview confirmed he had the abilities to do the job, but he had been marked down on his appearance. The others felt he was the right person for the job, but were concerned by his appearance: the company has quite a strict dress code. I felt the others were confusing matters and that Dylan's physical appearance was different to the way he dressed. Moreover, this dress code was an employment matter and nothing to do with his qualifications and experience. At the time, we could not agree on a selection decision.

I consulted with my boss, the deputy managing director, who said, 'I don't care what he looks like as long as he can do the job.' After receiving this reassurance, Dylan was offered the job, and he accepted. He's proved to be a first-class service engineer, who has performed and contributed significantly to our success.

In most organisations, it takes guts to say 'I don't know'. It is an admission of weakness that managers have been conditioned against. Many selection panels would have buckled beneath the regulation and red-lined Dylan. By being prepared to do extra work to find out what the rules mean and to ask the advice of a more senior person, these panel members demonstrated their understanding of the importance of their decision. These might sound like small things, but set in context, to my eyes they constitute actions 'above and beyond' from which many selectors would shy away.

This selection panel did more than avoid making a quick or 'easy' decision: they also confronted their prejudices. Confronting prejudices is a layered process. You must first realise that you have a prejudice. Then, the prejudice has to be voiced, which is quite a challenge in most organisational environments. Once voiced, the prejudice can be challenged. Glyn's documentation helped his panel realise the discord between the assessment of Dylan's knowledge and skills and his physical appearance. They found someone who satisfied the selection criteria, but who was in breach of a company rule. Rather than just 'obey orders', they thought through the logic: the selection panel needs to assess candidates' ability to do the job, not their conformity to rules that they may not know exist. Once they discover a candidate they wish to appoint based on alignment to the selection criteria, only then they should investigate whether or not that person is prepared to adhere to idiosyncratic company rules such as dress codes.

THINKING ON

1. How does the 'culture' of recruitment and selection sit with the culture of your organisation? Is the way selection decisions are made in your organisation in line with the way staff are managed?

2. Should selectors think about how they announce their selection decisions to a wider audience?

3. Imagine yourself on a selection panel. How would you react if a member of the panel seemed to have reached a decision on a candidate before the interview? How would you react if a panel member had made a prejudiced or unreasonable assessment? How would your reaction differ if the person was senior to you?

4. Can in-fighting on a selection panel be a force for good?

5. What is the relationship between the selection criteria and organisational rules and regulations? Should organisational rules and regulations be part of selection criteria? Should you recruit someone knowing that they will have to make changes to fit in with the company's rules and regulations?

6. Imagine the situation where a selection panel deliberately ignores an important organisational rule and offers the job to someone who is suitably qualified, but unlikely to be able to satisfy the rule. For example, imagine a job being offered to an excellent candidate who lives many miles away who is happy to commute the distance, but there is a company rule saying

that all employees have to live within 25 miles of the factory. What are the implications of this?

READING ON

Office politics is particularly well covered in the book by Fineman and Gabriel (1996) that inspired this book. They cover many different aspects of the reality of office politics, including empire building, insults, rumours, hidden agendas, blame and game playing. These issues are developed further in Fineman, Sims and Gabriel (2005). Some writers (e.g. Kanter, 1983) regard politicking as part of the normal run of events in organisational life, but few recruitment and selection scholars would hold that it should invade the organisational entry process. Indeed, the rational focus of the psychometric approach views such factors as distractions.

One aspect of recruitment and selection where politics and related issues have been studied is in assessment centre decision making. Such decision making has always been problematic given the fact that different tests often provide contrary indicators and the different perceptions of multiple assessors. Zedeck (1986) analysed group dynamics in these assessment centre decision makers. Dose (2003) has looked at the type of information that assessors discuss.

The issue of power in recruitment and selection is well covered in a chapter in Iles' (1999) book, *Managing Staff Selection and Assessment*. In this chapter he draws on the work of Foucault to explore power relationships within selection processes. Foucault, he notes, contrasts with Marxist approaches to power by asking 'how' questions rather than 'who' and 'why' questions. Drawing on the work of Townley (1994), Iles argues that the Foucauldian approach triggers questions of how an everyday, apolitical process can become a 'technology of power' (Iles, 1999, p. 110). In other words, he sees recruitment and selection processes as making employee behaviour visible, predictable, calculable and manageable. In doing so, this gives managers power over those they assess.

REFERENCES

Dose, J. J. (2003) 'Information exchange in personnel decision making'. *Applied Psychology: An International Review*, 52(2): 237–52.
Fineman, S. & Gabriel, Y. (1996) *Experiencing Organizations*, London: Sage.

Fineman, S., Sims, D. & Gabriel, Y. (2005) *Organizing and Organizations*, 3rd edn, London: Sage.

Iles, P. (1999) *Managing Staff Selection and Assessment*, Buckingham: Open University Press.

Kanter, R. M. (1983) *The Change Masters*, New York: Simon and Schuster.

Townley, B. (1994) *Reframing Human Resource Management*, London: Sage.

Zedeck, S. (1986) 'A process analysis of the assessment centre method', *Research in Organizational Behavior*, 8, 259–96.

CHAPTER 13

Case Study: The Prison Service Assessment Centre

This final chapter contains a series of stories about the Prison Service's Job Simulation Assessment Centre (JSAC). This assessment centre is particularly interesting to study for at least two reasons. It is one of the most professional and rigorous selection tests I have encountered. It was also designed by very able occupational psychologists who incorporated many cutting-edge selection technologies into the design. Studying this assessment centre therefore affords us an opportunity to consider people's reactions to a state-of-the-art process.

I was fortunate to receive a large number of stories about this assessment centre, which was the result of the Prison Service sending a large number of employees on Open University courses at the time the stories were being collected for my research. These stories come from two perspectives: internal applicants going for promotion and selectors involved in the running of the assessment centre.[1] Hence, we can do something that is quite rare in recruitment and selection research and that is to examine a selection intervention from multiple perspectives.

In this chapter, I have not added my own commentary after each story. I have omitted this because I hope you will treat this chapter as a treasury. I see this collection of stories as a resource for exploring people's experience

---

[1] Please note that as these stories were collected over a three-year period, they refer to differing versions of the assessment centre. Pavel's story, for example, is written about a very early version of the assessment centre that was used for external candidates rather than to assess internal applicants for promotion.

of recruitment and selection in depth. Many of the issues in these stories are themes that have been covered elsewhere in this book. By considering different perspectives on the same selection tool, I found that my understanding of these themes was enriched. Moreover, by reading these different perspectives on the same story, I found myself appreciating the complexity of recruitment and selection episodes.

The first story provides a detailed description of the assessment centre.

GARY'S STORY: HOOP DREAMS

The purpose of the Job Simulation Assessment Centre (JSAC) is to assess a candidate's suitability as a senior officer. First, the candidate needs to have successfully passed the Prison Officer's Promotion Examination. If they do this, they need to apply using the Prison Service application form for promotion/selection. This form needs to be completed by the applicant, endorsed by their line manager and countersigned by their manager's manager. If you are successful at the JSAC (i.e. obtain JSAC Accreditation), then you are eligible to apply for senior officers' posts advertised in the Prison Service Bulletin.

When I arrived at the assessment centre there were four other candidates in the room. The course administrator entered the room, and gave me a candidate number and a set of senior officer epaulets that I was asked to wear. I was also given a short briefing sheet that said I was to assume the role of a senior officer for the duration of the assessment. The sheet said that the assessment would take up to three hours to complete and would cover a variety of situations that I might face on a day-to-day basis. Each of these situations would be approximately 15 minutes in length and once I had tackled each one, I could not revisit it. I was then asked for my opinion of the process, to which I stated my disagreement to all of it, but that I wanted promotion and therefore had to jump through the required hoops. This did not go down too well!

Then it began. I was ushered into a prepared room that contained video cameras and microphones. I was presented with the following scenarios:

- *An office, which I was told was my office, and another senior officer to give me a 'handover' briefing. I began to take notes and asked what I felt were relevant questions. It did not seem real, partly because it felt that what was going on was simply what I already did as an officer; nevertheless, I had to play along. I was told that there was a pile of paperwork to be sorted out and that a member of staff was late. Then the other senior officer left.*

I began sorting through and prioritising the paperwork and attempting to get my bearings.

- *I was interrupted by a member of staff bursting through the door, who was unkempt and incorrectly dressed. I looked at the clock and asked the officer to sit down. We discussed his late attendance, his attire, and I asked him to return to me when he was correctly dressed and ready for his duties.*

- *The phone rang; you couldn't phone out, it only received incoming calls. I was asked for my wing roll; that is, the number of prisoners I had located on my wing, which I gave. The officer returned and requested that his detail (work schedule) be changed. I stated that as he was late the detail had been changed by the other senior officer, and I was not prepared to change it at this time. He would revert to his normal detail after lunch. He wasn't very happy when he left the office.*

- *I read a memo from the chaplain who stated that a certain prisoner had become withdrawn and he was extremely concerned. I was faced with a prisoner who was identified as a suicide risk; I needed to interview him as soon as possible. As I could not telephone out, I asked the facilitator at the door to see the prisoner, but he stated that it was not possible. I requested that he contacted the prisoner because of the serious nature of the situation. He blanked me! You were not able to speak to people when you wanted to (because they were role playing with other candidates), and the facilitator outside the room prevented you from leaving; he was not able to pass on any information of any kind.*

- *A member of staff who wanted the afternoon off came in, but would not tell me why. I also needed to speak to him in connection with a Board of Visitors' complaint (see later). I persevered, asking him about the reason he wanted the afternoon off. Eventually, after agreeing levels of confidentiality, he told me that his daughter had witnessed a traumatic car crash and had her first appointment with a counsellor. I obviously agreed.*

- *A persistently whinging prisoner entered, who wanted me to get him a knife, fork and spoon. I explained to him that this was the cleaning officer's responsibility. So I referred him to the cleaning officer, but he would not leave and kept on and on. I assured him that he would receive these items from the officer and asked him to leave.*

- *An irate manager, who had had a severe reprimand because a member of staff had not followed procedures, wanted to know what I had done to sort it out. I introduced myself. I tried to placate him by saying I had received a memo from the officer explaining his reasons. I had spoken to the officer and had his assurance that it would not happen again. He immediately left in the whirlwind that he had arrived in.*

- *I received a telephone call about a prisoner who was refusing to be transferred to another establishment and requesting my attendance. I went to 'reception' and spoke to the prisoner. He was extremely agitated, using abusive language and gesticulating. I asked him to calm down in a quiet voice, and asked what the problem was. He said that he did not want to transfer to 'X'. I explained that his transfer was happening that day, he was going overnight to 'X' and would be travelling on to 'Y' tomorrow. He said OK, but I am still not going. I asked why, and he replied that his mother was visiting him today and he wanted to see her. I asked if he had a number for her. He said he had. I said that if he gave it to the member of staff they would telephone her, ask her not to travel today and that he would be in touch soon. He said that he would transfer now!*

- *A prisoner entered, the same one the chaplain had mentioned, and said that he was in fear of his personal safety because he was in debt to two other prisoners. He would not disclose their names for fear of retribution. I managed to get him to tell me their names and reported this through the security information report system. I asked him about the chaplain's memo. He said that he was a bit down, but was OK; therefore I raised the appropriate paperwork. I also spoke to him about the board member's comments about the officer. He said that the officer was usually all right, and that he had interrupted the officer while he was speaking to someone else. He said there was no reason for the board member to get involved, 'everything was sweet'.*

- *A member of the Board of Visitors (an independent body) who had heard a member of staff use abusive language to a prisoner wanted to know what was being done. He was referring to the same member of staff I saw earlier. I said that I had interviewed the officer and the prisoner and both were OK. I said that the officer had apologised and said that he was having a bad day and that it wouldn't happen again. The board member asked what was wrong with the officer. I stated that I was not able to comment, except that the problem was now resolved. He left.*

Throughout the assessment there were interruptions, from staff, managers and prisoners. Finally it was over, and I was taken to a separate 'debriefing' room. Overall, I did not enjoy the assessment, mainly because I did not agree with the process, but also because the timing was poor: a member of my family had passed away only a few days before.

PAVEL'S STORY: FIRST ON SCENE

I would like to describe an incident that has taught me a lot about recruitment and selection. The incident in question was part of the recruitment process that I undertook when I first joined the Prison Service.

We first had to apply and that was on the normal application form and sifting process. Then we were asked to attend for psychometric testing and a medical, which was in turn followed by an interview. After this, and unknown to the remaining candidates, there was another test. This test was called 'first-on-scene hostage' and I now think that it is probably one of the scariest aspects of my job that I may have to deal with.

We were told that we were to report to a portacabin at 15-minute intervals and were to assume that it was a part of the interview process. Unfortunately, it was quite different to anything we had encountered before.

On entering, you are presented with a door and a lot of screaming. Once you have approached the door, you are informed that there is a hostage and unless demands are met, the hostage will be killed. There is a hidden camera above the door, which I was not immediately aware of, and a panel of assessors in a room above who are looking for your responses.

I approached the door with caution and had a conversation with the perpetrator. I soon learnt that the more I bluffed and talked, the less screaming was heard. I felt that I somehow had to show empathy with the hostage takers. It is a strange sensation to be in a position when you hold someone else's safety in your hands in the face of violence and adversity. It turned out to be something I dread even to this day, as to bargain for the life of a stranger is one thing, but to bargain for the life of a friend, associate or family member is quite another.

It felt as though it lasted an eternity, but in reality it was only 15 minutes and was designed to consolidate the interview process by making you demonstrate your claims of sound judgement and character. I felt almost traumatised at the time. Even now, I look back at it in awe as it could foreseeably have ended in rape, death, mutilation and misery and repercussions for the rest of your life if you could not justify your actions and someone was injured.

This is still something I contemplate daily, and it is etched into my memory forever.

I feel that the short- and long-term implications of this recruitment tool were to dispel any false ideas as to the nature of the prisoners I would be dealing with. Also, it made me think long and hard about pay and pensions, whether I would fit in, and about the danger I might face. It was also a guide about the level of performance I would be expected to achieve.

In retrospect, I feel that the incident fitted well into the bigger picture of the process, and was a stroke of genius in weeding out any misconceptions about the job. It was designed to test what we had promised in the interview and was designed to give our future employers an insight into how we would react in 'the real thing'. All in all it was, and still is, the best recruitment tool I have witnessed to date.

COLIN'S STORY: HARD LABOUR

I was involved in the recruitment process for prison officers. The service had just begun using a new system to assess potential officers, known as the Job Simulation Assessment Centre or JSAC for short. The old selection system included a battery of psychometric tests, with the successful candidates being interviewed by a panel of three prison governors. The new selection procedure took the form of role playing a number of different scenarios. Developed by psychologists, the idea is to test the range of skills possessed by the candidates against a pre-set scoring system. Each one of the tests takes place in a different room so the candidates are continually on the move. Outside each room there is a member of the recruitment team who gives the candidates an outline of the scenario that they have to play. Inside the room there are two assessors: one interacts with the candidate while the other one records the outcome using a video camera.

The test I was involved in was designed to assess whether the candidates were able to calm down an angry person (a good skill for any prison officer to possess), but the candidates didn't know how upset I would be. They had to come into the room and explain how my next-door neighbour had damaged my new car. The reason she had damaged my car was as she was driving home from work, a young child had run out into the road and she swerved to miss him; unfortunately for me she swerved into my new car. She was unable to come round herself, as she had been taken to hospital for a check-up and had asked her friend to come round and explain what had happened. They weren't to know that I would start shouting at them as soon as they mentioned that they had come about the car. If they did not try to interrupt me as I was shouting, then after a sentence or two, I would go quiet and give them chance to explain what had happened. If, however, they tried to shout me down or tried telling me to calm down, then I would just keep shouting until they stopped talking and listened to me. Throughout the role play I was told never to make a move towards the candidate, but to maintain the same distance between us.

I role played this scenario up to twenty times a day for three weeks with different results. The majority of people realised quite quickly that if they just let me say my piece I would go quiet and allow them the chance to explain everything to me. Three people began to show signs of being emotionally overcome and two attempted to physically grab me and had to be escorted out of the room. Both were ex-servicemen and one actually told one of the other recruiting members of staff that he had 'definitely passed that part of the assessment'. Needless to say, their services were not required.

Over the three weeks I acted as an assessor, there were times I could not stop laughing (I must stress this was after the candidates had left the room), like the time one of the candidates came into the room, forgot what he had to say, turned to the camera and shouted 'cut' as if he was directing some Hollywood movie. On the two occasions when it almost became physical, it was a little unsettling and numerous times I felt sorry for candidates who were totally out of their depth.

At the time, I remember thinking about the centrality of these skills to a prison officer and how quickly they need to produce the right response to calm a potentially explosive situation down. I also felt that the new system would produce a better standard of officer and that I was glad I was recruited through the interview process.

It's been over two years since I was involved in recruiting and I've not seen anything to support my initial thoughts that the assessment centres would produce a higher calibre of officer. As I was involved in one of the first JSACs to be run, I was asked by quite a few members of staff, including governor grades, what I thought of the new system. I believe it is a more comprehensive way of determining a person's suitability to become a Prison Officer. It also gives the candidate some insight into the many different roles they will be expected to cover in their day-to-day role as an officer.

ANNA'S STORY: REALITY BITES

I attended the first JSAC. They have been introduced by the Prison Service as a fair method of measuring competence for promotion. As one of the first officers to attend an assessment centre, there was very little information available as to what to expect and I was nervous and a bit apprehensive.

I was still nervous during the briefing when the procedure was explained to me, although the prospect of performing before the cameras did not worry me too much. I have had experience of being filmed while tutoring prisoners and staff, therefore the camera did not concern me. Once shown into my office, the simulation started and I waited for something to happen. I remember reading through all the available paperwork, trying to make sense of all the information; at this time it felt very artificial and the room felt empty and sterile. As soon as someone knocked at the door and entered the office, it all became real for me: I forgot that it was a role play and responded to the various individuals accordingly.

I remember feeling very warm; there were no windows to open and there was no water to drink. As the morning progressed, I became very uncomfortable at being confined to the office. The first time the telephone rang, I answered it, using my married name (at that time I had not changed my name, so I was registered in my single name). As soon as I said my married name, I realised my mistake and became completely flustered; it took me a while to regain my composure.

The time passed very quickly, and when I handed over to another member of staff, I was almost disappointed to be finished.

JON'S STORY: WHO WATCHES THE WATCHERS?

I had passed the promotion exam the year previously and had suddenly been told without prior warning that the route for senior officer had changed and would now entail an assessment of my abilities. I thought 'typical', but was not surprised as I had prior experience of processes and procedures changing without those affected being informed.

I received an invitation to attend an assessment centre to determine my suitability to take on the role of a senior officer. As usual I had very little information before the assessment of what this would entail. The Prison Service is terrible at not giving full information on new schemes to those concerned. However keeping secrets is not the Service's strongest point, especially 'in-house'. The assessment centre process meant that six officers attended the centre daily over a period of three months. This, in reality, meant that officers further down the list had prior knowledge of the role plays through listening to their colleagues who had taken the assessment the day or week before.

I tried as best I could to refrain from listening to those who had attended the assessment centre before so that my views would not be clouded or influenced. However, it was impossible and I thought, 'How can this be a true reflection of an individual's actions "on the day" when they already know what to expect?'

I arrived early at the assessment centre, all 'booted and spurred'. I was met at the reception by a woman who gave me a brief introduction that told me what to expect for the morning. I was then shown to my 'office' and then told that the assessment had started.

The role plays included many forms of interpersonal skills exercises such as dealing with angry prisoners and irate members of senior staff. There were seven role plays in total and each one lasted a maximum of ten minutes. They came thick and fast, with relatively little time to stop and think before the next actor came barging through the door. For example, a senior member of staff came storming in and shouted at me for something I was not responsible for. Having dealt with that, the next role play was dealing with a member of staff's personal family problem; so there was quite a swing in terms of emotion and stress. In between, there were some written tasks that had to be completed. However, these were less obvious and required some knowledge before they could be completed properly. At the time, I thought that, with the constant barrage of role plays, if this was a senior officer's typical day then they can 'stuff the job where the sun don't shine'.

After the role play had been concluded I was given a quick two-minute chat to ask any questions I might have had. I had no questions and could not think of any at the time as I was completely mentally stressed.

The feeling I had, after reflection, was quite terrible. There was no way of identifying how well or how badly I had done; there was no clear identification of what they wanted or how the assessment would be marked. With an interview I would have been able to say 'Yes, that went well' or 'I really messed that up'. With the assessment centre, there were so many variable factors that could have gone well or gone badly that it was impossible to gauge your own performance. Personally I thought I just did enough to pass. Very limited feedback was given in terms of a grade of either very strong, competent, needs training and perceived weakness.

The decision took over four months to come through. During that time I was constantly thinking have I or haven't I passed. I drove my friends and my family crazy over my constant pondering over the result. This deliberation and constant self-analysis of my performance have stayed throughout my time in the Service.

When I received the results, I found that I had passed. In fact, I was told that I was one of the highest passes in the country. My grades were so good that the role players and assessors believed me to be a plant or an assessor of the assessors. This has given me a lot of confidence and, as a result, I decided to take this one step further and try for accelerated promotion. I am thankful to say that I have been successful in this regard. This I owe to the assessment centre experience.

THINKING ON

1. How should selectors make sense of candidates' scores on a range of different tests? Does doing well on one test excuse doing poorly on another?

2. Assessors cannot predict every eventuality. To what extent should they control or force the actions of the assessed?

3. 'This is still something I contemplate daily, and it is etched into my memory forever.' What are the ethical limits of recruitment and selection? What would be unacceptable?

4. Does the inclusion of highly relevant work-simulation tests improve the quality of selection?

5. How do fatigue and other effects of prolonged bouts of selection influence the performance of selectors?

6. Role plays can become 'real' for both applicants and selectors. What are the risks associated with this? What are the advantages of this?

7. Are assessment centres more or less fair than other methods of selection?

8. How well do assessment centres replicate reality? Are they better than assessments of performance on the job?

9. 'As soon as I said my married name, I realised my mistake and became completely flustered; it took me a while to regain my composure.' What lessons can you draw from this sentence?

10. Do assessment centres have an aura? Put yourself in the place of someone who has been invited to attend an assessment centre. What are your preconceptions? How are these different to your preconceptions about

interviews? Do you think your preconceptions about assessment centres alter your behaviour during selection?

11. How can the success or failure of an assessment centre be determined? How can the success or failure of any selection device be assessed?

12. How long could the Prison Service continue to use the same assessment centre?

Some Concluding Thoughts

Reading these stories has been a journey that has transformed me. I began this project as a researcher who, like many others, was interested in the ways in which organisational selectors choose whom to appoint. I believed it was possible to assess people accurately for their job-related aptitude and I thought that selectors could be confident in their abilities to make rational decisions. I was also captured by the ideas of Peter Herriot (1989a, 1989b) about the social processes involved in recruitment and selection and the need for selectors to think about the manner of their interactions with applicants because of the way this influences future behaviour. I was fascinated by the ideas surrounding person–organisation fit and how selectors can recruit people who will grow and develop with the organisation, and also how recruitment and selection can be tailored to allow both sides (applicants and organisations) to make informed decisions about their futures. Now that I have read about 250 stories and thought deeply about 50 of them, I find that many of my thoughts about recruitment and selection have changed. I appreciate that these stories are individual recollections subject to all manner of biases, but nevertheless, they have changed my thinking. The purpose of this final chapter is to stand back from the detail of these stories and to consider broader issues.

THE STAGE

In *As You Like It*, Jaques says, 'All the world's a stage, and all the men and women merely players.' Shakespeare was saying that we all play roles: that everything we say and do is constructed by us for effect. Even when we try to behave 'normally' and 'be ourselves', we are acting a role. The notion of us acting roles seems particularly important in recruitment and selection. Not only is every person inhabiting their usual roles, they consciously take on another. Organisational selectors want to portray their organisation in the best light to make the organisation appear attractive so that they can 'land their catch'. Applicants, obviously, have a vested interest in making sure the selectors see their strengths and not their weaknesses. This 'acting' has always been known, but I was surprised just how extensive it is. I had not realised, for example, just how much external applicants misrepresent themselves. I had assumed that they applied for reasons of promotion and advancement, and for a fresh challenge. After reading these stories, I now think that although some people apply for these reasons, for most people these words are just rhetoric and a language they have learnt to portray themselves positively. They apply to work in other organisations because they need salvation from their current situation. They might be unemployed, they might be unhappy in their current job, or they might have personal reasons to move. But rarely do people move when they do not have to.

So I now think about recruitment and selection as a stage where performers act. It seems to me that most people are playing roles and, to some extent, misrepresenting themselves. We have always known that applicants emphasise their strengths and attempt to mask their weaknesses, but I had not realised that the misrepresentation had descended so deeply that it has created repertoires of language that are largely detached from the truth. Judging from some of these stories, organisational selectors are no better. They seem happy to extol the benefits of employment in their firm and avoid being drawn on many of the realities. They paint positive pictures of advancement and progression and, if they are really clever, will do so in such a way that applicants fill in the silences themselves with their own hopes.

If this is the reality of recruitment and selection, what chance does realistic recruitment have? Is it possible that selectors can get a full picture of each applicant? Can applicants find out what working in the organisation will really be like? Part of me feels resigned to accepting the inevitable that people will not be themselves in such important and strained situations. But another part of me wants to find a solution so that people explore opportunities with their eyes wide open. Sadly though, these stories do not give us a solution. Emma's story is a case in point. She was given a day to try out a job in the new employer, but was so excited about the opportunity and being treated decently that she saw everything through rose-tinted spectacles. One of two courses of action seems necessary for the parties to make sensible judgements about each other. Either there needs to be such prolonged contact between them to allow excitement to die away, masks to crumble and for reality to emerge; or initial contact between the parties should happen when recruitment and selection is not in the offing, so that behaviour and relationships are established that cannot later be deviated from without raising suspicion.

The first of these options, prolonged contact, is already recorded in the literature as a means of recruiting 'whole people' who will grow and develop with the organisation (Bowen, Ledford & Nathan, 1991). It has the major benefit that it prevents some of the flimsy, superficial recruitment and selection processes that not only fail to assess applicants properly, but also disappoint applicants with their lack of professionalism. The second option, pre-recruitment introduction, is inappropriate for many vacancies, but it does have wider relevance than might be first thought. It encourages a positive approach of searching for good people rather than the reactivity of the traditional approach, where recruiters sit back and wait for applicants to contact them. This might be conducted on a meta level with the use of headhunting and similar forms of recruitment; or it might work on a micro level with assessors actively expecting applicants to prove particular skills and abilities. Pre-recruitment introduction is also relevant in internal recruitment. To my eyes, it now seems profoundly wrong for selectors to deny themselves key information, such as performance and sickness records, simply because it is not available for every applicant. It would be better to acknowledge the information asymmetry and find ways to gather such information on people where it is absent, not exclude it where it is present.

THE DECISION

When selectors are trained they are taught how to make a rational decision. They learn how to construct a job description and a person (or job) specification. From these, selectors are shown how to infer a list of selection criteria that they can use to assess applicants. They are then shown how to generate applicants and taught ways to assess them against the criteria (interviews, assessment centres, analogous tests, personality tests and so on). This is a rational and structured process that relates the assessment of applicants to the qualities required to perform well in the role. One of the major benefits of the approach is that it helps selectors justify their decisions by surfacing the evidence they have used to judge people. They should be able to explain why they have selected or rejected each of the applicants.

After reading the stories in this database, I found myself wondering about this process. Can people act in the coldly rational way they are trained to do? Even when selection criteria are generated, selectors seem to rely on subjective judgement to rate people. They tend to seek the 'best' applicant rather than the applicant who best matches the selection criteria. Furthermore, while the selection criteria may guide what questions are asked, the responses are subjectively assessed. Unstructured and lightly structured interviews dominate the assessment of applicants. When other methods are included in the selection process, subjective interviews are used to make the 'final' decision. Even in elaborate assessment centres, interviews are the final set piece after which decisions are made. Given this dominance of subjective interviews, the impression management of applicants seems a fundamental flaw in the process. Is it possible to discover the 'real' person when they are acting a role?

The resistance of subjective interviews in this rational scheme of things is odd. Generally speaking, selectors are highly trained, highly competent managers who are assessed on their performance. They want to find the best person possible. So why do they fall back on subjective judgement and relegate more rational and scientific methods to a supportive role? Do they prefer to trust their judgement? Do they regard interpersonal interactions as more important than some of the objective measures? Is it just custom and practice? In reviewing these stories, I have noticed that these organisational selectors start the decision-making process by eliminating those applicants who are clearly unsuitable. After that, they have a problem and have to fall back on their own subjective impression of the applicants. Given the way in which the human brain processes information and the unrealistic atomisation of selection criteria, what else can they do? Who can say with any certainty that a slightly better answer on one interview question outweighs a slightly better score on another test? Once you whittle the field down to a group of people who have a thorough understanding of the job, who are all keen to do it and who all look like they will fit in, who can really say who the best applicant is? And this is a big problem for recruitment and selection: very often the differences between the better candidates are smaller than our ability as assessors to measure the differences meaningfully.

Going through the stories again, I gained a sense that the most successful selectors were those who appreciated the partiality of selection tests. They seemed to recognise their own limitations in understanding people and realised that the idea that they can quickly gain a full understanding of an applicant in an hour or so is ridiculous. As a result, they come over as humble people who respect applicants. Once they have this mindset, good decisions flow. It seems that once selectors realise that, at best, they can spot some hopeless applicants and can assess a few key skills and abilities, they begin to highlight what really matters. Moreover, because they realise that their own judgements are limited, they seek opportunities to draw other people into the decision, including the applicants. The decision makers become thoughtful, considered, respectful and aware of their limitations. And, ironically, their organisation becomes much more attractive to applicants, who associate this style of decision making with managerial behaviour in the organisation.

THE FIELD

Situations where internal and external candidates compete in the same group is a recurring theme throughout this book. It is a topic I had not previously considered and it is something I cannot recall seeing in the recruitment and selection literature. Such were the problems thrown up on these occasions that I now believe it is one of the key issues confronting recruiters and applicants alike.

To recap, at the time these stories were being written, it was commonplace in the UK, especially in not-for-profit organisations, for companies to adopt the 'level-playing-field approach', which allows internal and external applicants to compete for jobs on an equal footing. The idea is that only information introduced into the recruitment and selection process by applicants is included in the decision-making process. The main justifications for this approach are that it allows the recruiting organisation to 'benchmark' the knowledge, skills and salary of internal applicants against the market; it opens the door to applicants who might not otherwise be able to compete for these jobs; it prevents selectors making subjective decisions based on prior knowledge of some applicants; and it allows applicants to compete on an equal footing based on their knowledge and skills rather than their acquaintance with the job, the culture or the selectors. To my eyes, these are all worthy intentions and ones that I support. However, after reading these stories I find that the level playing field is poorly performed in practice and creates dissatisfaction in all camps: selectors realise that it is unachievable; internal applicants feel that their commitment and service are unappreciated; and external applicants feel that vacancies are already assigned to their internal rivals. As such, the approach creates as many issues of unfairness as it solves.

One of the main difficulties that the selector experiences in the level-playing-field approach was captured in Trevor's story. His panel interviewed a woman returning from maternity leave who gave 'a near-perfect interview'. However, the interview panel had personal experience of the applicant and 'knew' her to be abrasive and poor at supporting colleagues. As Trevor relates, two panel members simultaneously said something like 'That wasn't the Belinda we know and love'. These were selectors who were keenly aware of their responsibilities to exclude their past experience with applicants and to rely on their objective assessment of data introduced during the selection process. However, these selectors were caught in a bind. Not only were they unable to use their prior knowledge of the candidate in making their judgement, they were also unable to use this knowledge to form questions tailored to the individual. The result was that an hour's excellent performance in an interview could have got Belinda a job for which the selection panel knew she was a poor candidate. This panel did not ignore their prior knowledge of Belinda and did not offer her the job.

That raises further concerns. If this decision is made on prior knowledge of Belinda's abrasive style and this matter is not addressed in the interview, what chance does the applicant have to put her side across? Perhaps there were legitimate reasons for this style; perhaps it is a misreading of Belinda. If Belinda is not confronted with this preconception, she is being unfairly treated. This unfairness is compounded by the mystery concerning her non-selection. If she does not know the real reasons for her rejection, she cannot correct any problems. This example, which is typical of many, demonstrates the difficult situation in which the level-playing-field approach puts selectors. They are damned if they use prior knowledge of applicants in their decision making and they are damned if they do not. It forces selectors into an ethical dilemma by raising the possibility that they will have to make selection decisions that they know to be wrong, but are powerless to prevent.

The dissatisfaction of internal applicants has been another recurring theme in this book. When entering a level-playing-field-style recruitment and selection process, their disaffection is clear. Except for characters like Belinda, they are frustrated, even angered, that their past track record and commitment to the firm are not taken into account. When they are treated like external candidates, they feel devalued. They feel annoyed when they are in competition with other internal applicants but still have to prove themselves, and they have a sense that their employers are lazy in forcing them to introduce every piece of information they want considered into the process. By operating such a system, employers do not seem aware of the impact it has on internal applicants. By and large, internal applicants are good performers who decide to expose themselves for scrutiny. This is very risky, as the costs of disappointment are considerable. The stories in this book demonstrate that internal applicants are very aware of these risks and also of the tremendous negative impacts that failure can have, such as embarrassment, anger, illness and exit. It seems extraordinary to me that organisations have developed a promotion system that is likely to upset the majority of keen, ambitious employees who have to return to their jobs if they are unsuccessful. Reading between the lines of these stories, I sense these people are angry that their established record of performance is ignored by selectors in favour of the relatively superficial assessments. The employer has observed their performance in similar roles over the years, but throws out this data in favour of assessments in the impressionistic, artificial and stressful environment of a selection interview.

External applicants are dissatisfied by different things. They are concerned that, when competing against internal applicants, decisions are already made in favour of internal applicants against whom they feel disadvantaged. Their sense of disadvantage is often real. Yes, some internal applicants are already lined up for a vacancy and they will have an understanding of the culture, context and business environment of the employer. But when the prejudgements of internal applicants are negative or when the employer is actively looking for 'fresh blood', the advantage switches through 180 degrees. One of the main concerns of external applicants is the professionalism of the selection process. Are they given the opportunity to display their talents? Do the selectors focus on the important knowledge and skills to perform well? Are they dealt with courteously? Do the selectors use applicants' time appropriately? Their assessment of this professionalism shapes their decision whether or not to accept job offers. But when they feel disadvantaged, they differ from internal applicants because they can turn their backs on the unfairness or uncivil behaviour and put it down to experience.

Internal and external applicants are clearly different types of candidates. Internal applicants take a great risk in applying: they have a proven track record of performance (which the stories have shown can be good or bad) and they have given commitment to the organisation. External candidates, on the other hand, take no risks by applying (although it may take considerable time), are often a complete unknown to the employer, and usually have little relationship with the recruiting organisation. However, they may have new or different ideas (although this commonly heard justification has a hint of rhetoric to it), they symbolise the current state of the employment market, and they help change the balance of the existing workforce. These differences are important and provide categorically different profiles of applicants. Should these differences be recognised in the selection system?

I find several factors colliding. First, there are a range of good selection tools that, by and large, can only be used on internal applicants (performance reviews, peer assessments, sickness records, observation, career planning). Second, the impact of internal candidate failure is powerful and is often quite destructive to both the failed applicant and the employer. Third, I cannot help thinking that selection decisions should be made with the best information possible, not just the information that is available for every applicant. Consequently, I find myself questioning the wisdom of the level-playing-field approach to recruitment and selection. I cannot see how, in the normal run of events, such an approach is justifiable. It causes good people to make bad decisions. It favours 'performance' during recruitment and selection over 'performance' at work. It treats people like commodities. And it does little to help applicants assess the nature of the organisation.

Instead, I find myself thinking about a two-stage process in which vacancies are first opened up to internal candidates either through a selection or a promotion process. I would only open up the vacancy to external candidates if this internal trawl was unsuccessful. Although many organisations adopt this approach already, it is not without its drawbacks. It does not change the composition of the workforce and may reinforce the position of any dominant group. It also means that the quality and rewards of the organisation's labour force is not benchmarked against the market, although the benefits of this are questionable given the salvation-seeking nature of applicants. So there are some dangers with this approach. But for me, these problems are outweighed by the advantages of supporting, developing and appreciating existing employees.

I think we also need to consider how we make selection decisions. At present, the trend is to use the same methods for each applicant and in some countries, the USA for example, this approach is enshrined in law. However, it seems to me that the goal should be to assess each applicant against the selection criteria in the best way possible and, occasionally, this might mean using different tests and tools for different people. It will almost certainly mean that selectors will have different amounts and quality of information on each applicant. There have always been information asymmetries between applicants, but the current vogue of treating everyone identically means that selectors frequently ignore them. I believe that selectors should be forced to appreciate these differences and do what they can to close them. If they have to make selection decisions when there are large information asymmetries, they should be aware of these when making their decisions. Surely, the goal must be to use the best possible information to make the best possible decision. Isn't this best for everyone?

THE FIT

Another theme that ran through these stories was selectors' desire to select people who would 'fit in' and applicants' similar desire to join companies where they believe they will 'fit in'. These are themes that have concerned selectors and applicants since time began. But whereas the assessment of knowledge and skills has become a science, the assessment of fit largely remains a mystery. There are three main approaches. In the first two, the recruiting organisation transfers the fit decision to the applicants. The first approach is to give the applicants a realistic preview of work, such as a job trial, so that they can determine if they will get on with people and thrive in the new work environment. The second approach is to make applicants attend the company's premises on many occasions during the recruitment and selection process, and in doing so introduce them to a lot of different people. The third approach is for the recruiting organisation to make the fit decision itself based on contact with the applicants. This is commonly based on impressions formed in selection interviews or in informal interactions with other organisational members.

The stories in this book have demonstrated that all of these approaches are at best unsound, and at worst discriminatory. One problem is that both applicants and selectors are 'performing' roles and not being themselves. Another is that applicants often have too much at stake to refuse jobs where they are unsure they will fit in. In addition, when given the opportunity to assess their fit, they are often too excited by the opportunity to make good decisions, as exemplified by Emma's story. One way around these difficulties is to extend the amount of time applicants spend trying out the job and the organisation so that the job trial becomes 'real'. An example of this comes from football. Most clubs will take players on trial for prolonged periods. This allows both parties to assess their suitability and to walk away if necessary. It is made possible because the players can return to their current employers if the trial is unsuccessful. I find myself thinking how interesting and different recruitment and selection, particularly those aspects concerning fit, would become if people had a statutory right to return to their previous job within two months of leaving it. But, of course, this is a pipedream.

Both applicants and selectors remain concerned about the fit of new recruits. Interest in this field is increasing with a rapidly growing literature on fit. Parallel to this rise in academic interests are efforts to build selection tools to assess fit. Researchers are taking varying approaches. Some are looking at personality similarity, some at competence congruency. My own work is looking at fit across a range of domains. These tools are still years away, but we are moving in the right direction. In the meantime, the lesson from these stories is that selectors are unwise to make decisions about applicants' fit. Instead, they should be helping applicants find ways to assess their own fit.

FINAL THOUGHTS

Reading this database of stories has confirmed one thing for me: lightly structured interviews dominate selection. I always knew this, but reading these stories made me realise how interviews (and pre-screening by CV) are the norm. When there is a vacancy, selection panels swing into operation and create an interview schedule. Advertisements go out, applicants send in their CVs, four people are shortlisted, and then the interviews take place. Occasionally someone may suggest some form of enhancement such as an assessment centre, psychometric tests, presentations or a realistic job preview, but these are just variations on a theme. This process is so well established with 'normal' vacancies[1] that it has become a programmed decision that managers know how to tackle. Such is the embeddedness of this approach that recruitment and selection have become ritualised with job descriptions, person specifications, company promotion in advertisements, and a few moments at the end of the interview for the interviewee to ask questions. It is not merely organisational selectors who indulge in these rituals: applicants do so as well. They wear a dark suit, they arrive 10 minutes early, they adopt an overly demure persona, they stress the positives and they turn every negative into an opportunity.

These rituals have helped establish the interview as the way in which vacancies are filled. In doing so, I fear that we have lost our understanding of why we indulge in these selection practices. The goal for organisational selectors is to discover someone who will perform well in the vacant role. The best way to do this is to observe and analyse the people who want to do the job doing it for real over a prolonged period. Unfortunately, this is impractical for most jobs and so we have developed the selection practices we have now ritualised. Viewed in this way, modern selection practices are a substitute for the analysis of people doing real work in real situations. Instead, we use interviews that, at best, identify severe weaknesses, and, at worst, let applicants tell selectors how good they will be in the role and bear no relation to actual performance. It is an abstract environment populated by people not being themselves. Applicants spend all their time talking about themselves, which in more normal circumstances might be seen as sociopathic behaviour. With anything less than excellent interviewing, the successful candidates are

---

[1] I have highlighted the word 'normal' to differentiate this form of selection to the mass recruitment drives of large intakes such as graduates and soldiers. Such drives are commonly designed and managed by highly skilled recruitment and selection experts. They are very different to the single-post vacancies that most people encounter in their normal working life.

those with an 'everyman' quality who can think quickly on their feet and tell a good story.

The solution to this problem is first to recognise that selection procedures are a convenient, but not necessarily effective, substitute for real assessments of people doing the job for real over a prolonged period. Only once we realise that selection procedures are a poor substitute for more thorough ways of assessing people for work will we start to look for better ways of assessing people such as job trials, observation of work, trial periods, performance records and portfolio assessments.

REFERENCES

Bowen, D. E., Ledford G. E. & Nathan, B. R. (1991) 'Hiring for the organization, not the job', *Academy of Management Executive,* 5(4), 35–51.

Herriot, P. (1989a) *Recruitment in the 90s,* London: Institute of Personnel Management.

Herriot, P. (1989b) 'Selection as a social process', in M. Smith, & I. T. Robertson (eds), *Advances in Selection and Assessment*, Chichester: John Wiley & Sons Ltd, pp. 171–87.

Index